MIGRANT

WORLD

MAKING

MIGRANT WORLD MAKING

Edited by Sergio Fernando Juárez,

Julia Khrebtan-Hörhager, Michael Lechuga,

and Arthur D. Soto-Vásquez

MICHIGAN STATE UNIVERSITY PRESS | *East Lansing*

Michigan State University Press
East Lansing, Michigan 48823-5245

Library of Congress Cataloging-in-Publication Data

Names: Juárez, Sergio Fernando, editor. | Khrebtan-Hörhager, Julia, editor. | Lechuga,
Michael, editor. | Soto-Vásquez, Arthur D., editor.
Title: Migrant world making / Edited by Sergio Fernando Juárez, Julia Khrebtan-Hörhager,
Michael Lechuga, and Arthur D. Soto-Vásquez.
Description: East Lansing : Michigan State University Press, [2023] |
Includes bibliographical references.
Identifiers: LCCN 2023001801 | ISBN 9781611864687 (paperback) | ISBN 9781609177454 |
ISBN 9781628955101 (epub)
Subjects: LCSH: Emigration and immigration—Social aspects. | Mass media and immigrants.
| Immigrants—Social networks. | Immigrants—Language. | Communication in human
geography. | Transnationalism—Social aspects.
Classification: LCC JV6225 .M52 2023 | DDC 302.23086/912—dc23/eng/20230310
LC record available at https://lccn.loc.gov/2023001801

Cover design by Shaun Allshouse
Cover art: horizontal colorful abstract wave background by Nenone

———

Visit Michigan State University Press at *www.msupress.org*

Contents

Preface

Migrant World Making joins a growing body of research on the topic of transnational migration. As many scholars in migrant-destination countries have described, studying the phenomenon of migration can offer a glimpse at how migrant groups interact with state policies and citizenship codes that subject them to violence and exploitation. According to the World Economic Forum, there are more than 270 million people migrating today, more than triple the number of global migrants from 1970 (Edmund, 2020). The United Nations estimates that more than eighty-two million of those individuals can be categorized as refugees; more than forty-eight million as displaced peoples (United Nations High Commissioner for Refugees, 2021). As nationalism around the globe escalates and the effects of global climate change become more catastrophic, the number of global migrants and refugees arriving in destination countries will only increase.

Indeed, *Migrant World Making* joins the scholarly conversation at a turbulent time of yet another migration crisis, caused by Russia's brutal invasion of Ukraine. A prominent Ukrainian scholar on migration, Elena Makarova distinguishes two particularities of the current Ukrainian migration to the European countries after Russia's invasion on February 24, 2022: it is an extremely rapid process, and it is causing the unprecedented solidarity of the European Union (EU) countries with Ukraine, leading to the immediate legalization of permits for a temporary stay for war refugees from Ukraine with collective protection status. This collective protection status, Makarova explains, is different from normal refugee status, which is granted individually and takes much longer to verify and process. After the Russian war started, around eight million people had crossed the border from Ukraine by mid-June 2022 (Elena Makarova, personal communication, July 2022). The total number of war refugees has increased significantly day by day since the beginning of the war.

A large proportion of refugees, around 4.1 million, crossed the border into Poland. The reasons why Ukrainian refugees in Poland are so numerous compared to other neighboring countries are not only because most of the Ukrainian refugees are fleeing toward the Western borders of their country to escape the Russian invasion, but also because most of them have chosen Poland as their state of refuge due to historical sociocultural ties (especially in border regions). These migrations are also a result of linguistic similarities between the Ukrainian and Polish languages, as both languages are Slavic languages compared, for example, with the Hungarian language, which belongs to the Finno-Ugric language group and cannot be understood by Ukrainians without prior language knowledge (Elena Makarova, personal communication, July 2022). Iuliia Hoban, a Ukrainian scholar specializing in international relations and world history, elaborates:

> Poland and Ukraine share a complex past that involved rebellions, pogroms by both sides against their Jewish population, as well as ethnic cleansing and the forced removal of populations. Despite these historic traumas, Poland has demonstrated steadfast support to Ukrainians fleeing the war, showing that there are alternative ways to deal with complicated history. (personal communication, June 2022)

Migrant experiences are complex. They are characterized by a number of transitions, contradictions, and simultaneities that are not necessarily observable from a single political or economic orientation. For example, in 2015, a twenty-three-year-old university student named Shabir had to leave his native Pakistan and undertake a risky journey to Europe. Through Iran, Turkey, and Greece, Shabir made his way to Italy, where he was received by Casa Scalabrini

634, a migrant support center (the subject of Veronica De Sanctis and Julia Khrebtan-Hörhager's chapter in this volume). When asked about how the journey affected his identity and sense of the world, Shabir responded quizzically: "Identity? No, it hasn't changed, but I certainly have an additional identity that adds to the others." The migrant identity, as Shabir describes it, is multilayered, often compartmentalized, and plural. This book offers myriad narratives like Shabir's—mosaics of experiences that paint a picture of what it is like for traveling, transnational peoples to make a home in other places. We call this process *migrant world making*—a phenomenon of materially and discursively constructing a homeplace by creating a network of communication tools and strategies to navigate the tensions, contradictions, and range of emotions that characterize being transnational. This spirit invokes the words of author Toni Morrison, who encourages us to dialogue with the homeless, nomadic, and socially neglected migrant Others, in order to get their perspectives on the world: "Tell us what the world has been to you in the dark places and in the light . . . What moves at the margin. What is it like to have no home in this place" (2017). This volume centers such marginal migrant stories.

As scholars of migration, rhetoric, identity, and culture, we ask, What does the experience of migration mean to those who have lived it? To answer this question, this volume features research from transnational scholars in the fields of communication, media, and rhetorical studies who employ diverse research methods to describe how migrants and migrant communities carve out spaces of belonging in a hyper-nationalist world through storytelling via both traditional and new media communication technologies. This volume demonstrates that for migrants, developing communication strategies is a vital practice of finding social connections, navigating the pressures of assimilation, and maintaining links to various cultures. While migrants' experiences are uniquely their own, their resources for managing the experiences of being subjected as foreigners are similar: they build communities by telling stories, engage in social media activism, protest in the streets, write scholarly criticism, create art projects, and spread awareness about their cultures.

Migrant World Making approaches migration with the assumptions that migrants are not a monolithic group, a cultural totality with a certain meta-identity. Rather, we showcase the numerous practices of migrant communication and connection that allow migrants to thrive in globalized yet highly nationalistic societies. This approach "builds on the experiences of mobile communities in borderlands—those most affected by the rigid structures of belonging and exclusion" (Lechuga, 2019, p. 270). Thus, the aims of this volume are to both draw out a number of tensions through which migrants navigate in their experiences in transition between nations, and to highlight the communication practices and technologies that allow and enable migrants to build new homeplaces. Increased nationalistic tendencies of host countries, combined with negative representations of migrants and refugees, often contribute to absence of voice and agency by the affected demographics necessary for them to build communities, homes, and worlds of their own. Our volume aims to change that.

From a methodological perspective, this volume focuses on texts and interviews that center migrant voices and experiences. Three approaches dominate: qualitative content analysis of media, semi-structured interviews, and vernacular discourse analysis. In general, qualitative content analysis is used to approach texts as a rich source of information while employing a systemic collection procedure (Lindlof & Taylor, 2019). The resulting data is then coded and categorized to identify predominant themes, as the first three chapters do (Tracy, 2019). Chapters by Nathian Shae Rodriguez and Noor Ghazal Aswad rely on interviews with the participants to generate data. Using an interview guide with a series of questions, the interviewer tries to gain insight in the way a person sees and experiences a particular phenomenon (Lindlof & Taylor, 2019). Finally, chapters by Corinne Mitsuye Sugino, Victoria Cisneros and Sergio Fernando Juárez, and Anjana Mudambi utilize vernacular discourse analysis as a methodology. Vernacular discourse analysis is a critical rhetorical method is a critical rhetorical method that provides scholars a way to access the fluid discourses of groups, like migrants, who often simultaneously resist and embrace dominant discourses about citizenship, belonging, and what it means to have a homeplace (Lechuga, 2019).

Global Context: Migration and Nationalism

Since Shabir left Pakistan in 2015, there has been a rising swell of ethno-nationalism in countries where migration trends are concentrated. In Europe, the United States, and other places, such nationalistic fervor has led to the electoral success of right-wing parties and candidates whose primary rhetorical appeal is anti-migrant. Political violence toward migrants has also increased, both sanctioned by the states and committed by individuals in sporadic explosions of anger and hate. Partisan media, social media echo chambers, misinformation campaigns, and charismatic cynical leaders seem to only exacerbate this anti-immigrant sentiment. Of course, the economic precarity characteristic of the neoliberal world order also plays a large role in the disenfranchisement of migrant communities since the same forces that propel migrants to leave their homes in search of better lives also condition the violent reactions to their arrival.

Nationalism and populism have been instrumental in defining dominant anti-immigrant trends across the world, especially in Western societies. During the last decades, migration to Europe and the United States has been directly proportional to and productive of xenophobia, Islamophobia, and racism, rooted in colonialism, Eurocentrism, and the perception of the migrant Other according to the principle of the West and the Rest (Ahmed, 2010; Burg, 2019; Cretton, 2018; Drzewiecka & Steyn, 2012; Khrebtan-Hörhager, 2014, 2015, 2019; Morrison, 2017; Shi-Xu, 2009; Sommier, 2017; Stalker, 2002; Toffle, 2015). Examples of scholarly literature on the subject are thought-provoking and sobering. Examination of flows of migrants from developing countries to Europe, especially to Germany and the United Kingdom—ranging from undocumented migrants, to labor migration, and, eventually, to family members—reveals that in the future, immigration to the EU will only increase, especially given the destabilization of eastern Europe after the Russian invasion of Ukraine in February 2022.

Ongoing unrest in multiple locations in Africa and Asia will also spur new movements of people (Stalker, 2002). Similarly, the exportation of border enforcement to Turkey and Mexico complicates studies of borderlands and necessitates a moving away from the "binary differentiations" that characterize this area of study (Arriola Vega, 2020 p. 773). Neo-imperial and colonial systems of migratory regulation are also appearing outside the West, as global forces export borders to the periphery. For example, Brewer et al., (2022) report that "migrants and asylum seekers arriving in Tapachula—the city in southern Mexico where the vast majority of asylum claims are made—face what service providers repeatedly described to us as a 'system to wear people down' (política de desgaste)" (p. 1). Here, through various agreements with the United States, Mexico has enacted its own border regime.

Building on the work of Ahmed (2010), Flores (2003), and Morrison (1993), Brewer et al. (2022) emphasize the role of cultural Othering by host communities as central to the experiences of migrants, pointing out the "rhetorical framing of the immigrant Other as unworthy, threatening, and criminal" (p. 128). Studies of migration in other Western locations demonstrate that Swissness is usually synonymous with dominant whiteness and is productive not only of nationalism but also of normalized, institutional racism (Cretton, 2018), while the French notion of *laïcité* (separation of religion from public affairs) regularly adds to the existing complexity and controversy with regard to the discussion of national identity, and more specifically the non-white non-Christian migration to *la Grande Nation* (Sommier, 2017). Curiously, even the most recent development in Europe with regard to millions of refugees from the war-torn Ukraine reveals deeply Eurocentric and racist roots of Othering. Those roots are still normative in the Old World, and they result in the unprecedented solidarity with and an unconditional welcome given to the Ukrainian refugees, treated much better than the so-called other Others from non-European, non-white, non-Christian locations. The famous phrase of the president of the European Commission, Ursula von der Leyen, from March 2022, "Ukraine is one of us," explains and normalizes the status quo (McMahon, 2022). Yet selectivity of hospitality and humanity is another side of Othering.

Racism, Islamophobia, xenophobia, and highly selective humanity—all forms of cultural Othering—are simultaneously unique and universal, applied differently to various geopolitical locations, yet universally damaging in their effects and affects on the migrant Others. Toni Morrison reminds us how universal and ancient—timeless in fact—the phenomenon of creating borders is: "Our tendency to separate and judge those not in our clan as the enemy, as the vulnerable and the deficient needing control, has a long history not limited to the animal world and prehistoric man" (2017, p. 3). Klein also looks at the phenomenon historically and globally, and warns against the increasing tendencies of nationalism and multicultural selectivity:

If there is an overarching lesson to be drawn from the foul mood rising around the world, it may be this: we could never, ever underestimate the power of hate. Never underestimate the appeal of wielding power over "the Other," be they migrants, Muslims, Blacks, Mexicans, women, the other in any form. Especially during times of economic hardship, when a great many people have good reason to fear that the jobs that can support a decent life are disappearing for good. (2017, p. 84)

Nationalism, xenophobia, and anti-migrant Othering are powerful mechanisms of contemporary multicultural relations worldwide—but should not be the entire story of migration. Such Othering "extends beyond nationality, time, and space. It erects geographical and rhetorical borders between people and irreversibly changes the very essence of our democracy. It creates damaging divides and contributes to social isolation. Eventually, it takes humanity out of humans" (Khrebtan-Hörhager, 2019, p. 129). Instead, we choose in this volume to allow for a different series of stories to be told, those deriving from the multiple experiences of being a migrant amid the rising tides of nationalism, xenophobia, and climate disasters.

It must also be mentioned and emphasized that droughts, endless wildfires, severe monsoons, hurricanes, and other increasingly common climate disasters will harm and displace some of the most vulnerable human populations. Climate change is sociological and political. Foreign policy scholars are increasingly noting that it can lead to civil unrest and further displacement (Parenti, 2011). For example, Hallett (2019) contends that sustained droughts leading to lower food production in Central America have disrupted the developing economies and livelihoods of marginalized people, leading to more emigration pressure. In addition, a series of devastating hurricanes have pushed 3.5 million people to be food insecure (Narea, 2021). Drought conditions have also been associated with violent conflict in Syria (Linke & Ruether, 2021) and in Kenya (Koren et al., 2021). Catastrophic flooding in Pakistan in August 2022 (as the writing of this edited volume was being finalized) has killed hundreds and displaced nearly 30 million people, according to the United Nations High Commissioner for Refugees (2022).

It is certainly not the first time we are witnessing the rising tides of nationalism, increased numbers of displaced peoples, and extremist intellectual formations. These phenomena have been and ought to continue to be concerns of those in the fields of communication, rhetoric, and media studies. Many foundational theories to the study of culture, identity, and Othering can be traced back to the scholarship of "émigré intellectuals who had come close to the abyss" during the rise of Nazism in the 1930s (Katznelson, 2013, p. 13), the most prominent among them being Max Horkheimer, Theodor Adorno, and Herbert Marcuse. In the 1944 preface to *Dialectic of Enlightenment*, Adorno and Horkheimer note that "the theoretical work of German emigrants carried forward despite Hitler would not have been possible" (1997, p. xix) without the relocation of the Institute for Social Research to the United States, where—despite their lives in exile and their nostalgia for the home that irreversibly changed from the *Land der Dicher und Denker* to the realm of *Nationalsozialismus*—their voices were heard and their work continued. Their critiques of the culture industry and unchallenged dominant ideologies serve as a cautionary tale that encourages us to avoid repeating this history and making similar mistakes of cultural Othering again.

Ironically and alarmingly, history is repeating itself—in a different form and at a different place. Just like Nazi Germany, strategically and skillfully transformed by a charismatic leader into the realm of destructive fascism that led to the most horrific forms of genocide and resulted in a world war, contemporary Russia is the cradle of another form of culture-specific fascism, called *Russicm* (Snyder, 2022). Ukraine is among the first but certainly not the last victims of the regime. Iuliia Hoban elaborates:

> Russia's war against Ukraine is both a fascist and a colonial war, which is evident in Russia's claims that Ukraine as a nation does not exist and its tactics of mass killings, rape and deportation with intent to annihilate the country. (Personal communication, June 2022)

Russia's war against Ukraine, and the consequent refugee crises in the EU, reveal that the subjects of migration, Othering, and homeplace are not static but ebb and flow with the geopolitical forces that shape the world.

Tensions: Representation, Memory, and Place

The chapters in this volume each uniquely engage with different pushes and pulls that migrants face when materially and discursively constructing their worlds. We understand these sociocultural forces as tensions that, as Baxter and Montgomery (1996) suggest, pull communicators in different directions.

Social relations are thus "always in a state of flux, influenced by opposing forces or tensions within the individuals, context, and greater society" (Prentice & Kramer, 2006, p. 340). There are three tensions in particular that we explore in this volume: (1) between being represented versus representing oneself and the collection, (2) between memories of the past and the potential of the future, and (3) between belonging in a space and carrying culture from another place.

Representation

Negative portrayals of migrants in the news media and by demagogic politicians are countered by community media, alternative narratives on social media, and transmedia activism. The tension of migrant representation is even more complex: when responding to negative representations in the dominant mass media, migrants risk reinforcing narratives of unworthiness and reproducing discriminatory hegemony. In this way, the negative representation of migration also serves as an assimilatory force, socially conditioning normative behavior among migrants to avoid stigma or discrimination. As such, the tension of representation is also tied to tensions of nationalism and absence of voice.

The tension of representation is one of the most common phenomena in migrant communication and media studies. Unsurprisingly, the representation of migrants in mass media and journalism has historically been negative (Benson, 2013; Clark-Ibáñez & Swan, 2019; Rasinger, 2010). Migrants are constructed as pollutants and threats to the nation (Flores, 2003; Cisneros, 2008). Rhetorically, migration is also described with dehumanizing liquid metaphors, like a "wave" or "flood" (Abid et al., 2017). Dehumanizing language about migrants also leads to a negative popular opinion toward immigration (Utych, 2018). In the last decade, numerous right-wing politicians have seized upon such negative representations to mobilize their popular support in elections. For instance, Chavez (2013) shows how Latina/o/x migrants in the United States are constructed as threats to the nation, and Cisneros (2017) demonstrates how that same language was used by a right-wing populist like Donald Trump in his 2016 campaign for president of the United States.

Given the predominantly negative media framing, what can new and digital media offer migrants in regard to self-representation? On the one hand, media like social networks and online video promise a multitude of representation, with (arguably) less gatekeeping, centralization, and profit incentives than traditional mass media. For instance, migrants and refugees have used selfie-taking as a form of digital activism to counter increasing hostile attitudes in Europe (Nikunen, 2019; Risam, 2018). Visual digital platforms like Pinterest and Instagram have also been studied as sites where pro-immigrant content is created and shared (Guidry et al., 2018; Jaramillo-Dent and Pérez-Rodríguez, 2019). On the other hand, these studies also recognize the limits of migrant representation online. Nikunen (2019) notes how selfie-taking can also reinforce narratives of the "worthy immigrant" and contribute to a certain selectivity of representation. Similarly, the movement to extend legal status to DREAMers, undocumented migrants who were brought to the United States as children, has been criticized for creating narratives of the "perfect immigrant"—the one who goes to college and fits into the mainstream U.S. society (Lauby, 2016). The attempt to respond to negative portrayals through new media is a recurring theme in studies of migrant self-representation online. There is also a recognition in the literature that platforms like Instagram and Facebook are not neutral public spheres, and thus their politics (i.e., how content is impacted by an algorithm) contribute to shaping migrant representation.

Bringing socio-technical considerations to the tension of migrant representation is an urgent need. In the space of tensions between representation and voice, we must also ask whether the privileging of migrant voice must be complicated by the commercialized and commodified nature of privatized public spheres online. Can social movements, new ideas, and migrants' own voices truly prosper in online communication technology? After all, voice—and, in the case of migrants, its frequent absence—has always been representative of power and privilege, and directly correlated with the phenomena of exclusion, discrimination, and cultural Othering. Often, the scholarly impulse is to categorize and define the experiences of Others (Alcoff, 1991). This is especially true for migrating peoples, who are seen as already-Others. In an attempt to change the status quo, *Migrant World Making* highlights how migrants and migrant organizations utilize oral history and communication technologies to find and express their own voices, to build their own communities, and to craft a worthy, dignified existence in a globalized world.

Memory

Migrants often navigate new environments while carrying personal history, including memories of their family, relatives, friends, and community. Some, like undocumented Mexican migrants in the United States, craft a new world knowing they cannot go back to their home countries, and memories are all they have. We use the term "memory" not to engage memory studies or comment on collective memory; rather, we use this term to encapsulate how migrants negotiate tensions between remembering their past lives, who they were before having to migrate, the journey to another land, and the potential of the future in the process of world making.

Having faced displacement—in some cases triggered by political violence, economic devastation, and environmental catastrophes—all have left a past life and home. They face a tension Agnew describes as "the individual living in a diaspora experiences a dynamic tension everyday between living 'here' and 'remembering there'" (2005, p. 4). Later in "Social Identity in the Queer Diaspora," by Nathian Shae Rodriguez, readers will find these tensions are affecting Queer Middle Eastern migrants, who, while crafting new identities in online spaces, provide a sense of newness while also describing reservations when meeting people face-to-face. Self-identified Queer Middle Eastern males face a dilemma of revealing their sexual identity while being cautious of how they may be perceived by other Middle Eastern and non-Middle Eastern residents. It is a difficult tension to balance for these migrants who must navigate their identities around family, their community, and non-Middle Eastern communities.

Not only do migrants negotiate who they are individually, but they also remake who they are as a collective group. For example, Magan and Padgett (2021) cover the case of Bilal, a Somali migrant living in Chicago who exemplifies the process of identity negotiation when asked where they consider home. Bilal describes the United States as a second home and Somalia as a first home, stating, "The way I would define it is, first, it is your belonging. As long as someone is trying to make you as a second-class citizen, I don't consider it as a home" (Magan & Padgett, 2021, p. 107). Bilal exemplifies this tension of memory that migrants experience, negotiating who they were individually but also as a community in their homeland and who they will be in a new place.

Maintaining their culture while navigating a new culture, carrying their culture with them to new places, being able to practice who they are and who they will be—this is the migrant experience. Memories establish a connection between our individual past and our collective past (our origins, heritage, and history). The past is always with us, and it defines our present; it resonates in our voices, hovers over our silences, and explains how we came to be ourselves and to inhabit what we call our homes (Agnew, 2005).

Place

The final tension this volume engages with is place. As Cresswell (2009) writes, geographic locations become places when meaning is ascribed to them. The meaning of place is constructed personally and socially. However, there is disagreement over whether the rapid increase in human movement has destabilized static definitions of place, or is part of the process of defining place. For instance, New York City's image as a financial and cultural megacity is partially defined by its histories and legacy of migrations.

Beyond shaping the social meaning of a place, migrants also reshape the material conditions, landmarks, and relations of a place. For example, Alford et al. (2019) studied how migrant *manteros* (street vendor who sells their wares on a blanket) express agency as they source, compile, and sell merchandise on the *Barceloneta*, rearticulating their labor and place within global capitalism. In another case, Sun (2014) examines how the *nongmingong* (migrant workers from rural China) comprise a subaltern China, as they exert cultural influence in their new neighborhoods and even onto state media. Finally, material transformations and linkages occur even in the most quotidian of acts, such as cooking. Bailey (2017) notes how Indian migrants to the Netherlands literally carry their foodstuffs and develop a sense of belonging. In one case, Bailey cites the case of Varun, who is Indian, and his wife, who is Dutch. Varun literally intermixes foods so that "spice in his cooking is his way of place-making in a household that combines two cultures and two different foodscapes" (Bailey, 2017, p. 54).

Yet there is a tension in place—moving between places is treacherous, and new places can be unwelcoming and alienating spaces. Places left behind can be violent or destitute. At the same time, new places can hold promise while the nostalgic glow of former places grows as time passes. In many cases, there is an uncertain mixture. As the lyrics of the popular *corrido* by Los Tigres del Norte recite, "De que me sirve el dinero . . . Si estoy como prisionero . . . Dentro de esta gran nación . . . Cuando me acuerdo hasta lloro . . . Aunque la jaula sea de oro" (Franco, 1983). The song describes the pain of moving against the promise of prosperity, even if it's a cage made of gold. In unique and different ways, each chapter here deals with place—both in its material aspects and immaterially, through culture, online media, and the possibility of transformation.

Chapter Summaries: A Mosaic of Migrant World Building

The chapters included in the volume speak to the diversity of the migrant experiences across lines of time, space, and power and engage with the tensions discussed earlier in a variety of ways. In the first chapter, *"Ieri, Oggi, Domani*: Migrants' Being and Belonging beyond the Layers of Loss," De Sanctis and Khrebtan-Hörhager add European-African and European-Asian perspectives to the studies of migration. The chapter offers a rhetorical and cultural analysis of migrant narratives as an understudied area of European interculturality. Using open-ended, semi-structured interviews with migrants from refugee-welcoming center Casa Scalabrini 634 in Rome, the chapter addresses tensions of postcolonial, multiple linguistic and cultural realities. Here the tormenting past (country/culture of origin) versus the promising present (the host country) becomes an internal tension for the migrants with memoirs and longings of lost families and homes compared to aspirations and ambitions to build new communities in Italy. The authors analyze interviews with African (Senegal, Guinea-Bissau, Guinea, the Gambia) and Asian (Tibet and Pakistan) refugees. The chapter discusses the three main themes of the authors' narratives: homesickness and nostalgia about the past (*il passato*); challenges and opportunities of their Italian life (*la vita italiana*); and potentiality of moving forward with new identities (*andare avanti*).

In "Unengaged Presence: The Paradox of Refugee Voices on Humanitarian Organizations' Websites," Minkyung Kim and Melanie Kwestel address the tension between how humanitarian organizations instrumentalize refugees when communicating their institutional mission while actually excluding them from becoming engaged participants. Using a qualitative content analysis of organizational websites, the authors argue that while these organizations are doing the noble work of advocating for refugees, by virtue of having to appeal to funders and other institutions, their representation of refugees on their websites often extols the benefits of their organization in aiding the refugees in their resettlement.

In "*Por el Camino*: The Representation of Migrant Caravans on Instagram as an Aesthetics of Otherness," Fernanda R. Rosa and Arthur D. Soto-Vásquez address a different tension, between authentic migrant self-representation versus the common, almost stereotypical style of migrant presentation on Instagram. This style of Instagram representation is influenced by platform politics, such as using hashtags, seeking likes and followers, and hijacking trending topics, which the authors argue incentivizes a commodified, negative, and narrow representation. Using a qualitative content analysis of English and Spanish Instagram posts, Rosa and Soto-Vásquez define the aesthetics of Otherness as a process, resulting from the interaction between Instagram users' choices and the platform's features that establishes a distance from the migrants embedded in the design of the Instagram posts.

In "South Asian American Subjectivities: Searching for Agency among 'Forever Foreigners,'" Anjana Mudambi writes about responses to a controversial column in *Time Magazine*, which reproduced exoticized representations of South Asian Americans alongside anti-immigrant sentiments. Building on literature that seeks to understand nondominant subjectivities by examining the discourses of marginalized groups in the United States, Mudambi analyzes how the bloggers exercise agency to challenge exoticized representations that reinforce their positioning as "forever foreigners," in order to construct a collective subject position and to disrupts the existing colonialist framework. Through a vernacular discourse analysis, this chapter grapples with the tension of integration and belonging, as well as the representation of the complexities of how South Asian diasporic communities contest narratives of foreigners in the United States.

In "Transhistorical Resistance and Containment: Vernacular Discourses of Coalition at Fort Sill," Corinne Mitsuye Sugino deals with the use of Fort Sill in the state of Oklahoma to house immigrant children, detained on the U.S.-Mexico border. Community organizations decried the fact that the military base—which previously operated as a Japanese internment camp and relocation center for Indigenous people—would now incarcerate migrant children. Sugino considers the role of space and place in vernacular rhetoric and coalitional politics, arguing that the activism surrounding Fort Sill presented vernacular discourses of coalition that drew on a tension between recalling Fort Sill's history as a site of intergenerational and interracial violence and the present mode of migrant control. Also using vernacular discourse analysis, this chapter weaves histories of oppression and collective struggle across time that were staged at Fort Sill to tell a story about the United States as a hostile environment for today's migrants.

In "My Home/lands and Belonging beyond the Borderlines: An Oral History Performance of a Burmese Media Activist and Refugee in Diaspora," Eunbi Lee and Leda Cooks examine the ways in which M, a Burmese migrant worker, political refugee, and media activist in South Korea, narrates and negotiates various moments of his life. Through a post(de)colonial and performative reading of M's oral history, the chapter coalesces around three observations: the idea of "home/lands" for M as migrant worker and a refugee means something unique; M's development of a media network for himself and for the migrant community is a way to make meaning of the unique sense of home/lands; and that M's life both as a migrant and a media activist have shaped his sense of belonging. The authors demonstrate how M's life amplifies the prism of home/lands and belonging beyond borderlines, where the process of world making doesn't necessarily describe a migrant's transition between nations, but can define the ways in which migrants build local community while pushing against the violences of nationalism. Similar to the tensions of Mudambi and Cisneros's and Juárez's chapters, this chapter examines the struggles of integration, belonging, and representation for migrant world making.

In "Resisting Constructions of 'Refugee' Identity through Narrative Performances during a Colorado Refugee Speakers Bureau Event," Natasha Shrikant analyzes how refugee women from Iraq and Bosnia construct the "refugee" identity category through publicly performed personal narratives at a Colorado Refugee Speakers Bureau event. Through prioritizing the voices and narratives of refugees/asylum seekers, the chapter addresses tensions between ascribed versus self-constructed refugee/asylum seekers' identities, and the corresponding identity negotiations that typically result from such tensions. A discourse analysis of the speeches illustrates how these women voice a diversity of stances about moral obligations between themselves and certain hostile U.S. Americans they encounter and coexist with in daily life. The diversity of migrant voices and perspectives disrupts habitual discursive framings of "refugees" as homogenous invaders, victims, or illegitimate citizens, while sharing stories provides the narrators with an opportunity of building a sense of community among otherwise disconnected identities in contexts of displacement and hostility.

In "Online Latina/o/x Vernacular Discourse: CHIRLA's Crafting of Home and Resistance through Activism," Victoria A. Cisneros and Sergio Fernando Juárez explore the rhetoric of the Coalition for Humane Immigrant Rights Los Angeles (CHIRLA), a nonprofit that sprouted in 1986 in response to a national anti-immigrant movement that targeted broadly Latina/o/x communities. In this chapter, the authors analyze CHIRLA's Instagram posts and explore how their digital rhetoric works craft a home space and resist the negative perceptions espoused by anti-immigrant discourse while simultaneously affirming migrants' own identities and definitions of belonging and governance. Using Latina/o vernacular discourse, Cisneros and Juárez argue that Instagram serves as an example of pastiche, where Latina/o/x communities can deploy a syncretic rhetoric that provides a virtual home space, resists dominant notions of belonging, and creates opportunities to affirm migrant identities. In examining how CHIRLA crafts a home space for migrants online, this chapter highlights the tensions of representation and belonging.

In "Social Identity in the Queer Diaspora: The Use of Digital Media and the Middle Eastern Gay Refugee," Nathian Shae Rodriguez writes about Middle Eastern gay refugees/asylees in the queer diaspora of San Francisco who use a variety of digital media (social media, dating apps, and streaming services) to navigate tensions of national, ethnic, and sexual identity. Rodriguez finds that post-asylum, gay refugees/asylees negotiate pejorative and positive categorizations of a gay social identity and eventually articulate it online, even if unevenly to different audiences. Using in-depth, unstructured interviews, Rodriguez demonstrates how gay refugees/asylees preferred to build alliances with other gay men with similar Middle Eastern cultural backgrounds via digital media, although relationships were fostered in physical spaces. The chapter highlights the symbiotic relationship between the digital and the physical, showing a complex navigation of different spaces that are sometimes in conflict with each other.

In "You Are a Marked Body: Caught in the Fires of Racialization as an Arab Woman in the American Academy," Noor Ghazal Aswad uses a postcolonial autoethnography to call attention to the manner in which diasporic and transnational graduate students in the United States are implicated in pedagogical discussions of race, and problematizes how pedagogical spaces, while attempting to disrupt oppressions, invoke them. With a focus on belonging, she conceptualizes the academy as a border zone where racial constructions that regulate and define Others are legitimized and reproduced as othered bodies are interpellated as "subjects" of analysis. Pedagogical discussions of race encourage recentering U.S. notions of identity within a U.S. colonial imaginary. She contends that there is an ambivalence and quiescence that must accompany the praxis emanating from these academic spaces.

To end the volume, Walid Afifi and Michael Lechuga invite readers to champion migrant world making by focusing on the knowledge production and communication practices that emerge from the precariousness of non-belonging, both in scholarship and in our everyday lives. While the volume foregrounds the voices of migrants in current communication studies scholarship, the epilogue reminds readers that most migrants around the globe face a reality of economic and political exploitation along with cultural and social exclusion. This reality often remains obscure even to those in the fields of communication, rhetoric, and media studies who write about migrants and their experiences. Afifi and Lechuga demonstrate that nearly 99 percent of the most recent research in the respective fields lacks a migrant-centered methodology or epistemology. They offer ways that readers can engage in critical self-reflection and action on individual and collective levels in order to rethink our current research practices and relationships, prioritizing ones that champion migrant communities as they organize to create their own worlds.

REFERENCES

Abid, R. Z., Manan, S. A., & Rahman, Z. A. A. A. (2017). "'A Flood of Syrians Has Slowed to a Trickle': The Use of Metaphors in the Representation of Syrian Refugees in the Online Media News Reports of Host and Non-host Countries." *Discourse & Communication, 11*(2), 121–140.

Adorno, T. W., & Horkheimer, M. (1997). *Dialectic of Enlightenment* (Vol. 15). London: Verso.

Agnew, V. (2005). "Introduction." In *Diaspora, Memory, and Identity: A Search for Home,* edited by V. Agnew (pp. 3–18). Toronto: University of Toronto Press.

Ahmed, S. (2010). *Strange Encounters: Embodied Others in Post-Coloniality*. New York: Routledge.

Alcoff, L. (1991). "The Problem of Speaking for Others." *Cultural Critique, 20*, 5–32.

Alford, M., Kothari, U., & Pottinger, L. (2019). "Re-articulating Labour in Global Production Networks: The Case of Street Traders in Barcelona." *Environment and Planning D: Society and Space, 37*(6), 1081–1099.

Arriola Vega, L. A. (2020). "A New Agenda to Study the Guatemala–Mexico/Mexico–Guatemala Border (Lands) Region." *Journal of Borderlands Studies, 35*(5), 759–780.

Bailey, A. (2017). "The Migrant Suitcase: Food, Belonging and Commensality among Indian Migrants in the Netherlands." *Appetite, 110*, 51–60.

Baxter, L. A., & Montgomery, B. M. (1996). *Relating: Dialogues and Dialectics*. New York: Guilford Press.

Benson, R. (2013). *Shaping Immigration News*. Cambridge: Cambridge University Press.

Brewer, S., Tejada, L., & Meyer, M. (2022). "Struggling to Survive: The Situation of Asylum Seekers in Tapachula, Mexico." *WOLA*. https://www.wola.org/wp-content/uploads/2022/06/FINAL-Struggling-to-Survive-Asylum-Seekers-in-Tapachula.pdf.

Burg, A. V. (2019). "Citizenship Islands: The Ongoing Emergency in the Mediterranean Sea." *Media and Communication, 7*(2), 218–229.

Chavez, L. (2013). *The Latino Threat: Constructing Immigrants, Citizens, and the Nation*. Stanford, CA: Stanford University Press.

Cisneros, J. D. (2008). "Contaminated Communities: The Metaphor of 'Immigrant as Pollutant' in Media Representations of Immigration." *Rhetoric and Public Affairs*, 569–601.

Cisneros, J. D. (2017). "Racial Presidentialities: Narratives of Latinxs in the 2016 Campaign." *Rhetoric & Public Affairs, 20*(3), 511–524.

Clark-Ibáñez, M., & Swan, R. S. (2019). *Unauthorized: Portraits of Latino Immigrants*. Lanham, MD: Rowman & Littlefield Publishers.

Cresswell, T. (2009). "Place." *International Encyclopedia of Human Geography, 8*, 169–177.

Cretton, V. (2018). "Performing Whiteness: Racism, Skin Colour, and Identity in Western Switzerland." *Ethnic and Racial Studies, 41*(5), 842–859.

Drzewiecka, J. A., & Steyn, M. (2012). "Racial Immigrant Incorporation: Material-Symbolic Articulation of Identities." *Journal of International and Intercultural Communication, 5*(1), 1–19.

Edmund, C. (2020, January 10). "Global Migration, by the Numbers: Who Migrates, Where They Go and Why." *World Economic Forum*. https://www.weforum.org/

agenda/2020/01/iom-global-migration-report-international-migrants-2020/.

Flores, L. A. (2003). "Constructing Rhetorical Borders: Peons, Illegal Aliens, and Competing Narratives of Immigration." *Critical Studies in Media Communication, 20*(4), 362–387.

Franco, E. (1983). "Juala de oro" [recorded by Los Tigres del Norte]. On *Jaula de oro* [Cassette Tape]. Fonovisa Records.

Guidry, J. P., Austin, L. L., Carlyle, K. E., Freberg, K., Cacciatore, M., Meganck, S., Jin, Y., & Messner, M. (2018). "Welcome or Not: Comparing #Refugee Posts on Instagram and Pinterest." *American Behavioral Scientist, 62*(4), 512–531.

Hallett, M. C. (2019, September 8). "How Climate Change Is Driving Emigration from Central America." PBS News Hour Weekend, https://www.pbs.org/newshour/world/how-climate-change-is-driving- emigration-from-central-america.

Jaramillo-Dent, D., & Pérez-Rodríguez, M. A. (2019). "#MigrantCaravan: The Border Wall and the Establishment of Otherness on Instagram." *New Media & Society, 23*(1), pp. 1–21.

Katznelson, I. (2013). *Fear Itself: The New Deal and the Origins of Our Time.* New York: W. W. Norton & Company.

Khrebtan-Hörhager, J. (2015). "Italia–La Terra Promessa? Lampedusa and the Immigrant Crisis of the European Union." *Journal of Multicultural Discourses, 10*(1), 85–99.

Khrebtan-Hörhager, J. (2019). "Intersectional Othering and New Border Cultures: Lessons from Italy." *Women's Studies in Communication, 42*(2), 125–129.

Khrebtan-Hörhager, J. (2014). "Multiculturalism or Euroculturalism? 'Nomadism,' 'Passing,' and 'the West and the Rest' in German–Italian *Solino*." *Communication, Culture & Critique, 7*(4), 524–540.

Klein, N. (2017). *No Is Not Enough: Resisting Trump's Shock Politics and Winning the World We Need.* Chicago: Haymarket Books.

Koren, O., Bagozzi, B. E., & Benson, T. S. (2021). "Food and Water Insecurity as Causes of Social Unrest: Evidence from Geolocated Twitter Data." *Journal of Peace Research, 58*(1), 67–82.

Lauby, F. (2016). "Leaving the 'Perfect DREAMer' Behind? Narratives and Mobilization in Immigration Reform." *Social Movement Studies, 15*(4), 374–387.

Lechuga, M. (2019). "Mapping Migrant Vernacular Discourses: Mestiza Consciousness, Nomad Thought, and Latina/o/x Migrant Movement Politics in the United States." *Journal of International and Intercultural Communication, 13(3)*, 257–273.

Lindlof, T. R., & Taylor, B. C. (2019). *Qualitative Communication Research Methods.* Thousand Oaks: Sage Publications.

Linke, A. M., & Ruether, B. (2021). "Weather, Wheat, and War: Security Implications of Climate Variability for Conflict in Syria." *Journal of Peace Research*, 58(1), 114–131.

Magan, I. M., & Padgett, D. K. (2021). "'Home Is Where Your Root Is': Place Making, Belonging, and Community Building among Somalis in Chicago." *Social Work*, 66(2), 101–110.

McMahon, M. (2022, May 19). "Ukraine Is One of Us and We Want Them in EU, Ursula won der Leyen Tells Euronews." *Euronews*, https://www.euronews.com/2022/02/27/ukraine-is-one-of-us-and-we-want-them-in-eu-ursula-von-der-leyen-tells-euronews.

Morrison, T. (2017). *The Origin of Others*. Cambridge, MA: Harvard University Press.

Narea, N. (2021, March 22). "Migrants Are Heading North Because Central America Never Recovered from Last Year's Hurricanes." *Vox*. https://www.vox.com/policy-and-politics/2021/3/22/22335816/ border-crisis-migrant-hurricane-eta-iota.

Nikunen, K. (2019). "Once a Refugee: Selfie Activism, Visualized Citizenship and the Space of Appearance." *Popular Communication*, 17(2), 154–170.

Parenti, C. (2011). *Tropic of Chaos: Climate Change and the New Geography of Violence*. New York: Bold Type Books.

Prentice, C. M., & Kramer, M. W. (2006). "Dialectical Tensions in the Classroom: Managing Tensions through Communication." *Southern Communication Journal*, 71(4), 339–361.

Rasinger, S. M. (2010). "'Lithuanian Migrants Send Crime Rocketing': Representation of 'New' Migrants in Regional Print Media." *Media, Culture & Society*, 32(6), 1021–1030.

Risam, R. (2018). "Now You See Them: Self-Representation and the Refugee Selfie." *Popular Communication*, 16(1), 58–71.

Shi-Xu. (2009). "Reconstructing Eastern Paradigms of Discourse Studies." *Journal of Multicultural Discourses*, 4(1), 29–48.

Snyder, T. (2022, May 19). "We Should Say It. Russia Is Fascist." *New York Times*. https://www.nytimes.com/2022/05/19/opinion/russia-fascism-ukraine-putin.html.

Sommier, M. (2017). "Representations of Individuals in Discourses of Laïcité from Le Monde: Confirming or Challenging the Republican Framework of Identity?" *Social Identities*, 23(2), 232–247.

Stalker, P. (2002). "Migration Trends and Migration Policy in Europe." *International Migration*, 40(5), 151–179.

Sun, W. (2014). *Subaltern China: Rural Migrants, Media, and Cultural Practices*. Lanham: Rowman & Littlefield.

Toffle, M. E. (2015). "'Mal d'Afrique' in Italy: Translating African 'Cultural Idioms of Distress' for More Effective Treatment." *Procedia-Social and Behavioral Sciences*, 205,

445–456.

Tracy, S. J. (2019). *Qualitative Research Methods: Collecting Evidence, Crafting Analysis, Communicating Impact*. 2nd ed. New York: Wiley Blackwell.

United Nations High Commissioner for Refugees (UNHCR). (2021). "Figures at a Glance." https://www.unhcr.org/en-us/figures-at-a-glance.html.

United Nations High Commissioner for Refugees (UNHCR). (2022, August 30). "UNHCR Urges Immediate Support for Millions Caught in Pakistan Floods." https://www.unhcr.org/news/press/2022/8/630dcc744/unhcr-urges-immediate-support-millions-caught-pakistan-floods.html.

Utych, S. M. (2018). "How Dehumanization Influences Attitudes toward Immigrants." *Political Research Quarterly*, *71*(2), 440–452.

Acknowledgments

The editors of this volume would like to acknowledge the chapter authors who have contributed to this fascinating project. We are indebted to them for their insight, patience, diligence, and courtesy throughout the process. We would also like to thank the editorial team at Michigan State University Press for believing in this volume and providing the space for us to turn this collection of essays into a beautiful book. We especially thank editor in chief Catherine Cocks for her vision and guidance throughout the publishing process. We also would like to thank our copyeditor, Emily Dosch, for her work on the volume. We also have individual acknowledgments to make:

Sergio Fernando Juárez

I would like to thank my partner Lorane Bailon, stepdaughter Tatyana, and son Andrés for their love, support, and patience. I would also like to thank my parents, sisters, and friends for always being there for me. I'd like to thank Loyola

Marymount University Communication Studies Department for recognizing my passion and giving me an opportunity to do what I love. To my colleagues and friends Julia, Arthur, and Michael, thank you for your patience, commitment, and determination on this volume. Without each of you this book is at best significantly delayed and at worst completely stalled. Each of you have pushed this project to where we are now and I'm grateful for you.

Julia Khrebtan-Hörhager

My gratitude goes to my coeditors: esteemed colleagues and dear friends Michael, Arthur, and Sergio, for their professionalism, passion, and patience during this project. Thank you to my colleagues in the Department of Communication Studies, the Education Abroad Office at Colorado State University, and to the American University of Rome for supporting and encouraging unique opportunities of field work. I am thankful to the Scalabrini International Migration Institute in Rome and my amazing collaborator Dr. Veronica De Sanctis for their tireless efforts to make a warm welcome to refugee communities, and for enabling our cross-cultural dialogues. My profound gratitude goes to my beloved family, near and far, on both sides of the Atlantic—for granting me the power of multiple identities, for inspiring me to have many welcoming homes, and for always giving me their unconditional love.

Michael Lechuga

I could not do this work without the support from my first community, my family: Anais Lechuga, my partner, and my daughter, Maia Zen Yaretzi, thank you. I would like to thank my mom, Hilda Alarcon; she has always been my champion. My father and brothers—Tony Lechuga, Anthony Lechuga, and Chris Lechuga—thank you for loving and supporting me. Thank you to my colleagues in the Communication and Journalism Department at the University of New Mexico for supporting my work. Thanks to my coeditors, Arthur, Julia, and Sergio, for your patience and persistence over these challenging years. Finally, I want to thank those in my Albuquerque community for sharing their wisdom and teaching me about this land.

Arthur D. Soto-Vásquez

First and foremost, I thank God for the opportunity, health, and wisdom delivered to me through this project. I also must express my deepest thanks to my coeditors, who have become close friends in this long journey. To Sergio, Julia, and Michael—my sincere appreciation and gratitude. I also thank my colleagues at Texas A&M International University for their support of this project. Special thanks to my family—especially my wife, Allie Howland, my parents, Hector and Norma Soto, and my sister, Dr. Rebecca Soto, for their love, support, and patience. Finally, I honor my ancestors who migrated with dreams of opportunity, security, and a better life.

Finally, we acknowledge and honor the migrants whose journeys and stories help build a better world.

Ieri, Oggi, Domani

Migrants' Being and Belonging beyond the Layers of Loss

Veronica De Sanctis and Julia Khrebtan-Hörhager

O n the early morning of October 3, 2013, a boat carrying approximately 500 people sank a few meters off the coast of the Italian island of Lampedusa, leading to the deaths of 366 people. It was the worst maritime disaster in the Mediterranean Sea since World War II. Many more followed. In recent years, the processes of international mass migration have demonstrated an extraordinary evolution, both in the volume of flow and in their composition. The existing and growing body of evidence on migration and mobility shows that migration is related to broader global, economic, social, political, cultural, and technological transformations that are affecting a wide range of high-priority policy issues (*World Migration Report*, 2020). Within this complex scenario, over the last few years, Europe has faced the most dramatic refugee crisis in its recent history. It is a crisis of unprecedented magnitude that originates in Europe's neighborhoods, as well as the Middle East, and regions of Africa and Asia (and since 2022, Ukraine), leaving them rife with civil wars, violent conflicts, political instability, oppressive regimes, economic stagnation, and poverty (Carbone, 2017; European Commission, 2015, September 9). These factors have forced millions of people in troubled locations of the world to flee their homelands in search of protection and a decent life in more politically and economically stable locations, including the European Union.

In this context, southern Europe, especially Italy and Greece, has been faced with a steady flow of refugees and migrants. Italy is a case in point. Holding a position of crucial geographical importance in the Mediterranean, it is among the countries most directly affected by migration. Islands such as Lampedusa in Italy and Lesbos in Greece have come to be associated with the competing yet complementary political discourses of humanitarianism and securitization. The scale of the disaster on October 3, 2013, temporarily propelled Lampedusa to the center of global media attention and the European political debate (Dines et al., 2015; Khrebtan-Hörhager, 2015). Since then, immigration continues to be a contentious issue in Europe and remains on top of the political agenda across the region. While balanced debates on the issue are not absent, national rhetoric and public discourses on migration have often been dominated by anti-immigrant sentiments.

In addition to the de facto crisis of people being misplaced, and deprived of homes and hopes, there is an identity crisis they are facing—of losing agency, visibility, and voice—of becoming undesirable, stigmatized, and muted. Social integration and inclusion of migrants has always been an important part of the migration phenomenon; however, today it is a particularly complex issue. The relationship between migrants and the communities in which they reside forms an integral and fundamental part of the migration cycle. It is a process of reciprocal cultural adaptation of migrants and the respective receiving communities, which affects the degree of belonging that migrants eventually experience in the host country. That degree of belonging depends on not only migrants' activities within the host country but also the attitudes of the receiving communities, including their openness to the process of migration per se. In addition, the internet has enabled migrants to remain better connected to their sending communities (Chen & Choi, 2011). While the question of how to live together in increasingly diverse communities has become central in public debate and in "practices of everyday life" (de Certeau, 1984), it has also revealed an urgent and growing need for up-to-date academic scholarship on the subject of migration.

Various scholars have done a significant amount of work in the field of migration, focusing on the voices and identities of migrants (Aoki, 2000; Cisneros, 2012; Holling & Calafell, 2011; Juárez, 2019; Lechuga, 2020; Ono & Sloop, 1995; Soto-Vásquez, 2020). Despite their visionary contributions, the primary geopolitical foci of their respective scholarships have been in the Americas, often made synonymous with complexities of the U.S. southern border. We aim to contribute to the existing body of scholarship and enrich it by adding research about less-explored, understudied geopolitical localities, and the respective voices of migrant communities by adding European African and European Asian interculturality to the studies of migration. Specifically, we will examine and provide a comparative analysis of migrant narratives, originated from a series of interviews with a number of African (Senegal, Guinea-Bissau, Guinea, the Gambia) and Asian (Tibet and Pakistan) migrants and refugees in Rome, Italy.

Our chapter focuses on the general political, cultural, and historical context necessary for understanding the push-pull dynamics of migration, as well as the complexities and urgency of the current Humanitarian crisis. We use our research site—Casa Scalabrini 634 (CS634), a welcoming center in Rome concerned with issues of immigration and integration to provide the theoretical and methodological framework necessary for the interpretation and discussion of migrant narratives.[1] We present a collection of interviews centering the voices and the perspectives of the respective migrants (current and former guests of CS634), and focusing on three analytical categories:

1. *Ieri*/yesterday,[2] *il passato*: haunted and haunting memories, homesickness and nostalgia
2. *Oggi*/today, *la vita italiana*: challenges and opportunities in the new home
3. *Domani*/tomorrow, *andare avanti*: diasporic identities, community building, and cultural transformation

Those analytical sections are followed by a brief discussion of findings, and the project's implications for the studies of migration, the rhetoric of resistance, alternative epistemologies of studying multiculturalism, and communication studies at large.

The Context of Migration Controversies: The Old, the New, and the Mediterranean-Blue

Legacies of ruthless colonialism, political instabilities and oppressive regimes, major economic difficulties and extreme poverty, severe environmental threats and regularly occurring natural disasters have dramatically impacted rural economies of many West African nations. Places such as Senegal, the Gambia, Guinea-Bissau, and Guinea have driven many migrants to seek better opportunities in the *terra promessa* of Europe (Beauchemin et al., 2014). Considering that the Gambia is a former British colony, Guinea-Bissau is a former Portuguese colony, and Senegal and Guinea are former French colonies, it is necessary to acknowledge the significant role that European imperialism played in the frequent failure and the consequential postcolonial struggles of the respective West African nation-states. The Republic of Guinea-Bissau, for instance, has a history of political instability since its independence, resulting in the absolute deterioration of living conditions. In 1998 a civil war erupted in the country, contributing to the complete failure of state institutions and prompting tens of thousands to flee the country. National trajectories of other West African countries followed suit.

Similar push factors—political, economic, environmental, and cultural, intertwined with postcolonial legacies—regularly set Asian migrants on the move, as is the case of many refugees and labor workers from another former British colony, Pakistan (Yousef, 2013). In addition to the postcolonial complexities that trace back to European imperialism, Asia's own intracontinental tensions and controversies contribute to further instabilities in certain regions, such as Tibet, that have been occupied by the People's Republic of China since 1950 and have been producing significant migration flows. Systematic colonization and Sinicization of Tibet by the Chinese rule have manifested in a multitude of ways, including strategic Tibetan linguicism (with the purpose of Tibetan linguicide), ruthless religious suppression (despite the centuries of Buddhism, by 1965, out of more than six thousand Tibetan temples and monasteries, only a handful remained standing), and plundering of rich mineral resources and devastation of the delicate ecosystem. Nowadays, Tibetan youth are unable to read or write in their native tongue, and they are fully cut off from their cultural heritage (Craig, 2000; Goldstein, 1997; Klieger, 2002). As a result, more than 130,000 Tibetans have crossed the Himalayas to arrive in the neighboring countries of India, Nepal, Bhutan, and other parts of the world in the hope to save, and to continue practicing, their own cultural traditions. Similar to migrants from other parts of Asia (and Africa), many of them eventually reached the imagined El Dorado of the European Union. Sadly, an ancient European aphorism, "all that glitters is not gold," best characterizes Europe in its much debatable and arguably inclusive relationships with its countless migrant Others trying to reach its shores.

European multiculturalism and the very concept of fortress Europe have always been complicated (de Haas et al., 2020; Zanfrini, 2019). Even though often following the creation of the European Union (EU), many Europeans have hoped for a united, transnational, and multicultural totality, the reality of the EU revealed multiple issues, including hegemony of Eurocentricity as a defining principle of cultural inclusion, a lack of unified response to the questions of diversity, and immense (and increasing) intra-European differences in their response to the ongoing (and growing) humanitarian crises (e.g., Ahmed, 2000, 2013; Bhabha, 1994; Habermas & Derrida, 2006; Khrebtan-Hörhager, 2014, 2015, 2019; Modood, 2014; Ossewaarde, 2014; Wehler, 2005). The EU's attempt to be multicultural, unified, and inclusive failed on multiple levels and in various geopolitical locations. German *Willkommenskultur* (culture of open welcome) did not quite work as initially planned by German chancellor Angela Merkel and her overly optimistic *Wir schaffen das!* (We will manage this!). The crisis of Lampedusa was followed by a controversial period of *Salvinismo* and his infamous slogan *prima gli italiani* (Italians first). Great Britain chose a nationalistic course and insisted on Brexit. Orban's Hungary closed its borders to all non-Christian migrants, while former Austrian chancellor Sebastian Kurz declared that European open-door policy with respect to migrants was a grave mistake. Conservative French Marine Le Pen accused President Emmanuel Macron of promoting disastrous "*mondialisation sauvage*" (savage globalization) and suggested *Frexit*. In the meantime, thousands of migrants lost their lives on the way to Europe, especially in the Mediterranean, while the 2021 fire at the Moria refugee camp on the Greek island on Lesbos revealed once again both the salience and urgency of the topicality of migration in the EU. Located in the epicenter of the humanitarian disaster, Mediterranean Italy remains one of the most popular destinations for migrants from different corners of the world—and constitutes the geopolitical focus of this chapter.

Italy as a host country to major groups of migrants is a curious social phenomenon, given the historical transition of *il Belpaease* from the country of *emigration* to the country of *immigration*.[3] Throughout the nineteenth century and the first half of the twentieth century, Italy sent millions of working men, women, and children to virtually every corner of the globe. After World War

II, Italians found labor opportunities closer to home, shuttling back and forth to north and central Europe where they supplied the backbone of the industrial labor force for the postwar economic boom. By the late 1970s and 1980s, the migrant trends began to reverse and many former emigrants returned home due to the "economic miracle" that transformed Italy from an agricultural country to one of the biggest industrial powers in the world (Bevilacqua et al., 2001; Calavita, 2005; Colucci & Sanfilippo, 2015). Such change in economic structure had a direct influence on the country's traditional migration flows. Italy started attracting large numbers of migrants. The initial influx occurred at precisely the moment when northern European countries were closing their doors to economic migrants from poorer parts of the world. Quickly, Italy became the "back door" for migrants' intent to reach the rest of Europe, but it also became their alternative destination (Calavita, 2005). Especially when the EU-Turkey agreement (about the closure of the eastern Mediterranean route) came into force, Italy's location on the opposite coasts of the Maghreb region made it one of the most important arrival points in Europe within the central Mediterranean route (which goes from Egypt, Tunisia, and Libya to Italian shores).

Rapid transformation of Italy into the host country of mass migration resulted in an array of political, economic, and social issues. Typically, the Italian government intervened retroactively, after major humanitarian disasters and mass deaths already happened in the Mediterranean, and adopted a short-term "corrective" approach. In 2019, more than ever, conflict over the regulation of immigration was particularly dramatic, based on the restrictive approach of closing all the Italian ports to ships, carrying asylum seekers rescued at sea (Cesareo, 2020). The subject of controversial migration policies became a major topic in national rhetoric and public debates, and generated a polarization of Italian society, intensified by an oversimplified dualistic perception of migrants as either "good" or "bad" people, with arguable and highly disputable rights to sojourn in Italy or the EU at large (Ambrosini, 2020; Cesareo, 2020).

In light of the controversies, multiple organizations have attempted to respond to the challenging situation and to change the status quo with regard to migration (Zanfrini, 2020). Among them is CS634, whose mission is to promote the culture of open welcome and integration of migrants and refugees into the local community. Based in Rome, CS634 is a program of the Based in Rome, CS634 is a program of the Scalabrinian Agency for Cooperation and, run by the

Missionaries of St. Charles—Scalabrinians—a Roman Catholic religious order founded in 1887 by St. John Baptist Scalabrini that serves migrants and refugees in thirty-two countries worldwide (Baggio, 2019; Chiarello, 2013). Considering the urgent situation of the migration flows to Italy, and following the message by Pope Francis in which he urged Catholic Communities to open doors of churches, monasteries, and sanctuaries to refugees, Scalabrinians started in 2015 by transforming a former seminary into CS634. This organization leads a semi-autonomous program for refugees, including young adults and families. Independently run by the Italian government reception system, CS634 focuses on four imperatives, inspired by Pope Francis, regarding migrants: "Welcoming, Protecting, Promoting, and Integrating" (Pope Francis, 2017).

Since 2015, CS634 welcomed more than 260 beneficiaries and impacted more than 15,000 people through community outreach programs run at schools, various activities organized at CS634, and numerous fundraising campaigns. CS634 enables migrant education and integration by offering language courses (Italian and English), computer and web-radio literacy, driver's license training, sewing labs, and courses in social agriculture. CS634 also helps migrants create social networks with volunteers and local community members (Adeola et al., 2019; OECD, 2019). By doing so, CS634 attempts to provide an inclusive platform for refugees to share their own stories. Specifically, it aims to promote and encourage inclusive multicultural and intercultural dialogue in accordance with Pope Francis's message: "It is not about migrants. It is about all of us" (Pope Francis, 2019). Following the Pope's message, and in an attempt to avoid Alcoff's (1991) infamous problem of "speaking for others," we invited former and current beneficiaries of CS634—a group of migrants and refugees from African (Senegal, Guinea-Bissau, Guinea, the Gambia) and Asian (Tibet and Pakistan) countries—to share their stories with us in a series of interviews that provided rich and fruitful data for this project, and eventually enriched or extended the existing epistemologies and methodologies of migration studies.

Migration: Epistemologies and Methodologies

Migration studies have been at the heart of critical cultural and rhetorical theories, interlacing with the areas of performance ethnography, history, anthropology, political and media studies, and criminology. An impressive and growing number of scholars have studied and explored migrant discourses, with special foci on geographic and rhetorical border crossings and construction of immigrant bodies (Ambrosini, 2020; Calavita, 2005; Cisneros, 2012; Flores, 2003, 2020; Ono, 2012), intercultural identities and community building (Aoki, 2000; Ladegaard, 2012; Nakayama, 1997; Zanfrini, 2019, 2020), migrant voices and, more specifically, vernacular discourses (Holling & Calafell, 2011; Klieger, 2002; Lechuga, 2020; Ono & Sloop, 1995). Some scholars, actively engaged with migrant populations and ethnographic work, have prioritized—in Alcoff's terms—listening and speaking *to them*, instead of speaking *for them* (Alcoff, 1991), and have suggested new, inclusive epistemologies with regard to migrants (Delgado Bernal, 2001, 2002; Delgado Bernal & Villalpando, 2002; Yosso, 2005).

Aoki's (2000) and Lechuga's (2020) community-engaged scholarship, based on ethnographic work as well as collection, recoding, and interpretation of migrants' narratives as culturally rich texts that allow the reader to learn *from* and *with* others, greatly relates to our methodological approach, with a few differences. First of all, geopolitically, instead of the U.S.-Mexican topicality studied by the aforementioned scholars, and in communication studies at large, we concentrate on collecting, interpreting, and discussing a selection of stories of migrants from Africa and Asia. Furthermore, instead of examining narratives from a rather homogenous (ethnically and of nationality) migrant community, we provide a comparative discursive analysis of a cultural mélange of migrant stories from two continents, collected on a third one (their host). Our goal is not only to provide a diversity of voices and perspectives as well as their comparative cultural analysis, but also to examine social trajectories and identity transformations of the respective migrants over time. Therefore, we will be focusing on three time-segments of their lives and their stories: the past, the present, and the future.

The very process of collecting and recording the respective migrants' narratives has been challenging, given the sensitive nature of the matter. Many were reluctant to share their stories: some preferred to stay incognito, some were suspicious and skeptical, yet most of those who declined the invitation briefly explained that they simply did not want to relive the horrors of their previous experiences. Their pasts ranged from fleeing war-torn regimes, political persecutions, and social violence, to absolute poverty, loss of home, and hope. Ahmed reminds us that "the question of being-at-home or leaving home is always a question of memory, of the discontinuity between past and present" (2013 p. 91). In line with that, too often, in addition to that discontinuity, many migrants we approached chose a strategic amnesia about *un'altra vita*—a different life they lived and left in the past. Those who agreed to be interviewed, revealed that their *vita italiana*—a newly acquired Italian life—had a significant impact on their new, diasporic experiences and identities. For them, cultural bridging became a matter not just of living their lives differently but also of thinking differently about their identities.

Ultimately, the phenomenon of migration is not just about geographical dislocation of people; it is also about their emotional coexistence in multiple realities, the old (focusing on memory) and the new (focusing on community building). Bâ and Higbee (2010) explain the diasporic existence as a fluid consciousness between displacement (uprooting) and emplacement (regrounding). Mishra (2006) insists on cultural hybridity as a natural outcome of diasporic way of life, while Shome (2006, 2012) critiques hybridity as a sign of colonial power, in line with Bhabha's (1994) colonial critique of location of culture, and Ahmed's (2000) critique of the formula of "stranger-danger," in addition to other stigmas of postcoloniality. Dines et al. (2015) synonymize migration to the EU with a particular way of rethinking Lampedusa as the cradle of new, multicultural, plural consciousness. Anzaldúa's work (1987, 1990) invites the reader to consider a particular kind of *conocimiento* (embodied consciousness) and introduces a thought-provoking concept of a *mestiza* consciousness, while Braidotti (1994) focuses on the sense of perpetual movement of people and cultures and defines migrants as nomadic subjects. This theoretical and methodological framework informed our research project. Indeed, the stories of our interviewees illustrated various complexities and fluidities, as well as the potential of their cultural in-betweenness.

There is no "single story" (Adichie, 2009) of the thousands of destinies touched by CS634, and—although collected together—the narratives should not be read or interpreted as a rhetorical totality, given the diversity in the geopolitical, ethnic, socioeconomic, and demographic situations of the interviewees. Nonetheless, we clearly recognized three overlapping and almost universal themes repetitively addressed by our migrant narrators:

1. *Ieri*/yesterday, *il passato*: haunted and haunting memories, homesickness and nostalgia

2. *Oggi*/today, *la vita italiana*: challenges and opportunities in the new home
3. *Domani*/tomorrow, *andare avanti*: diasporic identities, community building, and cultural transformation

Ieri/Yesterday, *Il Passato*: Haunted and Haunting Memories, Homesickness, and Nostalgia

Sebald (1991) suggests that for those on the move, the very notion of home, or *Heimat*, eventually becomes a utopian and somewhat ephemeral construction, and notes that "home is unattainable not only because of the difficulties that arise from a confrontation between nostalgia and order, but also because home is nothing more than *le Chiffre* (a code) of a previous life" (p. 66).[4] The very title of Sebald's book is charged with an odd double meaning—that of a un-home-y home and, at the same time, an uncanny home.[5] Remarkably, migrants' narratives about their own places of origin—the homes they left, for various reasons, always out of necessity, prior to arriving in Italy—had distinct features of both, intensified through haunted memories, a hint of homesickness, and an almost infallible nostalgia. A thirty-eight-year-old Senegalese refugee Ndiaye, for example, confides that back in Senegal, despite her good education, her job as a nurse in a clinic, and two additional part-time jobs at two major hospitals (and being in charge of everything from vaccinations to assisting in a neonatal department), both her salary and job security were so low that eventually she saw no other choice than giving herself a chance abroad, in Italy.[6] Ndiaye recalls, "I had a good life in my country as I was living with my family. However, we were poor and we did not have many financial possibilities . . . so, in agreement with my family I decided to leave my country to look for a better life in Italy" (Ndiaye, personal communication, October 2020).

For twenty-eight-year-old Pakistani refugee Shabir, the idea of searching for better opportunities, combined with economic necessity and political turmoil in his own country has been the primary motivation to migrate to the EU. Like many other of his countrymen—Shabir reveals—the young man left his parents and siblings, and traveled to Europe via Iran, Turkey, and Greece, to join a relatively large and growing Pakistani community in Italy. He left Pakistan as a college student in 2015, because in addition to the realities of a stagnating economy, he and his peers experienced political repressions that forced them to leave the college—and for many, to leave the country and never come back.

Although forty-three-year-old Oumar comes from Guinea, a very different part of the world, his story is quite similar to that of Shabir and Ndiaye. When asked about *l'altra vita*, or his life prior to his departure, Oumar recalls: "I studied with the hope to work in my country, but I know that there was no future there. We wanted to stay, but there was no future. I liked literature, I wanted to become a writer. I also played football. I alternated those two passions." Oumar also worked as a warehouse keeper at a cargo and container port, both in Guinea and in Senegal. His situation changed drastically in 2007, during a national strike against the government. Oumar recalls:

> We united to demonstrate, but the government sent the military to stop the demonstrations. From that moment on, the problems started. A political party came to us to invite us to work with them. I collaborated with them. When there were demonstrations, we went to demonstrate. The military killed many people. The military entered various neighborhoods to arrest some movement leaders. (Oumar, personal communication, October 2020)

As a political activist, Oumar risked being persecuted by the government. In the midst of political and social disorder, Oumar's close friend, a policeman, urged him to leave immediately, to save his life: "My policeman-friend advised me to leave the country to avoid being arrested. Thanks to him and the people in Senegal, I escaped. I learned that some friends who remained in Guinea were arrested and killed, I know nothing about others" (Oumar, personal communication, October 2020). Oumar also explains that at that point, his destination was irrelevant to him; the only thing that mattered was to leave. In Italy, Oumar was granted political asylum and eventually received a political refugee residence permit. Today, Oumar does not think back about his country: in his mind, it did become *die unheimliche Heimat*—the uncanny, dangerous homeplace, synonymous with death.

For a nineteen-year-old Malam, from Guinea-Bissau, not only the potential of death but the actual death of his family became the signifier for his old home and old life. Initially, he wanted to study and live a happy life as a single child of doting parents. Malam explains:

> I did not want to leave my country. I was studying and living with my family, but after losing my family I decided to leave. I knew it was risky, but I couldn't do otherwise. I would rather not talk about it. (Malam, personal communication, October 2020)

He did not know much about Italy, except for its football (nowadays, *gli Azzurri*, the Italy national football team and four-time world champions), but did not think about it as a potential home. Assassination of his parents changed things, robbing Malam of two things simultaneously: his home and his childhood. Blicke reminds us that home is "a deeply sentimental nostalgia for one's own personal childhood; and the attachment to one's childhood shows itself in many ways" (2004, p. 133). In order to move on, Malam chose suppressing, forgetting, and letting go of the past.

For twenty-one-year-old Lamin, an educated trilingual migrant from the Gambia, the decision to leave his home was sentimentally difficult, because he left behind his baby sister and his doting parents. Lamin explained that unlike for others at CS634, in his case it was not economic and political reasons to leave, but problems with his family. At the same time, coming from a very community- and family-based collectivistic culture, Lamin used to work at his family restaurant back home, so problems with his family also meant problems with his employment. Lamin left home and traveled across seven different countries to Libya, with the help from his dear uncle. At that time Lamin's uncle worked as a baker in Libya, who gladly gave his then teenage nephew a warm welcome and a good job at the bakery. Yet, soon after, in 2014, the Second Libyan Civil War started, and Lamin's uncle was killed. A then sixteen-year-old Lamin left the country and traveled to Italy, crossing the moody Mediterranean in an overfilled dingy. What connects him to his past and to his former home is his close relationship with his *mamma*, who had encouraged Lamin to leave (Lamin, personal communication, October 2020).

For thirty-five-year-old Tashi, from Tibet, the reasons to leave his beloved home were numerous. He left Tibet for the first time when he was only eight years old. A son of Tibetan shepherds, Tashi considers himself fortunate because he had a chance to study at a Tibetan monastery, and when he was about to turn eight years old, he went to India to continue his education at a Tibetan school. After that, he returned to his home country, where suddenly everything changed after the Chinese invasion. Tashi recalls, "Chinese government officials thought I had returned to 'bring/promote democracy.' They doubted everyone, especially the Tibetans who had studied outside and were returning to the country." Naturally, the Chinese became suspicious of Tashi, so he was advised to flee, and his family paid an agency to get him out of Tibet. "They put me in a truck and let me out after we crossed the Indian border" (Tashi, personal communication, October 2020). With a falsified document, Tashi flew to Italy and arrived in Rome.

A passionate artist with a university degree in hotel and hospitality management, in addition to his native Tibetan, Tashi speaks English, Italian, Hindi, and seven other Indian languages. Leaving his "beloved and beautiful" Tibet was very difficult for him, but the challenging political circumstances left him no other choice. He further explains how after the Chinese occupation, the situation increasingly became unbearable for the Tibetans. "In many places, Tibetan schools have been closed and in their place there are now Chinese schools. Tibetan language and culture are increasingly marginalized" (Tashi, personal communication, October 2020). Today, Tibet is facing a multilayered cultural erasure—a fact that makes Tashi's homesickness and nostalgia grow stronger. When asked what he misses about Tibet, Tashi shared:

> Everything: The landscape, the culture, the ice that turns into water, the scent of flowers, the prayers from the monastery. The bells of the shepherds, the barking of dogs at animals, the beautiful colors of the flags on the mountain tops, the bridges colored with the five colors of the flags, the fresh, clean water. The green grass and above all the black curtain, which is home, our true home. (Tashi, personal communication, October 2020)

In a sobering volume with a self-explanatory title, *No Place like Home*, Von Moltke explains how the true value of home "can only be known by those who have left it" (2005, p. 5). Migrants' narratives in general, and Tashi's story in particular, are lived testimonies of this statement. Serving as a source of inspiration, homesickness, or painful memories, it is always the loss of home that defines social positions and voices of the displaced. Agnew's (2005) view of diasporic existence as deeply rooted in memory of home, careful self-reflexivity, and constant negotiation of identity, is also helpful for realizing that—deprived of their old homes—migrants have to rethink, reimagine, and recreate new ones. Therefore, instead of thinking about diaspora as displacement, the focus of discussion should be shifted toward connectivity; instead of imagining diasporic communities as mere extensions of ethnic or national groups, such communities should be constantly reconstructed and reinvented (Tsagarousianou, 2004). Although our interviewees came from very different geopolitical, cultural, and social backgrounds, and represented different demographics, religious affiliations, and even continents, they all shared the inevitability of homelessness and the consequent necessity to build a new home under the Mediterranean sun.

Oggi/Today, *La Vita Italiana*: Challenges and Opportunities in the New Home

Italy is famous for a myriad of components, ranging from fine arts, jurisdictional and economic institutions, to the world-famous cuisine and phenomenal football victories (Khrebtan-Hörhager & Burgchardt, 2019). Italy's history of the humanities and arts is contrasted with the frequent presence of discriminatory, often inhumane treatment of migrants in the country, trying to build their new lives. Racism has been named as one of the primary challenges in the way of building new communities. Senegalese Ndiaye has often felt discriminated against and intimidated in Italy. She recalls:

> On the bus, people get up if you sit down, they would not sit down next to you. I felt offended because someone also told me to go back home. One day I was in Tiburtina [the main train station in Rome] and I entered the bus, and a person was shouting at me on the bus, and I was with my baby in a stroller. Later, I cried a lot. (Ndiaye, personal communication, October 2020)

The youngest of our interviewees, Guinea-Bissauan nineteen-year-old Malam, also confessed that racism has followed him all the way throughout his journey, and not only in Italy. He describes the phenomenon as a habitual part of his existence, and emphasizes how racism "happens all over the world. Practiced by white people, I can't just say Italians, but also Americans and whites in general" (Malam, personal communication, October 2020). Guinean Omar's story also reveals a solid amount of racist treatment that he experiences in Italy, yet also demonstrates a different, welcoming side of Italy. While describing the way he experiences racism, Oumar recalls:

> I experienced racism many times, through people's glances, words, and gestures. Once on the bus, two elderly people accused me of not paying for the ticket, just because I was African. I replied in Italian, because I learned it well, and I also showed the season ticket. There were some Italian boys who called me 'brother' and welcomed me among them. (Oumar, personal communication, October 2020)

Oumar's story is particularly reflective of the complexities and controversies of Italy with regard to migration—the social phenomena that, like in many other countries of the West, including France, Great Britain, and the United States, starkly radicalized between the hardened fronts of those pro and contra migration. Therefore, the politics of racism—as undeniable and inhumane as it has been for many migrants—should not be generalized and understood as an Italian cultural axiom equally applicable to all migrants. When speaking about Italy, Pakistani Shabir, on the contrary, describes how "some people are a little tough, but I have never directly experienced episodes of racism" (Shabir, personal communication, October 2020).

Tashi's reflections about racisms in Italy are particularly curious, in relation to the current COVID-19 pandemic around the world, and given the fact that it originated in China. When asked whether there were times when he felt uncomfortable and/or experienced racism in Italy, Tashi admits: "Yes, but only in the period of the coronavirus pandemic, because I am often mistaken for a Chinese [person] and therefore blamed, at least at the beginning, for the spread of the virus. They treated me badly in a clothing store, saying not to touch the clothes." At the same time, Tashi also admits that he considers himself a very fortunate person—fortunate to be in a democratic country, with the values Tashi holds close to his heart, such as "the freedom of speech, and the respect of human rights" (Tashi, personal communication, October 2020). Although Tashi did not know much about Italy except a bit of history of the Roman Empire, football, admiration for the city of Rome as one of the world wonders, and found Italian an incredibly difficult language to master—especially given the drastically different language structure from that of his mother tongue—he still has only one word to describe his current, new, Italian life: "marvelous."

Commonsensically, the language barrier has been identified as a major obstacle by all the interviewees. Having to master that hurdle naturally lowered their chances of a smooth integration. In addition to that came another predictable by-product of integration—that of a social "demotion." Whether students, artists, bakers, or nurse practitioners, in their new environment of Italy, without sufficient knowledge of the language, society, and culture, and even their diplomas not being recognized by the host country (and the EU at large), they became a single demographic category: needy migrants—in need of food and shelter, social protection, integration, jobs, home, and hope.

Using Critical Race Theory, Yosso (2005) introduces the concept of cultural capital, which is different for various demographics, and argues that people of color have traditionally been deprived of cultural validity, agency, and power to enter the rhetoric. Building upon the scholarship by Anzaldúa (1987, 1990), who criticizes the lack of entry into the public sphere, certain professions, and academia for various marginalized groups; Delgado Bernal (2001, 2002), who urges to recognize students of color as holders and creators of knowledge; and Delgado Bernal and Villalpando (2002), who critically address the struggle of faculty of color to legitimize their knowledge in academia, Yosso urges the reader to acknowledge the discriminatory absence of voices of marginalized groups. The scholar also encourages to perceive those atypical rhetors as cultural assets, who can educate and empower traditionally marginalized communities through their stories. Those stories, in turn, can create inclusive communities and "nurture a culture of possibility" (Yosso, 2005, p. 78).

Sadly, as if to provide additional proof to Yosso's (2005) theory, the narratives of our interviewees reveal their original social, cultural, and discursive marginality in the host country. Building a new home in Italy has not been easy for any of them. Still, they often recall many acts of kindness and a warm welcome. In addition to the macro level of Italy as a host country, our interviewees referred to the micro level—CS634—as a particularly important place of social and cultural transition between their new, European sojourn, and the turbulent lives they had left behind. Oumar explains:

When I arrived in Italy in 2008, the reception system was less prepared and developed than today. I went through several centers until CS634 was open. I was the second beneficiary. Eventually, I had safe accommodation and the necessary help to move forward. I still visit them [CS634] regularly. I am Muslim, but I have been with them to see Pope Francis. (Oumar, personal communication, October 2020)

For Ndiaye, it was initially very difficult to stay at reception centers, where one could not cook independently and had a very limited autonomy. She tells us how the situation was particularly difficult at the beginning, when she did not have a job, yet she considers herself lucky to be joined by her husband, since many centers received families. When she and her husband eventually arrived at CS634, their situation changed significantly: "It is a place where one is independent in cooking and in the entrances and exits. There are always social workers who help clarify things. This is why we feel more protected" (Ndiaye, personal communication, October 2020).

The center is active in arranging various activities for its inhabitants, with the idea of providing them with professional training and social opportunities for better cultural integration. Ndiaye recalls: "They also helped me to find work and thanks to the activities and courses they organize there are many friendships with people of different nationalities and cultures" (Ndiaye, personal communication, October 2020). Tashi's memories of his time at the migration center are similar. They provide further details that allow us to imagine how what de Certeau (1984) defines as "practices of everyday life" are created and carried out by CS634. Tashi explains:

I had greater freedom of movement in and out of the building compared to others' reception centers and the possibility of cooking independently. There were many useful education and training programs and a room where you could play table tennis and be with the volunteers and friends of the house. Above all, events and activities organized by CS634 allow beneficiaries to gain confidence in establishing relations with local people. They also taught us how to save the money earned before leaving the house and thus be completely autonomous. (Tashi, personal communication, October 2020)

Practices of everyday life are so mundane, so taken for granted—we seldom think about their value, unless—like in the case of our interviewees—we drastically change that life. With it, the practices simply have to change— everything from a simple greeting in the morning, to a complex process of redefining oneself professionally on the job market, and all of that—in addition to being different—nationally, racially, culturally. And—as all our interviewees immediately admitted—linguistically. After all, in a discursively constructed world around us, language is not simply the means of communication and expression; it is also one of the focal constituents of culture, and an active agent of social construction of reality (Ladegaard, 2012; Thurlow, 2010; Xu, 2013; Zhou-min, 2013). Unlike English, whose usage is widely spread around the world, Italian is not an international language, and is a difficult one, too. For the migrants, mastering it becomes a necessity. They end up embracing—not only linguistically but also culturally and psychologically, often with great difficulties—what Nakayama (1997) in his work on diasporic communities wisely defined as *les voix de l'Autre* (the voices of the powerful *Other*)—in their case, Italy. The process is particularly challenging, given that—as our interviewees revealed—African and Asian migrants are often racially Othered by the host communities, and treated according to Ahmed's formula of "stranger-danger" from her groundbreaking book *Strange Encounters* (2000). Although there is still a strong tendency among the Italians and Europeans at large to see the world as the West and the Rest, migrants continue their linguistic, social, and cultural transformation in the host country. That transformation irreversibly changes their identities, their positionalities, and their voices—and promises a better future in their European home.

Domani/Tomorrow, *Andare Avanti*: Diasporic Identities, Community Building, and Cultural Transformation

For migrants, there is no universal formula of integrational success in Italy, the EU, or anywhere in the world. Universal is only migrants' attempts—to find, to negotiate, and to define—their post-migration identities, values, social positionalities, and aspirations. *Per andare avanti*—to move forward. That inevitable sense of *il movimento avanti* is usually accompanied by complex phenomena of cultural assimilation, fragmentation and partial loss of identity, or cultural in-between-ness and hybridity. Shabir tells us that he tries to live in two parallel worlds, in order to preserve his original Pakistani identity, that is why he purposefully chose a country with one of the biggest Pakistani communities in Europe. "I know many Italians, but I mostly surround myself with Pakistanis," he says. When asked about his identity and whether or not it has changed, Shabir responds, "Identity? No, it hasn't changed, but I certainly have an additional identity that adds to the others. I try to preserve my culture and not mix it with others, but I like to know other cultures." He then adds that his way of socializing massively changed: "When I lived in Pakistan I did not talk to people I did not know, now here I have learned to also relate to people I do not know" (Shabir, personal communication, October 2020). Shabir's perspective can be eye-opening, even inspirational for any migrants, who often pay a high price of literal and symbolic homelessness, and whose sense of belonging and cultural integrity are frequently compromised. Instead of the frustrating denial of their old selves for the sake of acculturation and cultural assimilation, the idea of plural and skillfully compartmentalized identities provides a more humanistic, more inclusive way of being and belonging.

Tashi's sentiments about identity are similar: the thirty-five-year-old Tibetan reveals, "I feel much more confident about everything. I learned a lot about Italian culture. That is why I feel much safer." Remarkably, regardless of his impressive accomplishments, Tashi is very humble, and in fact dislikes the very notion of pride: "I hate the word 'proud' because it means to be yourself above everything. So, you separate yourself from others, but this is not right. I am happy to be myself." And indeed, Tashi lives what he preaches, happy to be himself with others—and not above them. He actively participates in cultural events, organized by migration centers, contributing to "major activities on migrants and refugees together with the Italians, which also involve other reception centers; events on the culture of various countries, on food, on clothes." Tashi sees his main mission in preserving and promoting his native culture: "I work to protect Tibetan culture." His new community is multiethnic; he spends time with many Italians and other Europeans. In many ways, Tashi is the ultimate embodiment of a successful cultural mélange of mutually benefiting and enriching layers of identity. A talented artist and gifted calligrapher, Tashi acts like a cultural ambassador, representing and providing awareness about his original Tibetan culture.

Oumar's story also focuses on multiple layers of identity as the result of connectivity with Italian culture—and, in his case, with a new, Italianized understanding of self. He explains, "I spend time with a few Africans and many Italians. I often talk to Africans on the phone, but we meet very rarely." He also confesses to be very proud of his journey, everything he has learned in Italy, to arrive—in all senses of the word—where he is today, while understanding that the journey is an ongoing process: "I know that the Italians have worked very hard to get to where they are. The path I have chosen is not easy and for this reason I am proud, I am proud of the path I have mastered. And there are still many bridges that I have to cross." Oumar's reflections about his identity transformation and his "practices of everyday life" are fascinating:

> I became more mature than before; with experience, with greater patience; higher quality of life; I changed the way of doing, the way of talking; even my identity. Another continent, another life, different behaviors. In Guinea, we say: "Where you live reflects on you/The environment determines the man." (Oumar, personal communication, October 2020).

Oumar himself personifies the aforementioned Guinean proverb in his successful cultural adjustability, almost cultural chameleon-ism (Khrebtan-Hörhager, 2014). Today, he considers himself a cultural mix, with *italianità* being stronger than his original, purely African self. He identifies as "70% Italian and the rest African, because I took the ways of saying and doing; even when I talk to my friends, I realize how much my mentality has changed, but I don't mention it to them" (Oumar, personal communication, October 2020). Similar to others, Oumar's identities do not exclude but rather complete each other, enabling his still-belonging in his community of origin, and his already-belonging in the new, Italian public sphere.

Gambian Lamin also admits that his identity is changing, culturally in general and linguistically in particular, revealing the same complementary plurality: "Sometimes when I talk to my mother, I find myself mixing my own dialect with Italian. She teases me and tells me I'm becoming Italian" (Lamin, personal communication, October 2020). The fact that Lamin's own mother gladly acknowledges her son's cultural becoming and his successful embracing of *italianità* is particularly telling, since, metaphorically speaking, she personifies Gambian-ness, Lamin's original homeplace. Malam from Guinea-Bissau shares that he actively seeks and creates communities of local, Italian friends, explaining, "Yes, because I'm trying to integrate my culture with the Italian one and get to know Italy better" (Malam, personal communication, October 2020). As the youngest of our interviewees, and an orphan, haunted by horrible memories from the past, Malam sees Italy as one and only home, as—metaphorically speaking—the bridges to his past were brutally and irreversibly burned. In Malam's case, we still see the multilayered and compartmentalized identity—only in his case, he chooses to actively distinguish the compartment of his painful past, since he has no person and no place to return to, and the memories are too unbearable. In other words, Malam chooses to let go of the ties to his past and fully invest into building his present and his future.

Senegalese Ndiaye, on the contrary, embodies a more cultural rather than multilayered identity. This is not only because she still has a loving and caring community back in Senegal to get back to, since her "push factor" was primarily economic in nature—but also because, in addition to the significant difference in age with Malam (thirty-eight versus nineteen), Ndiaye did not come to Italy alone; she came with her husband. That allowed her to create a microcosmos of her beloved Senegal in the very heart of Rome. Their daughter was born in Rome and is growing up bilingual and bicultural. With regard to two homes and two cultures, Ndiaye best exemplifies a proverbial wisdom of "take the best, leave the rest." In fact, in her native Senegalese culture, there is a proverb that helps her make smart and sensitive cultural choices:

> A Senegalese proverb says 'Whenever you go to a new country, copy its culture well, but don't change the culture of your own.' For example, an Italian woman who drinks and smokes is not a problem, but if I get into this habit it's not good if I bring it back into my culture. (Ndiaye, personal communication, October 2020)

Ndiaye's understanding of her own, transformed identity is unique, yet at the same time similar to that of all other migrants, in its diasporic bicultural and bilingual features, its cultural chameleon-ism, and its performative compartmentalization.

To an extent, when in Italy, all our interviewees—and, as they told us, many others from their native communities—end up living what Mishra (2006) defines as diasporic living, a dual—or even triple and multiple—territoriality, combined with the creation of intra- and inter-diasporic relations, a fine cultural and psychological balance of living in-between. Some identities are a bit more hybrid than others (like those of Ndiaye, Lamin, and Oumar); some attempt to preserve their most original, most authentic self (like Shabir and Tashi), and others have no other choice but to give in to the power of *italianità* (like Malam). The politics of emotion always adds a significant dimension to their positionalities, reminding us about the intersections between places, memories, and nostalgia (Dickinson, 2015); the salient role of affect in relation to home and belonging (Ahmed, 2000, 2013); and a profoundly fluid consciousness of diasporic identities (Bâ & Higbee, 2010). Some of the migrants, haunted by that fluidity, become eternal "nomadic subjects" (Braidotti, 1994), while others skillfully master the fine art of cultural "passing" (Ahmed, 2000) and even "cultural chameleon-ism" (Khrebtan-Hörhager, 2014). More often than not, cultural multiplicity of migrant identities does not mean their mutual exclusions, or denial of one for the sake of another—rather, it implies mastering the fine art of embracing the old and the new, and finding a fine balance between the two. The stories of the interviewees also revealed the salience of creating inclusive spaces where human interaction brings migrant and local communities closer together, to move forward together: *per andare avanti, insieme.*

Migrants' stories, identities, and voices are unique and diverse. The bottom line is in the globalized and demographically turbulent society we live in, especially in the powerful *West* (represented by Italy and the EU at large, but also the United States and Canada), it is important not to treat all migrants as the undesirable and inferior Others from the world's *Rest*, in chronic need of Western pity. Communication is at the very heart of humanity, and inclusive multicultural dialogue is what defines true democracies, like Italy and other Western countries claim—and strive—to be, and to build.

Migration: Toward Human Faces and Human Voices

Today's Italy and Europe at large are at the crossroads of an immense and fast-growing migration of peoples and cultures, a challenging and complex cultural phenomenon that many historians, politicians, and rhetorical and cultural scholars consider the biggest European humanitarian crisis of modern times. Within this context, although there is a certain consensus that migratory pressure on the EU borders is the "new normal" in European border policy (European Commission, 2016, June 7), the immigration and asylum policies are overwhelmingly addressed only through the logic of emergency. While this feature is particularly compelling in Italian politics, the same holds true across many other European countries, where national governments have followed and embraced—rather than opposed—growing anti-immigration tendencies, often accompanied by populist propaganda. Based on that permanent state of emergency—and given the de facto multicultural moment in European history—the handling of the refugee crisis might have dramatic consequences for future actions, shaping the ways in which European societies cope with the forthcoming crises, transforming relationship between states and citizens, and contributing to the progressive erosion of fundamental democratic rights (Castelli Gattinara, 2017). In short, our core values of humanity and democracy are at stake.

In order to embrace the multicultural moment as a democracy, it is important to examine and extend the common epistemology of our global coexistence, as well as our relations between Selves and Others. Italian and European at-large epistemologies about Others are rooted in Eurocentricity and carry a solid amount of discriminatory colonial binaries. Naturally, in Italy and other countries across Europe, various news outlets routinely produce stories that create repetitive narratives of border security being at risk, perpetrated by countless migrants and refugees. The news often portrays the Mediterranean Sea as the cemetery of Europe, and detention centers as places of suffering of migrants and refugees, of endless human misery. According to the European Commission (2011), these narratives are considered to be the key sources of the common European epistemology, through which the continent's collective perception of migrants and refugees emerge.

Using CS634 as a social and cultural research site and locus of our case study, we have offered an alternative epistemic approach, focused on listening and learning *from* and *with* the migrants, instead of speaking *for* them. The chapter presents a discursive analysis of migrant voices as an underrepresented and understudied area of Italian and largely European interculturality. Through interviews with former and current beneficiaries of CS634, this chapter provided a snapshot of experiences of migrants and refugees, concentrating on three periods of their lives: their past in their countries of origin, their present situations in Italy, and their aspirations for the future. Through a thorough analysis of migrants' trajectories and their narratives, this chapter became a written testimony of brief oral histories, reflections about community building and inclusive multicultural practices, and a new understanding of migration: migration with a multitude of human faces and a multitude of human voices.

NOTES

1. For more information about the center, please visit the Casa Scalabrini 634 official website: https://www.ascs.it/en/scalabrini-house-634/.

2. Authors' research positionalities played a key role in their fruitful collaboration and a successful completion of this project. Dr. Veronica De Sanctis is a project manager/researcher at the Scalabrini International Migration Institute (SIMI) and a researcher at the Historical Institute of the Scalabrinian Congregation. Since 2017 she has assisted migrants and refugees in Italy with CS634 and in Mexico at the Casa del Migrante Nazareth (Nuevo Laredo). Given her continuous engagement with CS634, Dr. De Sanctis has established a relationship of care and trust with the interviewees as the premise for the successful collection of the interviews. Multicultural and multilingual scholar Dr. Julia Khrebtan-Hörhager is associate professor of communication studies at Colorado State University (CSU), and a director of the "Communication in Rome" Educational Program at the American University in Rome (AUR). Her expertise in the subjects of intercultural communication, cultural Othering, international conflict, and European multiculturalism, together with her prior experience as an interpreter have been instrumental for the interpretation and analysis of migrant narratives and voices.

3. Literally, "the beautiful country," the classical poetical appellative for Italy, commonly used since the Middle Ages, in the county and Europe at large to honor cultural, artistic, and geographical beauty.

4. *Die unheimliche Heimat* has a double meaning in German and can be translated as either "the un-home-y home" or "the uncanny home."

5. Authors' translation from the German language.

6. All the names of the interviewees have been changed in order to protect their privacy and to enable a larger degree of openness and trust.

REFERENCES

Adeola, R., Nyarko, M. G., Okeowo, A., & Viljoen, F. (Eds.). (2019). *The Art of Human Rights: Commingling Art, Human Rights and the Law in Africa*. Cham: Springer.

Adichie, C. N. (2009). *The Danger of a Single Story*. New York: Ted Talk.

Agnew, V. (Ed.). (2005). *Diaspora, Memory and Identity: A Search for Home*. Toronto: University of Toronto Press.

Ahmed, S. (2000). *Strange Encounters: Embodied Others in Post-coloniality*. New York: Routledge.

Ahmed, S. (2013). *The Cultural Politics of Emotion*. New York: Routledge.

Alcoff, L. (1991). "The Problem of Speaking for Others." *Cultural Critique, 20*, 5–32.

Ambrosini, M. (2020). *L'invasione immaginaria: L'immigrazione oltre i luoghi comuni*. Laterza.

Anzaldúa, G. (1987). *Borderlands/La Frontera: The New Mestiza*. San Francisco: Aunt Lute Press.

Anzaldúa, G. (1990). *Haciendo Caras/Making Face, Making Soul: Creative and Critical Perspectives by Women of Color*. San Francisco: Aunt Lute Press.

Aoki, E. (2000). "Mexican American Ethnicity in Biola, CA: An Ethnographic Account of Hard Work, Family, and Religion." *Howard Journal of Communication, 11*(3), 207–227.

Bâ, S. M., & Higbee, W. (2010). "Re-presenting Diasporas in Cinema and New (Digital) Media: Introduction." *Journal of Media Practice, 11*(1), 3–10.

Baggio, F. (2019). "L'opera della Congregazione Scalabriniana a favore di una migliore govenance delle migrazioni dal 1945 a oggi." *Studi Emigrazione, 56*(215), 453–466.

Beauchemin, C., Sakho, P., Schoumaker, B., Flahaux, M.-L. (2014). *From Senegal and Back (1975–2008): Trends and Routes of Migrants in Times of Restrictions*. (MAFE Working Paper 21, New Patterns of Migration between Senegal and Europe).

Bevilacqua, P., De Clementi, A., & Franzina, E. (Eds.). (2001). *Storia dell'emigrazione italiana*. Vol. 2. Rome: Donzelli Editore.

Bhabha, H. K. (1994). *The Location of Culture*. New York: Routledge Classics.

Blicke, P. (2004). *Heimat: A Critical Theory of the German Idea of Homeland*. Rochester: Camden House.

Braidotti, R. (1994). *Nomadic Subjects: Embodiment and Sexual Difference in Contemporary Feminist Theory*. New York: Columbia University Press.

Calavita, K. (2005). "Law, Citizenship, and the Construction of (Some) Immigrant 'Others.'" *Law & Social Inquiry, 30*(2), 401–420.

Carbone, G. (2017). *Out of Africa: Why People Migrate*. Rome: ISPI.

Castelli Gattinara, P. (2017). "The 'Refugee Crisis' in Italy As a Crisis of Legitimacy." *Contemporary Italian Politics, 9*(3), 318–331.

Cesareo, V. (Ed.). (2020). *The Twenty-Fifth Italian Report on Migrations 2019*. Milan: Fondazione ISMU.

Chen, W., & Choi, A. S. K. (2011). "Internet and Social Support among Chinese Migrants in Singapore." *New Media & Society, 13*(7), 1067–1084.

Chiarello, L. M. (2013). "Protecting and Promoting Dignity and Rights of Children and Youth Migrants Worldwide. The Best Practice of the Scalabrini International Migration Network (SIMN)." *Studi Emigrazione, 50*(192), 623–650.

Cisneros, J. D. (2012). "Reclaiming the Rhetoric of Reies López Tijerina: Border Identity and Agency in 'The Land Grant Question.'" *Communication Quarterly, 60*(5), 561–587.

Colucci, M., & Sanfilippo, M. (2005). *Le migrazioni: Un'introduzione storica*. Rome: Carocci.

Craig, M. (2000). *Tears of Blood: A Cry for Tibet*. New York: Counterpoint.

de Certeau, M. (1984). *The Practice of Everyday Life*. Berkeley: University of California Press.

de Haas, H., Castles, S., & Miller, M. J. (2020). *The Age of Migration: International Population Movements in the Modern World*. 6th ed. New York: Guilford Press.

Delgado Bernal, D. (2001). "Living and Learning Pedagogies of the Home: The Mestiza Consciousness of Chicana Students." *International Journal of Qualitative Studies in Education, 14*(5), 623–639.

Delgado Bernal, D. (2002). "Critical Race Theory, LatCrit Theory and Critical Raced-Gendered Epistemologies: Recognizing Students of Color as Holders and Creators of Knowledge." *Qualitative Inquiry, 8*(1), 105–126.

Delgado Bernal, D., & Villalpando, O. (2002). "An Apartheid of Knowledge in Academia: The Struggle over the 'Legitimate' Knowledge of Faculty of Color." *Equity and Excellence in Education, 35*(2), 169–180.

Dickinson, G. (2015). *Suburban Dreams: Imagining and Building the Good Life*. Tuscaloosa: University of Alabama Press.

Dines, N., Montagna, N., & Ruggiero, V. (2015). "Debates and Developments: Thinking Lampedusa; Border Construction, the Spectacle of Bare File and the Productivity of Migrants." *Ethnic and Racial Studies, 3*(38), 430–445.

European Commission. (2011). *A Dialogue for Migration, Mobility and Security with the Southern Mediterranean Countries*. Brussels: European Commission.

European Commission. (2015, September 9). *Joint Communication to the European Parliament and the Council Addressing the Refugee Crisis in Europe: The Role of EU*

External Action. Brussels: European Commission.

European Commission. (2016, June 7). *Communication from the Commission to the European Parliament, the European Council, the Council and the European Investment Bank on Establishing a New Partnership Framework with Third Countries under the European Agenda on Migration*. Brussels: European Commission.

Flores, L. A. (2003). "Constructing Rhetorical Borders: Peons, Illegal Aliens, and Competing Narratives of Immigration." *Critical Studies in Media Communication, 20*(4), 362–387.

Flores, L. A. (2020). *Deportable and Disposable: Public Rhetoric and the Making of the "Illegal" Immigrant*. State College: Penn State University Press.

Goldstein, M. C. (1997). *The Snow Lion and the Dragon: China, Tibet and the Dalai Lama*. Berkeley: University of California Press.

Habermas, J., & Derrida, J. (2006). "February 15, or What Binds Europeans Together: A Plea for a Common Foreign Policy in the Core of Europe." In *The Derrida-Habermas Reader*, edited by L. Thomasse (pp. 291–297). Chicago: University of Chicago Press.

Holling, M. A., & Calafell, B. M. (2011). "Vernaculars in Studies of Latin@ Communication." In *Latina/o Discourse in Vernacular Spaces: Somos de Una Voz, 17* (pp. 17–29). New York: Rowman & Littlefield.

International Migration Organization. (2020). *World Migration Report*. https://publications.iom.int/system/files/pdf/wmr_2020.pdf.

Juárez, S. F. (2019). "Chicana Feminist Ontologies and the Social Process of Constructing Knowledge." *Review of Communication, 19*(4), 291–308.

Khrebtan-Hörhager, J. (2014). "Multiculturalism or Euroculturalism? 'Nomadism,' 'Passing,' and 'the West and the Rest' in German–Italian Solino." *Communication, Culture & Critique, 7*(4), 524–540.

Khrebtan-Hörhager, J. (2015). "Italia–La Terra Promessa? Lampedusa and the Immigrant Crisis of the European Union." *Journal of Multicultural Discourses, 10*(1), 85–99.

Khrebtan-Hörhager, J. (2019). "Intersectional Othering and New Border Cultures: Lessons from Italy." *Women's Studies in Communication, 42*(2), 125–129.

Khrebtan-Hörhager, J., & Burgchardt, C. (2019). "Exhibiting Italianità: Anna Magnani and Sophia Loren as *Madri della Patria*." *Communication, Culture and Critique*.

Klieger, P. C. (Ed.). (2002). *Tibet, Self and the Tibetan Diaspora: Voices of Difference*. Leiden: Brill.

Ladegaard, H. J. (2012). "Discourses of Identity: Outgroup Stereotypes and Strategies of Discursive Boundary-Making in Chinese Students' Online Discussions about 'the Other.'" *Journal of Multicultural Discourses, 7*(1), 59–79.

Lechuga, M. (2020). "Mapping Migrant Vernacular Discourses: Mestiza Consciousness, Nomad Thought, and Latina/o/x Migrant Movement Politics in the United States." *Journal of International and Intercultural Communication, 13*(3), 257–273.

Mishra, S. (2006). *Diaspora Criticism.* Edinburgh: Edinburgh University Press.

Modood, T. (2014). "Understanding 'Death of Multiculturalism' Discourse Means Understanding Multiculturalism." *Journal of Multicultural Discourses, 9*(3), 201–211.

Nakayama, T. K. (1997). "Les voix de L'Autre." *Western Journal of Communication, 61*(2), 235–242.

OECD. (2019). *Working Together for Local Integration of Migrants and Refugees in Rome.* Paris: OECD Publishing.

Ono, K. A. (2012). "Borders That Travel: Matters of the Figural Border." In *Border Rhetorics: Citizenship and Identity on the US-Mexico Frontier,* edited by D. Robert DeChaine (pp. 19–32). Tuscaloosa: University of Alabama Press.

Ono, K. A., & Sloop, J. M. (1995). "The Critique of Vernacular Discourse." *Communications Monographs, 62*(1), 19–46.

Ossewaarde, M. (2014). "The National Identities of the 'Death of Multiculturalism' Discourse in Western Europe." *Journal of Multicultural Discourses, 9*(3), 173–189.

Pope Francis. (2017). "Welcoming, Protecting, Promoting and Integrating Migrants and Refugees." In *Message for the 104th World Day of Migrants and Refugees 2018.* Vatican City: Libreria Editrice Vaticana.

Pope Francis. (2019). "It Is Not Just about Migrants." In *Message for the 105th World Day of Migrants and Refugees 2019.* Vatican City: Libreria Editrice Vaticana.

Sebald, W. G. (1991). *Unheimliche Heimat: Essays zur österreichen Literatur.* Salzburg-Wien: Residenz Verlag GmbH.

Shome, R. (2006). "Thinking through the Diaspora: Call Centers, India, and a New Politics of Hybridity." *International Journal of Cultural Studies, 9*(1), 105–124.

Shome, R. (2012). "Mapping the Limits of Multiculturalism in the Context of Globalization." *International Journal of Communication, 6*(22).

Soto-Vásquez, A. D. (2020). *Mobilizing the US Latinx Vote: Media, Identity, and Politics.* New York: Routledge.

Thurlow, C. (2010). "Speaking of Difference: Language, Inequality and Interculturality." In *The Handbook of Critical Intercultural Communication,* edited by T. K. Nakayama & R. T. Halualani (pp. 227–247). New York: Wiley Blackwell.

Tsagarousianou, R. (2004). "Rethinking the Concept of Diaspora: Mobility, Connectivity and Communication in a Globalised World." *Westminster Papers in Communication and Culture, 1*(1), 52–65.

Von Moltke, J. (2005). *No Place like Home: Locations of Heimat in German Cinema*. Berkeley: University of California Press.

Wehler, H.-U. (2005). "Let the United States Be Strong! Europe Remains a Mid-size Power; A Response to Jürgen Habermas." In *Old Europe, New Europe, Core Europe: Transatlantic Relations after the Iraq War*, edited by D. Levy, M. Pensky & J. Torpey (pp. 120–127). London: Verso.

IOM UN Migration. (2020). *World Migration Report*. Geneva: International Organization for Migration. https://publications.iom.int/system/files/pdf/wmr_2020.pdf.

Xu, K. (2013). "Theorizing Difference in Intercultural Communication: A Critical Dialogic Perspective." *Communication Monographs, 80*(3), 379–397.

Yosso, T. J. (2005). "Whose Culture Has Capital? A Critical Race Theory Discussion of Community Cultural Wealth." *Race Ethnicity and Education, 8*(1), 69–91.

Yousef, K. (2013). *The Vicious Circle of Irregular Migration from Pakistan to Greece and Back to Pakistan*. Athens: Hellenic Foundation for European and Foreign Policy (ELIAMEP).

Zanfrini, L. (2019). *The Challenge of Migration in a Janus-Faced Europe*. Cham: Palgrave Macmillan.

Zanfrini, L. (2020). *Migrants and Religion: Paths, Issues, and Lenses: A Multidisciplinary and Multi-sited Study on the Role of Religious Belongings in Migratory and Integration Processes*. Leiden: Brill.

Zhou-min, Y. (2013). "Understanding Identity Discourse: A Critical and Sociolinguistic Perspective." *Journal of Multicultural Discourses, 8*(1), 79–85.

Unengaged Presence

The Paradox of Refugee Voices on Humanitarian Organizations' Websites

Minkyung Kim and Melanie Kwestel

I n the United States, nonprofit refugee organizations offer critical assistance to refugees during long and arduous migration and resettlement processes. These are organizations with "power" (Karam & Jamali, 2017, p. 461) to directly affect the lives of refugees through direct services (e.g., financial, social, and educational aid) (Andretta & Pavan, 2018; Ferris, 2005). In addition to assisting refugees' community settlement and integration, humanitarian nonprofit organizations (HNPOs) also advocate for refugees' welfare through participating in policy-related initiatives (Benson, 2019; Trudeau, 2008; Wolch, 1990; Yang & Saffer, 2018). These organizations may be locally based, with leadership and volunteers drawn from the cities in which they are situated, or they can be national or international in scope and leadership. As nonprofit organizations with 501(c)(3) status, they must compete for limited social and financial resources to fund their programs (Haski-Leventhal & Mejis, 2010).

As one of the primary means of digital communication, HNPOs and their organizational websites serve multiple purposes and are directed to various stakeholders. Among their aims are increased donor engagement and public awareness (Di Lauro et al., 2019; Saxton & Guo, 2011). Fundraising campaigns often include website components that highlight stories of refugee experiences with the organization (Audette et al., 2020). Within these spaces, the hardships and the experiences of marginalization that refugees face upon entry to the United States are shown only in relation to successful agency intervention. Their narratives, as published in these highly mediated spaces, can impact how other stakeholders view refugees (Yang, 2013).

We argue that highly mediated versions of the refugee experiences on these websites center the organization and its intervention rather than those that highlight agency in the resettlement process. In doing so, organizational websites keep refugees at the margins in mediated spaces, representing them as present yet unengaged. This chapter aims to add to our understanding of how HNPOs serving refugees communicate to other stakeholders on their websites, where refugee voices are only reflected to underscore their vulnerable position instead of being represented as empowered, self-sufficient individuals. The chapter is foregrounded in the question, How are the voices of refugees represented on HNPOs' mediated digital spaces, the websites, when organizations communicate about them to other stakeholders?

Refugees in the United States and HNPOs

Political upheavals, wars, and ethnic conflicts have led to waves of refugee migration for several decades (Castles, 2003; Edwards, 2016; Lacroix et al., 2015; UNHCR, 2015). Although the number of refugee admission grew significantly between 2008 and 2016, accepting and resettling refugees remains a political and social controversy (Krogstad, 2019). The refugees themselves are expected to navigate basic life necessities, laws and regulations, and the community (Andrade & Doolin, 2016) without the benefit of language skills, sufficient income, or knowledge of the culture of their new homes. Refugees often face social and cultural marginalization (Andrade & Doolin, 2016; Simmonds et al., 1983) and the increased possibility of community exclusion. In the United States, refugee migration and resettlement remains a controversial and politically charged issue.

The first refugee resettlement law was enacted in the United States in 1948 to provide a mechanism for legal immigration of refugees following World War II. Despite waves of refugees arriving to American shores, the first federal resettlement system was not put into place until 1960 (Zucker, 1983). Over the years, ad hoc efforts gave way to systematic, institutionalized resettlement programs that brought together private nonprofit voluntary agencies and the public sector in cross-sector, multilevel networks (Zucker, 1983). The enactment of the U.S. Refugee Admissions Program further systematized resettlement in the United States, and more than three million refugees have been admitted since the passing of the Refugee Act of 1980 (Kerwin, 2018). The high early employment rates, demonstrating the ability of refugees to become economically self-sufficient, revitalization of economically depressed communities in the United States by refugees (e.g., Akron, Ohio), and tax payments that outweighed monies received in public benefits (UNHCR, 2016), are among the reasons the U.S. refugee program is considered "one of the most successful humanitarian programs in U.S. history" (Kerwin, 2018, p. 207). However, for refugees the process of integrating into and becoming part of the settlement community is slow, and the need for HNPOs that offer financial and social assistance and advocate for public policies to benefit resettlement is great.

The perception of refugees changed with the election of President Donald J. Trump in 2016. In 2017, refugees were publicly described as "a burden and a potential threat" to the United States rather than as a source of "strength, renewal and inspiration" notes Kerwin (2017, p. 205). Furthermore, public stigma was intensified when refugees were framed as "terrorists and criminals," which questioned their willingness and ability to integrate into the United States (Kerwin, 2017, p. 209). The change in frames from asset to liability has made HNPO advocacy even more crucial. HNPOs successfully keep the issue in the public eye and generate funding from government and other sources (Ramarajan, 2008). Thus, they are critical collective action organizations (CAOs), advocating for refugee welfare and human rights, coordinating community services, and mobilizing diverse stakeholders to act on behalf of a vulnerable population (Collins-Jarvis, 1997; Knoke, 1990).

HNPOs and Collective Action

CAOs are enmeshed in networks that exist in the larger ecology of cross-sectoral relationships among different entities (Monge & Contractor, 2003) within the collective action space (Flanagin et al., 2006). These networks are the key contributors within the larger communities where individuals, organizations, and the media and policy systems coexist (Kim & Ball-Rokeach, 2006). In the United States, HNPOs that have taken on the cause of refugee resettlement include humanitarian organizations like faith-based organizations, government bodies, and local or international nongovernmental organizations (NGOs). The organizations have evolved from a collection of individuals advocating for a social cause to highly bureaucratized institutions mediated through the larger media landscape (Collins-Jarvis, 1997; Salem et al., 2002). Advocacy is a collective action endeavor in which NGOs and nonprofit organizations (NPOs) are key actors (Prakash & Gugerty, 2010). When collective action movements arise to advocate for refugees, they also affect community narratives about refugees and how they are perceived or accepted. For instance, Doerfel and Taylor (2017) showed that among social society organizations in Croatia, networks relied on international institutions such as USAID and the George Soros Fund to perpetuate narratives germane to their initiatives, thus serving vital roles in reproducing pro-democracy narratives during a period of political change.

However, a paradox emerges within organizations that take the dual role of an on-the-ground advocate and service provider dedicated to empowering refugees to move from helpless to independent, and a bureaucratized organization that relies on sophisticated stakeholder management of patrons, donors, settlement community members, and public agencies to sustain itself. To attract sufficient resources, they must present the organization as the agent of change. However, for refugees to successfully settle in their new homes, they need to change from service recipients to responsible, independent citizens.

In the pre-internet era, CAOs could control the narrative, because collective action initiatives that required high levels of commitment on the part of individuals or organizations were relegated to organizations that controlled sufficient resources to mount expensive collective action programs (Flanagin et al., 2006; Karpf, 2012). CAOs were able to frame the issues to benefit themselves and communicate them to evoke the desired response (Snow, 2013; Snow & Benford, 1992; Snow et al., 2014). The advent of social media facilitated a paradigmatic change in collective action. Instead of depending on organizations to develop frames, social media allows individuals to craft their own frames of discontent through their stories and lived experiences. The dynamics of social media have created a new, networked public sphere where these frames are generated, communicated, discussed, and acted upon without the mediation of CAOs (Bennett & Segerberg, 2011). Individuals can now choose how to interact and engage with CAOs, "crossing between private and public domains" (Flanagin et al., 2006, p. 365). They also have the option to decide on modes of interaction and engagement not previously available within the traditional collective action space. While two-way social media affords refugees the opportunity to control the narrative of their own stories—and organizational websites, which are highly curated online spaces controlled by organizations—may deny them that opportunity if the organization privileges stakeholders like funders over the refugees who are the recipients of their services. This prioritization often leads to unengaged participation of refugees within the collective action context.

Refugee Representation

Despite the success of HNPOS in resettling refugees, refugees are often the object of collective action without the benefit of becoming active actors in endeavors meant to assist them in their own resettlement. They are simultaneously portrayed as important social actors in the resettlement community while their voices are often marginalized (Chouliaraki & Zaborowski, 2017). Refugees, especially in media, are depicted as subjects of concern, needing assistance, often vilified, stereotyped, and viewed as hapless, passive victims (Anand, 2012). Malkki's seminal work on refugees of Tanzania revealed that refugees are considered "speechless" within political, historical, and cultural spaces (1996, p. 377). Refugees lack agency particularly in political contexts, and are "objects of migration policies, beneficiaries of assistance or individuals with traumatic stories" (Godin & Doná, 2016, p. 61). They live on the margins of the nation-state, where they are inhabitants but not citizens; they are key producers in the economy but not an official part of it (de Genova & Peutz, 2010). The prolonged silencing of refugees and their voices has reconfigured their position in society as "muted victims" (Rajaram, 2002, p. 248). Existing research underscores the unfair marginalization of refugees by the media, which inevitably affects perception of the settlement community (e.g., Horstmann, 2011). We assert that organizational websites, which provide information and shape narratives of refugee experiences, are similarly able to affect community perceptions.

Refugees on Organizational Websites

While refugees are empowered by HNPOs' direct services, their images on organizational websites are often out of their control. Despite the ubiquity of social media, which gives individuals the ability to post about their own lives and experiences, websites have yet to achieve the same interactivity (Lambiase, 2018). Instead, they remain highly curated spaces where collective action activities are largely framed by the organizations and where refugee representation can be limited and restricted to organizational frames. Websites are often used as outreach channels for organizations because they are direct and controllable (Coombs, 1998); provide organization-centered information and resources for the public (Callison, 2003); are spaces for communication with the public (Yang, 2013); and are where information about organizational activities are publicly displayed (Hayes-Smith & Hayes-Smith, 2009; Bennett & Segerberg, 2011).

From their earliest iterations, nonprofit organizations' (NPO) websites have been the public face of the agency and are an essential tool for reaching external stakeholders (Saxton & Guo, 2011). Waters (2007) identified information on programs and missions, a donation link, transparency (i.e., IRS forms and annual reports that show how donor money is used), and security as major portions of NPO websites. For instance, by 2016, fundraising content was found to be both visible and accessible from NPO home pages (Shin & Chen, 2016). Researchers have argued that mediated channels controlled by non-refugee-managed organizations serve to silence and marginalize refugees (e.g., Dahlvik, 2018; Leudar et al., 2008). While HNPOs advocating for refugees build their refugee aid agenda by mobilizing global networks via online spaces like their websites (Yang & Saffer, 2018), these spaces often create narratives that depict refugees as helpless and lost (Martens, 2002; Rajaram, 2002), or otherwise mute their voices (Sigona, 2014). For example, in many organizations' online spaces, refugees are primarily just the service recipients (Hahn & Holzscheiter, 2013). Their stories are mediated and curated by the organizations to underscore the agency's good intentions and successful interventions for refugees. It seems ironic that

HNPOS, which do such important and good work in helping refugees resettle in the United States, unintentionally portray refugees as passive actors when they appear on organizational websites. Organizational websites can be a powerful tool to bring refugee voices to the center of their narratives by showcasing them as capable, self-sufficient individuals who can benefit the settlement community.

Methods

To explore how HNPOS in the United States use their websites to highlight resettlement efforts, we conducted a qualitative content analysis of the websites of nineteen nonprofit organizations that provide refugee resettlement services. Content analysis is particularly useful to exploring the voices of refugees because they appear through texts of narratives that are situated within the larger organizational space. To explore the virtual organizational space, we limited the analysis to websites whose content is current, curated by the organization, and available without a paywall (Hayes-Smith & Hayes-Smith, 2009; Kousis et al., 2018).

Sampling

Our sample consisted of cross-sectoral humanitarian organizations (governmental, nongovernmental, nonprofit, religious, secular) operating in the United States that serve and aid refugees in a number of ways from migration to resettlement. We extracted a list of U.S.-based HNPOS (*n*=19) from Google's search engine (see appendix 1 for a list of the organizations studied). There is existing research on refugee centers in the EU context; though the United States has also admitted a soaring number of refugees since 1980 (Office of the Spokesperson—U.S. Department of State, 2016). This study focused on organizations headquartered in the United States to understand how their websites represent refugees when communicating with other U.S.-based community stakeholders who may hold resources important to HNPO sustainability. To identify our sample, the keywords we utilized in Google search engine included "refugee organizations," "human rights organizations," "humanitarian organizations," and "refugee aid organizations." We limited our sample to organizations that provide direct, on-the-ground services for refugees.[1]

Data Collection

The data collection stages were twofold. First, after we identified and finalized the list of organizations to study, we began with a general survey of the organizations' websites. This preliminary step enhanced our understanding about the overall landscape and configurations of the websites. We then began collecting narratives of and about refugees from the websites through a keyword search within each organization's websites, using the following terms: "story," "refugee story," "my story," "our story," "who we are," "what we do," "activities," "service," "leadership," and "values." We specifically looked for the cases of already settled refugees in the United States to restrict our cases to the resettlement community context. We also collected publicly available formal structures and records on the websites (e.g., board structures, annual reports, press materials).

Themes and Operationalization

After the initial website observation and discussion of our impression, we began to identify emerging themes. Through debating themes of our initial observations, we categorized and made decisions to "drop or retain choices" on consensus (Leonardi et al., 2010, p. 90). Then, for theoretical conceptualizations, we employed Thorbjørnsrud and Figenschou's (2016) work on migrants' voices in the news media and Johnston's (2016) conceptualization of engagement. Thorbjøsngund and Figeischou's (2016) work reviewed how the voices of forced migrants were published in news articles encompassing traditional to progressive media. Johnston (2016) views engagement as involvement and participation in organizational dialogue.

Based on the existing work, we operationalized voice as the stories that appear on organizational websites about refugees. We parsed out *organizational* stories of refugees and *refugee* stories of themselves. For instance, organizations tell two-mode stories where refugees are represented in two perspectives:

first-person (I) and third-person narratives (he/his/him, she/her/hers). By examining the voice representation, we examined the perspectives of their voice within the online organizational space. Next, we operationalized engagement based on the refugee involvement and activities within the organizational space. We specifically reviewed organizational activities and positions in the organizations (e.g., leadership, board members) to evaluate how involved refugees are in organizational spaces (see appendix 2).

Unit of Analysis

We analyzed a total of 772 stories (79 first-person stories; 693 third-person organizational stories). The unit of analysis was the entire story, regardless of length. Stories varied in length from a few sentences to a few paragraphs. In order to focus on the narratives and the contents, we analyzed the entire story rather than chunks of sentences or paragraphs that could skew the tone or message, or fail to capture the full range of representation. We excluded visual images or non-textual contents in our analysis. While photos are critical aspects of the storytelling process (Sánchez & Lillie, 2019), we focused on textual data to better understand the dialogic communication. We also excluded contents written in languages other than English because the primary stakeholders and aimed audiences of these websites are English-speaking settlement communities.

Coding and Reliability

We reviewed the data several times to identify key themes. We highlighted key quotes and developed theoretical memos that reflected our findings and the unique observed patterns of voices and engagement. The coding continued until theoretical saturation was reached and no new codes could be found. After multiple rounds of coding, the authors resolved disagreements and ambiguity through constant comparison technique (Glaser & Strauss, 1967) and discussion at each stage. To ensure we were in consensus about understanding the data, we continuously addressed any unique cases or further clarified any discrepancy in understanding each unit of the data (Leonardi et al., 2010). Through iterative comparison of each other's notes and findings from the coding, the constant comparative method gave us confidence that our coding is reliable.

Results

Our research question asked how HNPOs represent and engage refugee voices on websites. Our findings suggest that the depiction of refugee voices contains a paradox: refugee voices are present but not engaged. The engagement is limited only to endorse organizational agendas rather than to represent refugees' own experiences.

Refugee Voices as Storytelling for Organizations

Our findings suggest that refugee voices are present yet unengaged on organizational websites. The websites represent refugees as endorsers of organizational agendas. The websites relay stories of refugees, complete with descriptions of their migration experiences and the hardships they endure. However, such stories emphasize the role of the organization and its intervention at the price of the person's independent actions. For instance, a refugee portrayed on Church World Services said, "I received a lot of help from Church World Service. They introduced me to the Lancaster people and showed me how to apply for work. They helped me to improve my English." Refugees, even when they seem like they have a voice (i.e., speaking about their story via first-person voice), are transmitting an organizational message as recipients of services.

Featured stories include what the organizations did for refugees (e.g., house building, community outreach programs that organizations devised). Even refugees' "thank you" stories highlight the work organizations did for them, once again, self-portraying as grateful recipients of organizational services. One refugee said, "With resilience, ambition, strength within ourselves and support from LIRS, we got back on our feet." The organization's assistance is highlighted as crucial to the narrative, minimizing the refugees' own contributions to their successful acclimation to a new country and life. Even if the refugees share their narratives about their migration experiences or the difficult backgrounds they left behind, they reorient the focus to organizations and their agenda. For example, a teenage refugee from the Congo who received aid from Refuge Point said, "Ever since I was young, I loved education. When I met Refuge Point, they helped me to enroll in my final year of primary school." Refugees might be telling the story, seemingly having a voice in the online space; however, they deliver a message that is more about the organization, demonstrating the presence of voices yet unengaged.

When organizations tell the story using third-person perspectives to share the refugee narratives, these narratives are framed in terms of what services the organization provided and how refugees were saved by their work, mission, and commitment. For example, International Refugee Assistance Project published the following account on their website:

> IRAP helped him apply for resettlement via UNHCR and the Canadian government, drafting his referral documents, attending his interview with him, and submitting follow-up requests to expedite his case. . . . *We* referred him to a local organization that provides psychological assistance for survivors of torture. And *we* assisted in his application for a Canadian conjugal partner visa, including submitting a letter attesting to his relationship and the extreme urgency of his situation, which would enable him to escape to Canada to finally reunite with his long-term partner. (International Refugee Assistance Project)

Even when organizations depict a particular refugee and attempt to highlight the horrible conditions they endured, the focus remains on the organizations:

> Estefany, a 17 year-old transgender girl, was a victim of sex trafficking. . . . This is where USCRI stepped in. Afterward, Estefany was thrilled to receive a birth certificate and an identity card. Estefany's traffickers received a 16-year prison sentence. Today, Estefany is happy and safe. (U.S. Committee for Refugees and Immigrants)

The refugees do not possess full ownership of their voice or agency; instead, they are portrayed as grateful recipients, endorsing organizational agendas and promoting the organizations' well-intended missions.

Refugees Endorse the United States

Another pattern we found was the loyal voice of refugees in support of the United States. In their narratives, refugees endorsed the United States as the country in which they are free to realize dreams and accomplish goals that would be impossible in their home countries. Exodus Refugee Immigration stated, "Helene knew that coming to the U.S. meant an opportunity at a better life." World Relief wrote, "Because of the World Relief staff, volunteers and church partners, Jose feels empowered to pursue his dream of having a stable and secure life here in the U.S." Emphasizing the United States as a place for stable and secure life connects refugees and the organization to national ideals and insinuates that the organization is linked to a bureaucratized national agenda. In addition, such emphasis also alludes to the refugees as "good" immigrants who are assimilable. Upwardly Global quoted a refugee as stating, "I feel loyalty to the country that accepted and protected me, and I want to make life better for everyone by applying my skills. I am sure that a lot of immigrant job seekers feel the same." Similarly, LIRS published, "America opened its doors and welcomed us to its shores. With resilience, ambition, strength within ourselves and support from LIRS, we got back on our feet." These statements demonstrate how the importance of patriotic displays to organizational agendas becomes a narrative of refugees' loyalty and devotion to the host country (the United States). In return it becomes a public rhetoric that acknowledges refugees as continuing recipients and beneficiaries rather than as engaged, participating members in the organizational endeavors and spaces. While this may be a strategic control of messages for stakeholders— particularly funders and donors—it reifies the organizational agenda that excludes refugees as a meaningful partner.

Between Presence and Unengagement

Through our review of documents shared by HNPOs on their websites (e.g., annual reports, activity reports, leadership records), we found that refugees are often unengaged in organizational life in roles other than grateful supplicants. Only a very small number of organizations from our sample (one out of nineteen) engaged refugees as empowered residents of their new country. For example,

HIAS highlights how refugees can be active agents in their assimilation. A HIAS post talked about already settled refugees who obtained professional licenses to practice medicine and who now practice within their refugee communities. This type of coverage positions refugees as more involved and engaged partners of the organizations with active presence, voices, and the capacity to help newer immigrants within their community. The extensive coverage on their outreach endeavors demonstrate that they are not being co-opted for organizational gain but actually offering practical, more hands-on assistance to those who go through the same challenges they once had.

Refugees are often neglected in key decision-making roles, such as holding leadership positions or being part of the board. Only one organization, LIRS, has a former civil war refugee as the president of the organization. We could find no other instances of refugees serving as board members or in other leadership positions where they would have decision-making capabilities responsible for programming or operations. The organizations were led by homogenous groups of non-refugees. Moreover, white American leaders outnumber other leaders or board members. Lists display noticeably Western names that reflect the reality of limited opportunities of refugee engagement in decision-making positions.

The homogeneity of leadership is also reflected through their displayed qualifications. Professional leadership and board members are mostly individuals with advanced academic degrees with tenure and expertise in migration policy, refugee studies, and transnational governance; they are not refugees themselves. Church-based organizations' board members also included religious leaders (e.g., rabbi, reverend, pastor). Leadership may be diverse, but these individuals do not have personal experience as refugees. Findings show that perhaps the lack of refugee engagement is also structural and requires reconsideration of refugee representations on the websites. Ultimately, our findings demonstrate that refugee voices are present in restricted and unengaged ways, suggesting a number of organizational, cultural, and communicative implications.

Discussion

This study extends the ongoing arguments about marginalization and lack of voice among refugees in their new communities, particularly on websites, specific mediated collective action spaces. Results showed that refugee voices on these websites are present yet unengaged. The paradox is that while their presence underscores the organizations' mission-driven work to assimilate refugees into American communities, the refugees themselves are presented as passive, grateful service recipients rather than active participants within the organizational narratives. By focusing on websites where the narratives are carefully curated *by* and *through* the HNPOs, we seek to advance how such collective action space needs to be leveraged more effectively to truly *engage* refugee voices in a meaningful way. The work HNPOs do for the refugees is undoubtedly valuable and needed. Despite the HNPOs' important advocacy work and collective action participation, oftentimes such marginalized public display or representation could skew the refugee identity and narratives driven by organizational storytelling (Boje, 1991).

The Paradox of Voice and Engagement

Our findings suggest that organizational websites portray refugee voices as present but unengaged while the success of the organization is moving refugees toward independent living in their new country. HNPOs seem to sacrifice mission while prioritizing the donors and funders with means to support organizations' collective action endeavors to meet organizational needs for resources necessary for sustainability. However, we assert that organizations would also benefit from engaging refugees as active participants and engaged members on websites intended for fundraising and awareness. Website narratives could emphasize the success of the HNPOs' mission and advocacy work by showing how their work extends deeper into long-term refugee experiences. Nikunen asserts that the digital era can "challenge the dominant discourses of fear and the position of migrants and refugees as voiceless" (2019, p. 155). HNPOs can utilize their websites to encourage inclusive dialogue about refugees, facilitating engagement between the settlement community, funders and donors, and refugees. Alcoff argues that "speaking for others has come under increasing criticism, and in some communities, it is being rejected" (1991, p. 6). Our findings show that refugee voices are still caught in these in-between spaces where they are encouraged to tell a story without full engagement, suppressing their capacity as integrated, self-sufficient, and empowered community members. Right now, organizations speak for refugees, but they can shift so that refugees own their voices as active organizational participants and community members.

Refugee voice is complicated (Anand, 2012). A recent work on the marginalized voices of comfort women suggests voices need to be *invited* (Khrebtan-Hörhager & Kim, 2021). We do not argue that refugee voices are completely marginalized or silenced on HNPOs' websites. Rather, their voices are still mediated *by and for* organizational needs only. We contend that merely telling a story is not the same as having a voice. Echoing Colvin's (2018) argument, refugees experience an identity shift that alters the voice of their being and experiences, and only the refugees themselves can negotiate such identity transformation. Without the power to intervene, organizational portrayal on a curated website does not equate to enabling a voice to be heard. Engagement entails active participation in the dialogue between organizations and refugees (Lane & Kent, 2018), inviting them to be part of even the most goal-driven, curated spaces like the websites. HNPOs can engage refugees in the virtual spaces through recognizing them as partners and key organizational actors. Many HNPOs curate their mediated spaces to tell the organization's stories, mission, and accomplishments. Of course, such work serves refugees by enabling organizations to acquire needed resources. At the same time, however, curating stories in service of the organization redirects the focus back onto the HNPOs, reinforcing the hegemonic position of refugees as service recipients rather than partners. Hence, refugees remain as subjects of collective action instead of active participants. As a result, despite well-intended missions of HNPOs, refugee voices are co-opted for them and experience unintended marginalization and disempowerment.

Organizational websites and their representation of refugees and narratives are an important and influential communication channel. Narratives are an important tool for hearing "authentic lived experiences" of refugees (Colvin & Munz, 2020, p. 156). Representations are established through "language, in signs and symbols" that create shared meaning and understanding that provide a sense of identity and belonging (Hall, 1997, p. 3). For refugees, voice is a critical tool for their narratives to be recognized as equal and valuable (Chouliaraki & Zaborowski, 2017). Although strategically curated, the HNPOs mediated, digital refugee representation reveals how the refugee voice is revised, which becomes the hegemonic norm for organizations.

Organizational Hegemony and Mediated Websites

HNPOs' mediated organizational spaces demonstrate hegemonic norms of refugee voices and representation. Hegemony is a complex concept that exposes power imbalances in our society. It refers to the normalization of socially constructed ideas so that they become thought of as "common sense, common knowledge, human nature, and even normal" (Griffin, 2020, p. 234). Hegemony demonstrates the way certain concepts are defined as normal, then dominate societal thinking (Hoare, 1971). For example, media and organizations tend to have more power and control over identities of community members (Georgiou, 2006), which became the norm.

HNPOs in the United States exert hegemonic control of refugee voices as present while yet unengaged. Refugees do not possess the same agency to participate in organizational narratives. They are not fully involved in organizational framing within the collective action space and have little power to change how their lives are described online. The narration of refugee experiences has become the "prerogative of Western experts" where their ways of knowing and thinking are placed upon the refugees (Rajaram, 2002, p. 259). For instance, Dahlvik's (2018) work reveals that organizations have more power as resource-holding institutions and asylum granters. The power-driven relationship has denied refugees' representations in public discourse (Szörényi, 2006). Dutta argues that international organizations and their efforts in developing communities aiming for local empowerment and community-based participation actually work to "systematically erase subaltern communities" (2015, p. 123). For example, labeling subaltern communities as "undeveloped" suggested that they would be improved by Western interventions that "modernized" their lives (p. 125). Similarly, despite their good intentions, HNPOs still exert hegemonic organizational and cultural control over refugee narratives. As a result, the service-receiving perception becomes the norm and organizational hegemony is maintained.

These hegemonic norms of HNPOs result from the clash between organizational advocacy principles and external pressures for resources (Prakash & Gugerty, 2010). Many humanitarian organizations are driven by the interests of donors and political stakeholders (Risse, 2010); their need for financial, human, and political capital can compromise their advocacy-driven missions. These tensions have been documented in NPOs dedicated to serving clients with disabilities (Segal, 1970), or advocating for education (Gittell, 1980) or women's rights (Riger, 1984). Donnelly (2007) argues that humanitarian organizations have become ideologically hegemonic in international society. What we witness on their websites highlights the complicated dilemma HNPOs face between advocacy and systematic and structural irony. To support their organizational endeavors, refugees become the vessel for HNPOs to continue collective action work that appeals to a selected group of stakeholders. While HNPOs are expected to challenge the status quo of social injustice, their unengaged representation of refugee voices becomes a trade-off for organizations. We argue that to break the hegemonic norms, organizations must *engage* refugees in their communication and their programming.

Engaging refugees in organizational agendas is not a new idea. International NGOs and local organizations have long advocated for refugee participation in governance because the experiences of refugees are crucial in policy making (Johnson, 2016; Nyers, 2006; Panizzon & van Riemsdijk, 2019). However, cultural and language barriers make this goal difficult to achieve for grassroots and local refugee organizations (Clarke, 2014; Griffith et al., 2005). Yet their challenging migration and resettlement journeys suggest that refugees can be critical contributors to their new communities and the resettlement process (Kerwin, 2010, 2017, 2018). A recent study on refugee resettlement organizations revealed that seasoned refugees are indispensable brokers to organizing through offering cultural and language assistance (Kim, 2022). For instance, in South Korean refugee organizations, HNPOs focus on the organizational involvement of refugees on their social media, creating a discourse of empowerment, engagement, and inclusivity. Such efforts perpetuate HNPOs as powerful community integration mechanisms as multiple stakeholder groups are active audiences and consumers of digital spaces.

Websites, which disseminate information and burnish organizational reputations (Saxton et al., 2007), can become a critical space to represent refugees in meaningful ways that enhance other mission-driven activities. Such engagement suggests a promising leap forward for both HNPOs and refugees. HNPOs can leverage their websites to facilitate engaged communication between the settlement community and refugees, extending their ability to portray accomplishments for funders and donors. For refugees, the organizations can offer a space to be active participants and actors of collective action. For example,

Wright (2014) suggests that active refugee engagement could reconfigure their voice and agency as civic brokers in their own communities instead of becoming the subject of curated media coverage. Additionally, Morland and Levine's (2016) report revealed that refugees tend to be excluded in organizational planning (e.g., education) even when they are the ones receiving the services in the settled communities. Thus, HNPOs can facilitate engagement by encouraging refugees to take on programmatic and leadership roles that include them in decision-making. Ultimately, these new levels of engagement can be reflected on websites and in social media, demonstrating the active engagement of refugees and their voices. These mediated efforts can change the status quo portrayal of refugees as vulnerable and powerless. This in turn can facilitate inclusive communication among the resettlement community, media, and the larger society in which refugees live.

Conclusion

HNPOs do noble work for refugees. They are critical facilitators and brokers for successful refugee resettlement and community integration. By extending the efforts to their mediated spaces, they invite refugees to emerge from margins to centers as active members of a collective action community. Voice is a complicated process whereby individuals attempt to speak for themselves and be recognized (Nikunen, 2019). The thin line between present but unengaged refugee voices on organizational websites echoes what Alcoff (1991) defines as the problem of "speaking for others." Scholars have argued that humanitarian organizations should recognize that refugees are critical social actors with their own agency (Hynes, 2003; Korac, 2003; Trethewey, 1997). While refugees should be able to express their own goals and voices, presently they are unempowered on HNPO websites, requiring others to speak on their behalf (Steimel, 2017).

This is the dilemma facing HNPOs. They must make refugee experiences sympathetic and relatable to the settlement community and funders. Yet the mediation of refugee voices has inadvertently created stereotypes of who refugees are and should be, which ultimately marginalizes them. Our study suggests that HNPOs can more effectively utilize their websites as mechanisms to showcase refugee engagement to debunk stereotypical media narratives. Engaged organizing for refugees can challenge the status quo and reconfigure their voices so that they are no longer just social minorities needing assistance. Furthermore, such a step will help HNPOs to challenge the hegemonic norms of organizational bureaucracy and combat the unintended paradox of refugee voices. Refugees remain vulnerable to this day, and despite decades of research on their voice, we see little change. Organizational websites are critical platforms to invite refugees as engaged participants of collective action and organizing. HNPOs do meaningful work, and embracing refugee voices through engagement on mediated digital spaces can also empower their mission and the social causes to which they contribute.

Appendix 1. List of Refugee Organizations

- HIAS (Hebrew Immigrant Aid Society)
- Church World Service
- World Relief
- Lutheran Immigration and Refugee Service
- U.S. Committee for Refugees and Immigrants
- International Refuge Assistance Project
- Refugees International
- Human Rights First
- National Immigration Forum
- Upwardly Global
- National Immigration Law Center
- Exodus Refugee Immigration
- American Immigration Council
- Institutional Institute of New England
- Refuge Point
- Islamic Relief USA
- Women's Refugee Commission
- USA for UNHCR
- UNHCR

Appendix 2. Coding Scheme

THEMES	CODES	CODED FOR	EXAMPLE
Voice (Thorbjørnsrud & Figenschou, 2016)	First Voice	Use of first-person voice • Refugees telling their story (e.g., their life, background, family, interests, goals, and aspirations) • Refugees telling their experiences as refugees (e.g., migration journey, life before coming to the United States, the challenges that refugees experienced) • Refugees telling stories about the organizations (e.g., how the organization helped them, what the organizations do for them, how organizations were part of during their transition)	"RefugeePoint helped me to resettle to Australia in 2013. Here in Australia, I went to university and studied for a Masters in Nursing."
	Third Voice	Use of third-person voice • Organizations telling the refugees' stories (e.g., who/how they helped, what services they provided for refugees, how they were part of refugees' lives) • Organizations promoting their work through refugee storytelling. • Request for donation	"Abdullah and his family have begun to start their new lives, but they are many more families still in limbo all over the world. By taking advantage of Dropbox's services, IRAP is able to assist refugees, no matter where they are located."
Engagement (Johnston, 2016)	Engagement	Engaged as part of organizations through involvement and participation • Activity involvement (e.g., planning, decision-making) • Refugees' part of advocacy • Leadership participation (e.g., board member, organizational leader)	"Four decades ago, my parents fled a civil war in Sri Lanka. I was 9 months old . . ." (President of LIRS as a former refugee).

NOTE

1. An initial Google search yielded mixed results: nongovernmental, governmental, research centers on refugees, and policy institutions appeared. Research and policy institutions were excluded from the study as their interaction with refugees are in a different context.

REFERENCES

Alcoff, L. (1991). "The Problem of Speaking for Others." *Cultural Critique, 20*, 5–32.

Anand, V. Z. J. (2012). "The Complexity of Refugee Voice." In *Refugees Worldwide*, edited by D. Elliott & U. A. Segal (Vol. 1, pp. 19–38). Santa Barbara: Praeger.

Andrade, A. D., & Doolin, B. (2016). "Information and Communication Technology and the Social Inclusion of Refugees." *MIS Quarterly, 40*(2), 405–416.

Andretta, M., & Pavan, E. (2018). "Mapping Protest on the Refugee Crisis: Insights from Online Protest Event Analysis." In *Solidarity Mobilizations in the "Refugee Crisis": Contentious Moves*, edited by C. Ruzza & H.-J. Trenz (pp. 299–324). Cham: Palgrave Macmillan.

Audette, N., Horowitz, J., & Michelitch, K. (2020). "Personal Narratives Reduce Negative Attitudes toward Refugees and Immigrant Outgroups: Evidence from Kenya." *Working Paper*. https://cpb-us-el.wpmucdn.com/sites.dartmouth.edu/dist/9/452/files/2020/07/Personal-Narratives.pdf.

Bennett, W. L., & Segerberg, A. (2011). "Digital Media and the Personalization of Collective Action: Social Technology and the Organization of Protests against the Global Economic Crisis." *Information, Communication and Society, 14*(6), 770–799.

Benson, O. G. (2019). "Refugee-Run Grassroots Organizations: Responsive Assistance beyond the Constraints of US Resettlement Policy." *Journal of Refugee Studies, 34*(2), 1–18.

Boje, D. (1991). "The Storytelling Organization: A Study of Story Performance in an Office-Supply Firm." *Administrative Science Quarterly, 36*(1), 106–126.

Callison, C. (2003). "Media Relations and the Internet: How Fortune 500 Company Web Sites Assist Journalists in News Gathering." *Public relations Review, 29*(1), 29–41.

Castles, S. (2003). "Towards a Sociology of Forced Migration and Social Transformation." *Sociology, 37*(1), 13–34.

Chouliaraki, L., & Zaborowski, R. (2017). "Voice and Community in the 2015 Refugee Crisis: A Content Analysis of News Coverage in Eight European Countries." *The International Communication Gazette, 79*(6–7), 613–635.

Clarke, J. (2014). "Beyond Social Capital: A Capability Approach to Understanding Refugee Community Organisations and Other Providers for 'Hard to Reach' Groups." *International Journal of Migration, Health and Social Care, 10*(2), 61–72.

Collins-Jarvis, L. (1997). "Participation and Consensus in Collective Action Organizations: The Influence of Interpersonal versus Mass-Mediated Channels." *Journal of Applied Communication Research, 25*(1), 1–16.

Colvin, J. W. (2018). "Voices of Newly Arrived Refugee Women." *Journal of Intercultural Communication Research, 47*(6), 581–595.

Colvin, J. W., & Munz, S. M. (2020). "Voices of Refugee Women: Adaptation and Identification." *Journal of Intercultural Communication Research, 49*(2), 156–171.

Coombs, W. T. (1998). "An Analytic Framework for Crisis Situations: Better Responses from a Better Understanding of the Situation." *Journal of Public Relations Research, 10*(3), 177–191.

Dahlvik, J. (2018). *Inside Asylum Bureaucracy: Organizing Refugee Status Determination in Austria.* Cham: Springer.

de Genova, N., & Peutz, N. (Eds.). (2010). *The Deportation Regime: Sovereignty, Space, and the Freedom of Movement.* Durham: Duke University Press.

Di Lauro, S., Tursunbayeva, A., & Antonelli, G. (2019). "How Nonprofit Organizations Use Social Media for Fundraising: A Systematic Literature Review." *International Journal of Business and Management, 14*(7), 1–22.

Doerfel, M. L., & Taylor, M. (2017). "The Story of Collective Action: The Emergence of Ideological Leaders, Collective Action Network Leaders, and Cross-Sector Network Partners in Civil Society." *Journal of Communication, 67*, 820–943.

Donnelly, J. (2007). "The Relative Universality of Human Rights." *Human Rights Quarterly, 29*(2), 281–306.

Dutta, M. J. (2015). "Decolonizing Communication for Social Change: A Culture-Centered Approach." *Communication Theory, 25*, 123–143.

Edwards, A. (2016). "Global Forced Displacement Hits Record High." Brussels: *United Nations Refugee Agency (UNHCR) News.*

Ferris, E. (2005). "Faith-Based and Secular Humanitarian Organizations." *International Review of the Red Cross, 87*(858), 311–326.

Flanagin, A. J., Stohl, C., & Bimber, B. (2006). "Modeling the Structure of Collective Action." *Communication Monographs, 73*(1), 29–54.

Georgiou, M. (2006). "Diasporic Media across Europe: Multicultural Societies and the Universalism-Particularism Continuum." *Journal of Ethnic and Migration Studies, 31*(3), 481–498.

Gittell, M. (1980). *Limits to Citizen Participation: The Decline of Community Organizations.* Thousand Oaks: SAGE.

Glaser, B., & Strauss, A. L. (1967). *The Discovery of Grounded Theory: Strategies for Qualitative Research.* New Brunswick: Aldine.

Godin, M., & Doná, G. (2016). "'Refugee Voices,' New Social Media and Politics of Representation: Young Congolese in the Diaspora and Beyond." *Canada's Journal on*

Refugees, 32(1), 60–71.

Griffin, C. L. (2020). *Beyond Gender Binaries: An Intersectional Orientation to Communication and Identities.* Berkeley: University of California Press.

Griffith, D. N., Sigona, N., & Zetter, R. (2005). *Refugee Community Organisations and Dispersal: Networks, Resources and Social Capital.* Bristol: Policy Press.

Hahn, K., & Holzscheiter, A. (2013). "The Ambivalence of Advocacy: Representation and Contestation in Global NGO Advocacy for Child Workers and Sex Workers." *Global Society, 27*(4), 497–520.

Hall, S. (1997). *Representation: Cultural Representations and Signifying Practices.* Thousand Oaks: SAGE.

Haski-Leventhal, D., & Mejis, L. S. P. M. (2010). "The Volunteer Matrix: Positioning of Volunteer Organizations." *Journal of Philanthropy and Marketing, 16*(2), 127–137.

Hayes-Smith, R., & Hayes-Smith, J. (2009). "A Website Content Analysis of Women's Resources and Sexual Assault Literature on College Campuses." *Crit Crim, 17,* 109–123.

Hoare, Q. (Ed.). (1971). *Selections from the Prison Notebooks,* trans. N. Smith. London: Lawrence & Wishart.

Horstmann, A. (2011). "Ethical Dilemma and Identifications of Faith-Based Humanitarian Organizations in the Karen Refugee Crisis." *Journal of Religious Studies, 24*(3), 513–532.

Hynes, T. (2003). *The Issues of "Trust" or "Mistrust" in Research with Refugees: Choices, Caveats and Considerations for Researchers* (Evaluation and Policy Analysis Unit). Brussels: United Nations High Commissioner for Refugees (UNHCR).

Johnson, H. L. (2016). "Narrating Entanglements: Rethinking the Local/Global Divide in Ethnographic Migration Research." *International Political Sociology, 10*(4), 383–397.

Johnston, K. A. (2016). "Engagement." In *Encyclopedia of Corporate Reputation,* edited by C. Carroll (pp. 272–275). Thousand Oaks: SAGE.

Karam, C. M., & Jamali, D. A. (2017). "A Cross-Cultural and Feminist Perspective on CSR in Developing Countries: Uncovering Latent Power Dynamics." *Journal of Business Ethics, 14*(2), 461–477.

Karpf, D. (2012). *The MoveOn Effect: The Unexpected Transformation of American Political Advocacy.* Oxford: Oxford University Press.

Kerwin, D. (2010). *More than IRCA: US Legalization Programs and the Current Policy Debate.* Washington, DC: Migration Policy Institute.

Kerwin, D. (2017). *The Besieged US Refugee Protection System: Why Temporary Protected Status Matters.* New York: Center for Migration Studies.

Kerwin, D. (2018). "The US Refugee Resettlement Program—A Return to First Principles: How Refugees Help to Define, Strengthen, and Revitalize the United States." *Journal on Migration and Human Security, 6*(3), 205–225.

Khrebtan-Hörhager, J., & Kim, M. (2021, February 18). "The Invitation to Learn the Uncomfortable Truth about Comfort Women" [Online Post]. National Communication Association Communication Currents. https://www.natcom.org/communication-currents/invitation-learn-uncomfortable-truth-about-comfort-women.

Kim, M. (2022). "From Challenges to Opportunities: Interorganizational Resilience Brokering for Refugee Communities during COVID-19." Dissertation. New Brunswick: Rutgers University.

Kim, Y., & Ball-Rokeach, S. (2006). "Civic Engagement from a Communication Infrastructure Perspective." *Communication Theory, 16*, 173–197.

Knoke, D. (1990). *Organizing for Collective Action: The Political Economies of Associations.* New York: Aldine de Gruyter.

Korac, M. (2003). "Integration and How We Facilitate It: A Comparative Study of the Settlement Experiences of Refugees in Italy and the Netherlands." *Sociology, 37*(1), 51–68.

Kousis, M., Giugni, M., & Lahusen, C. (2018). "Action Organization Analysis: Extending Protest Event Analysis Using Hubs-Retrieved Websites." *American Behavioral Scientist, 62*(6), 739–757.

Krogstad, J. M. (2019). "Key Facts about Refugees to the U.S." Pew Research Center. https://www.pewresearch.org/fact-tank/2019/10/07/key-facts-about-refugees-to-the-u-s/.

Lacroix, M., Baffoe, M., & Liguori, M. (2015). "Refugee Community Organizations in Canada: From the Margins to the Mainstream? A Challenge and Opportunity for Social Workers." *International Journal of Social Welfare, 34*, 62–72.

Lambiase, J. J. (2018). "Searching for City Hall, Digital Democracy, and Public-Making Rhetoric: U.S. Municipal Websites and Citizen Engagement." *Journal of Public Interest Communications, 2*(1), 85–106.

Lane, A., & Kent, M. L. (2018). "Dialogic Engagement." In *The Handbook of Communication Engagement*, edited by K. A. Johnston & M. Taylor (pp. 61–72). Hoboken: John Wiley & Sons, Inc.

Leonardi, P. M., Treem, J. W., & Jackson, M. H. (2010). "The Connectivity Paradox: Using Technology to Both Decrease and Increase Perceptions of Distance in Distributed Work Arrangements." *Journal of Applied Communication Research, 38*(1), 85–105.

Leudar, I., Hayes, J., Nekvapil, J., & Turner-Baker, J. (2008). "Hostility Themes in Media, Community and Refugee Narratives." *Discourse & Society, 19*(2), 187–221.

Malkki, L. H. (1996). "Speechless Emissaries: Refugees, Humanitarianism, and Dehistoricization." *Cultural Anthropology, 11*(3), 377–404.

Martens, K. (2002). "Mission Impossible? Defining Nongovernmental Organizations." *Voluntas: International Journal of Voluntary and Nonprofit Organizations, 13*(3), 271–285.

Monge, P. R., & Contractor, N. S. (2003). *Theories of Communication Networks.* Oxford: Oxford University Press.

Morland, L., & Levine, T. (2016). "Collaborating with Refugee Resettlement Organizations." *YC Young Children, 71*(4), 69–75.

Nikunen, K. (2019). "Once a Refugee: Selfie Activism, Visualized Citizenship and the Space of Appearance." *Popular Communication, 17*(2), 154–170.

Nyers, P. (2006). *Rethinking Refugees: Beyond States of Emergency.* New York: Routledge.

Office of the Spokesperson. U.S. Department of State. (2016, January 13). [Government Website]. U.S. Department of State. https://2009-2017.state.gov/secretary/ remarks/2016/01/251185.htm.

Panizzon, M., & van Riemsdijk, M. (2019). "Introduction to Special Issue: Migration Governance in an Era of Large Movements: A Multi-level Approach." *Journal of Ethnic and Migration Studies, 45*(8), 1225–1241.

Prakash, A., & Gugerty, M. K. (2010). "Advocacy Organizations and Collective Action: An Introduction." In *Advocacy Organizations and Collective Action,* edited by A. Prakash & M. K. Gugerty (pp. 1–28). Cambridge: Cambridge University Press.

Rajaram, P. K. (2002). "Humanitarianism and Representations of the Refugees." *Journal of Refugee Studies, 15*(3), 247–264.

Ramarajan, L. (2008). "In the Space between Employees and Clients: The Impact of Organizational Context on a Refugee Program in Sierra Leone." *Refugee, 25*(1), 35–43.

Riger, S. (1984). "Vehicles for Empowerment: The Case of Feminist Movement Organizations." *Prevention in Human Services, 9,* 99–117.

Risse, T. (2010). "Rethinking Advocacy Organizations? A Critical Comment." In *Advocacy Organizations and Collective Action,* edited by A. Prakash & M. K. Gugerty (pp. 238–294). Cambridge: Cambridge University Press.

Salem, D. A., Foster-Fishman, P. G., & Goodkind, J. R. (2002). "The Adoption of Innovation in Collective Action Organizations." *American Journal of Community Psychology, 30*(5), 681–710.

Sánchez, V. S., & Lillie, H. (2019). "And Then the War Came: A Content Analysis of

Resilience Processes in the Narratives of Refugees from Humans of New York." *International Journal of Communication, 13,* 4240–4260.

Saxton, G. D., & Guo, C. (2011). "Accountability Online: Understanding the Web-Based Accountability Practices of Nonprofit Organizations." *Nonprofit and Voluntary Sector Quarterly, 40*(2), 270–295.

Saxton, G. D., Guo, S. C., & Brown, W. A. (2007). "New Dimensions of Nonprofit Responsiveness: The Application and Promise of Internet-Based Technologies." *Public Performance & Management Review, 31*(2), 144–173.

Segal, R. M. (1970). *Mental Retardation and Social Action: A Study of the Associations for Retarded Children as a Force for Social Change.* Springfield: Thomas Books.

Shin, N., & Chen, Q. (2016). "An Exploratory Study of Nonprofit Organisation's Use of the Internet for Communication and Fundraising." *International Journal of Technology, Policy, & Management, 16*(1), 32–44.

Sigona, N. (2014). "The Politics of Refugee Voices: Representations, Narratives and Memories." In *The Oxford Handbook of Refugee and Forced Migration Studies,* edited by E. Fiddian-Qasmiyeh, G. Loescher & N. Sigona (pp. 369–382). Oxford: Oxford University Press.

Simmonds, S., Vaughan, P., & Gunn, S. W. (Eds.). (1983). *Refugee Community Health Care.* Oxford: Oxford University Press.

Snow, D. A. (2013). "Framing Processes, Ideology, and Discursive Fields: The Blackwell Companion to Social Movements." In *The Wiley-Blackwell Encyclopedia of Social and Political Movements,* edited by D. A. Snow, D. della Porta, B. Klandermans & D. McAdam (pp. 1–6). London: Blackwell Publishing Ltd.

Snow, D. A., & Benford, R. D. (1992). *Frontiers in Social Movement Theory.* New Haven: Yale University Press.

Snow, D. A., Benford, R. D., McCammon, H. J., Hewitt, L., & Fitzgerald, S. (2014). "The Emergence, Development, and Future of the Framing Perspective: 25+ Years since 'Frame Alignment.'" *An International Quarterly, 19*(1), 23–45.

Steimel, S. (2017). *Negotiating Refugee Empowerment(s) in Resettlement Organizations.* Lincoln: Digital Commons at University of Nebraska-Lincoln.

Szörényi, A. (2006). "The Images Speak for Themselves? Reading Refugee Coffee-Table Books." *Visual Studies, 21*(1), 24–41.

Thorbjørnsrud, K., & Figenschou, T. U. (2016). "Do Marginalized Sources Matter? A Comparative Analysis of Irregular Migrant Voice in Western Media." *Journalism Studies, 17*(3), 337–355.

Trethewey, A. (1997). "Resistance, Identity, and Empowerment: A Postmodern Feminist

Analysis of Clients in a Human Service Organization." *Communication Monographs*, 64(4), 281–301.

Trudeau, D. (2008). "Junior Partner or Empowered Community? The Role of Non-profit Social Service Providers amidst State Restructuring in the U.S." *Urban Studies*, 45(13), 2805–2927.

UNHCR. (2015). *UNHCR Projected Global Resettlement Needs: 2016*. Brussels: United Nations High Commissioner for Refugees (UNHCR).

UNHCR. (2016). *Global Trends: Forced Displacement in 2015*. Brussels: United Nations High Commissioner for Refugees (UNHCR).

Waters, R. D. (2007). "Building the Nonprofit Organization-Donor Relationship Online." In *New Media in Public Relations*, 3rd ed., edited by S. C. Duhé (pp. 299–312). New York: Peter Lang.

Wolch, J. (1990). *The Shadow State: Government and Voluntary Sector in Transition*. New York: Foundation Center.

Wright, T. (2014). "The Media and Representations of Refugees and Other Forced Migrants." In *The Oxford Handbook of Refugee and Forced Migration Studies*, edited by E. Fiddian-Qasmiyeh, G. Loescher & N. Sigona (pp. 460–472). Oxford: Oxford University Press.

Yang, A. (2013). "Building Global Strategic Alliances in the Virtual Space: A Structural Analysis of International Nonprofit and Nongovernmental Organizations' Transnational Relationship Networks." *Journal of Public Affairs*, 13(3), 239–250.

Yang, A., & Saffer, A. (2018). "NGO's Advocacy in the 2015 Refugee Crisis: A Study of Agenda Building in the Digital Age." *American Behavioral Scientist*, 62(4), 421–439.

Zucker, N. L. (1983). "Refugee Resettlement in the United States: Policy and Problems." *The Annals of the American Academy of Political and Social Science*, 467(1), 172–186.

Por el Camino

The Representation of Migrant Caravans on Instagram
as an Aesthetics of Otherness

Fernanda R. Rosa and Arthur D. Soto-Vásquez

In this chapter, we untangle the politics of (in)visibility among migrants on their way from Central to North America, as they move not only through systems of border and state control but also through the sociotechnical architecture of Instagram. The migrant caravan gained public attention in 2018, especially after tweets from then U.S. president Donald Trump, defending stronger border control in the United States and in neighboring Mexico to prevent people from reaching the country (Semple, 2018). In search of safety and security, these people have organized themselves through social media, intending to travel thousands of kilometers together in a way to collectively support each other and protect themselves from the risks on the way. On social media two hashtags have been widely used to represent this movement: #caravanamigrante and #migrantcaravan. We understand both hashtags as a public shaped not only by users but also by the features of the platforms used, which is the focus of this chapter.

While one can argue that borders are increasingly becoming invisible, as surveillance technologies are utilized to make migrants visible and track them (Lechuga, 2017), borders clearly stand out in social media discourses that politically address migration, in a way that conversely raises their visibility. In this regard, we start from the assumption that social media cannot be taken for granted in the discussion of migrants' representations, but needs to be considered part of it, to allow for a better understanding of its co-productive role in the phenomenon (Jasanoff, 2004). Metaphorical and figurative borders also become enmeshed into the digitally mediated journey of the migrant caravan (Ono, 2012).

Our goal is to understand how Instagram users represent the migrant caravan utilizing the English and Spanish hashtags and how the affordances of the platform play a role in this representation. Our research reveals that these hashtags form parallel communicative spaces in which the migrant caravan representation is mostly mediated by professionals and organizations interested in promoting their own work. In association with Instagram affordances, there is a representation primarily based on an aesthetics of otherness that encompasses specific choices in photography and video editing, hashtag citations, and connection with other publics that expand the limits of the caravan while also demonstrating the role of the platform in shaping the movement. In the following sections, we begin by presenting the recent results of studies on migrants in traditional news media and social media, and then we explain our intervention in the methodology section. Afterward, we discuss the findings of a three-month qualitative content analysis of the hashtags #migrantcaravan and #caravanamigrante on Instagram in early 2020, which partly coincided with the COVID-19 pandemic.

(In)visible Migrants

Many of the tensions of migrant representation discussed in this volume's introduction are relevant to this chapter. In addition, there are visual aspects of representation that scholars have identified that both appear in news coverage and shape representation on social media. A content analysis of front pages of Australian newspapers finds that refugees are often depicted in medium to large groups (Bleiker et al., 2013). In contrast, "photographs of individual refugees with clearly recognisable facial features" (p. 413) accounted for only 2 percent of images, which the authors argue visually dehumanizes the refugees. Lind and Meltzer find "that women migrants are generally underrepresented in migration news coverage compared to their real share in the German population" (2020, p. 14). This trend also extends to U.S. entertainment television, where representation of migrant women is also disproportionately low (Immigration Nation, 2018, p. 8). Finally, while migrants are visualized in the mass media as threats and pollutants to the nation (Chavez, 2013; Cisneros, 2016), they are also simultaneously made invisible as credible sources and information assets for journalism. Thorbjørnsrud and Figenschou (2016) find that less than 10 percent of stories on immigration in the United States, France, and Norway include a migrant as a quoted source. These dominant ways of depicting the migrant experiences surely influence the digitally mediated representation of migrants; however, there is limited academic focus on the subject.

Studies of immigration and racial representation on social media have started to connect issues related to platforms' affordances and the shaping of migrant representation. Guidry et al. (2018) look at the differences between Syrian refugees' representation on Instagram and Pinterest and find that Pinterest posts tended to employ security frames, positioning refugees as threats to the nation, while Instagram posts were more humanistic. The authors identify the differences between the platforms as functions of the architecture and user bases of each social media site. For example, Instagram has a more diverse user base and a more robust commenting interface than Pinterest. Many of the Pinterest posts were not commented on, suggesting that they were ignored or unseen by the user base of Pinterest.

In another study, Jaramillo-Dent and Pérez-Rodríguez (2019) collected Instagram posts, using the same hashtags as our work, during the fall of 2018, a period when the migrant caravan was a high-salience issue in the public agenda. They found that the juxtaposition of representation was common on Instagram posts. The majority of posts sampled had a seemingly positive sentiment toward migrants. For example, many positive posts attempted to shift the view of major news events toward a pro-immigrant narrative, tending to adopt a humanitarian frame, as in the previously discussed study. Despite that, pro-immigrant posts on Instagram also reinforced the otherness of migrants through these representational choices. In the authors' words, otherness is constructed when "images are always taken from the perspective of an individual who is not part of the migrant community, or at least not explicitly," and then is used as a "device to victimize the (im)migrant and appeal to the guilt or compassion of the reader" (2019, p. 16). In addition, they argue, the prominence of the border wall in positive immigration posts also signified otherness by delineating spatial difference.

Regarding the effects of Instagram on the posts, Jaramillo-Dent and Pérez-Rodríguez (2019) assert that since the platform is popularly understood as one for self-representation and for performance of identity, it leads to users posting about migration so they can present themselves as good and caring people. It is less understood how the interaction between users' intentions and Instagram platform affordances relates to representation, though. Aesthetics of otherness has been used to describe the representation of nation-states at museums disregarding the voices of immigrants (Naguib, 2004), and although not named as such, also examined as the reproduction of colonial discourses by Instagram influencers in their travel photography of the Global South (Smith, 2018).

Medium-specific considerations are pivotal, as not only the content addressed but also the medium used to address it has a role in the study of representation. In their study on racial representation of Asian, Black, and Latina/o/x people on YouTube in the United States, Guo and Harlow (2014) not only found that racial stereotypes, commonly portrayed in the mainstream media, were reproduced by most (85 percent) of the content analyzed on the video-sharing platform; they also found that such content obtained more views and interactions. Furthermore, the authors warn that "the recommendation system and popularity-based search function on YouTube usually make the popular content even more popular," which illustrates the algorithmic affordance further entrenching racial stereotypes (p. 299). The recommendation algorithms are key for YouTube functioning, as they keep user attention longer on the platform. It also affects which content is seen on the platform and which is not. It also affects which content is seen on the platform and which is not—70 percent of the time spent in the platform is determined by the algorithm (Mozilla, 2021).

Instagram as a Site of Representation

Instagram-focused scholarship is an emerging topic in communication studies, as the platform can be studied from a variety of perspectives, including but not limited to culture, commerce, and aesthetics (Leaver et al., 2020). Instagram is an application used to share photos and videos, especially known for the popularization of travel story sharing and the emergence of professional travelers and travel influencers who get thousands and even millions of followers converted into money through brand sponsorships (Fitzmaurice, 2017; Smith, 2018). The app is owned by Facebook and has more than one billion users per month worldwide. As of May 2020, almost 18 percent of its users are from the United States, where 38 percent of Latina/o/x internet users are also Instagram users (Clement, 2020; Duggan, 2015). In Latin America, Mexico accounts for the second largest number of users, with more than 26 million, which represents the eightieth largest user base in the world. In Central America, the Dominican Republic, with more than 3.2 million users, and Guatemala, with more than 1.9 million users, are the countries that stand out (Navarro, 2020).

Following the scholarship concerned with the politics of social media platforms (DeNardis & Hackl, 2015; Gillespie, 2010; Massanari, 2017), we argue #caravanamigrante and #migrantcaravan should not be dissociated from the current uses of Instagram and its economy. We understand these hashtags as communicative spaces that allow for the creation of content about migrants while being also associated with widespread topics present on the platform, especially travel and advocacy. While the migrant caravan is unlikely to be framed as conventional travel and tourism, migration is necessarily related to travel and mobility, and as such, it is by no means distant from the popular user-generated content on Instagram. Similarly, Instagram has also been used for activism purposes, a parallel trend to the turn of social media from text to images in web 2.0 (Gupta, 2013; Muñoz & Towner, 2017). For instance, in June 2020 #blackouttuesday took over Instagram, combining activism with visual performance (Griffin, 2020). Certainly, such diverse uses of Instagram contribute to other metrics that attest to its success in the market, such as the time that users spend daily on the app, twenty-five to thirty minutes on average (Chowdhry, 2018; Newberry, 2019), and the engagement generated, known for being considerably higher than that of Facebook (Muñoz & Towner, 2017).

Importantly, Instagram posts are not about images or videos only; they also include captions as long as twenty-two hundred characters and a considerable hashtag limit—as many as thirty. Our object of analysis is thus neither exclusively text nor visual elements. Rather, it is deeply entangled with the holistic politics and design of the platform. In this regard, we follow the call for "media-specific analysis" (Hayles, 2004) when analyzing text, understanding that a caption or geotag is not detachable from the other elements of the post. Examining the form, possibilities, and constraints of the medium will allow for a richer analysis of the content. Regarding photographs, algorithms have a key role in digital photo-making and photo-sharing apps (Gillespie, 2014; Manovich, 2017). Gillespie notes that in the case of Flickr, most users have a desire for the photographs to be seen, either for personal or professional reasons. As a result, "photographers have an interest in being sensitive to the algorithm," and therefore the site may "induce subtle reorientations of photographers' practices towards its own constructed logics" (2014, p. 184). As Instagram responds to a logic of quantifying the maximum followers, likes, and interactions, it is possible to suggest that the motivations generated by the algorithms will be embedded in Instagram posts.

Finally, hashtags were added to Instagram one year after its release in 2011 as a feature to "help users discover photos and other users" (Manovich, 2017, p. 145). On the web there are numerous guides for Instagram users to boost their posts and use hashtags strategically, including lists to find daily hashtags, numbers advised per post, and advice on where to place the hashtags to make posts more appealing (Aynsley, 2018; Newberry, 2020). As of May 2022, the most common is to use three to four hashtags per post (Dixon, 2022). We understand the use of hashtags not only as a way to integrate the posts into a major public but also as a way to connect such publics. Furthermore, hashtags have been studied as a way of forming political counter-publics with the phenomenon named "hijacking" (Jackson & Foucault Welles, 2015). We use this work to explain other types of hijacking that contribute to the representation of the migrant caravan within hashtags. The theme of representation of migrants is reframed here to move beyond mere representation. That is, we attempt to move beyond the methods of mass media studies of representation toward considering how Instagram users and the sociotechnical aspects of Instagram shape representation amid state border and mobility control.

Methodology

Qualitative analysis of Instagram posts associated by hashtags is an emerging area of communication research (Laestadius, 2018). While computational "big data" methods of analyzing Instagram posts can shed light on mass usage patterns in tagging, likes, and network dynamics (Ferrara et al., 2014; Jang et al., 2015), the qualitative analysis of the so-called small batches of Instagram posts can show depth in the cultural practices associated with the platform (Kitchin & Lauriault, 2015; Losh, 2015). These new qualitative methodologies of Instagram analysis are very much in flux and will continue to change as, on the one hand, the platform adds new features that alter the user experience and, on the other, users "domesticate" them by adding meanings and incorporating the tools in their daily use (Boczkowski & Lievrouw, 2008).

Following small-batch qualitative studies of cultural practices on Instagram (Gibbs et al., 2014; Jaramillo-Dent & Pérez-Rodríguez, 2019; Lamont & Ross, 2019; Soto-Vásquez, 2021), we adopted the common procedure of (1) collecting posts by determining a relevant hashtag, and (2) developing overarching thematic categories and codes using variations of open-axial coding (Charmaz, 2008). Data collection was done manually from February 1, 2020, through April 30, 2020, using the hashtags #caravanamigrante and #migrantcaravan. The data collected included the link to the post, the date posted, the caption, and the hashtags. Our procedures of seeking out the hashtags as they are used and read at face value on Instagram replicate the experience of a user encountering the hashtags. The total amount of posts collected during the time range was 302, with 171 posts collected from #migrantcaravan and 131 from #caravanamigrante.

We then randomly selected a hundred-post sample for an in-depth qualitative analysis, resulting in a total of fifty posts for each hashtag. We ensured that posts were not duplicated between the two hashtag samples. Unlike Jaramillo-Dent and Pérez-Rodríguez (2019), who employed a purposive sampling technique to filter migrant caravan posts not depicting walls, we chose to analyze the entirety of content associated with the hashtags to capture the nature of representations of the migrant caravan in English and Spanish. Also, different from this previous work, we chose to study the hashtags not at the peak of the salience of their issue, but in a period when they were very low on the public agenda. As a consultation of "migrant caravan" on mediacloud.org demonstrates, few news pieces in the mainstream media covered the caravan between February and April 2020, with most days having zero stories. This was also a period that unintentionally coincided with the COVID-19 pandemic, which was addressed as one of the topics associated with the movement, among others. Finally, our data is more demographically diverse and global in nature, with posts from the Americas, Europe, and Asia.

Following the topics that emerged in the literature on media representation, we generated a number of provisional descriptive codes to guide our first analysis of the posts, encompassing the photos, the captions, and the hashtags—the visuality and the texts. The initial goal was to see and determine to what extent the literature was able to capture the content, and what was left behind. The codes selected to be further polished were "depict a migrant," "men depicted," "women depicted," "migrant bio informed," "borders depicted," "sympathy to the migrant caravan," and "promotion of own work." Based on a general examination of the posts, we also added codes to help distinguish what was related to migration, what was related to the pandemic, and the location of the profile: migration-, COVID-19-, and country-related. In this first round, we also generated word clouds in English and Spanish to identify their respective differences and similarities and guide further analysis.

With this material and a list of observations recorded while coding, we synthesized and refined five thematic categories that accounted for the elements that stood out from the data. With our set of categories defined, we undertook one more reading of the Instagram posts to develop and refine subtheme codes in each category. We then used these subtheme codes to separately and independently code the hundred-post random sample, with fifty posts from each hashtag. When coding, we read each post holistically, using the caption, the image, and the hashtag. In some cases, we also read the user's profile to determine whether applying the code was appropriate, as a user profile could provide context—just as knowing which media company produced and broadcast a news piece is useful. In all cases, we adopted a conservative coding approach, meaning that if the post was not clear enough, we would code it as null.

We used ReCal (Freelon, 2010) to determine the percent agreement between the two coders, then the two authors conferred to reach agreement on each subtheme code. During code realignment, codes were discarded, reorganized, and refined, and new codes were created. The most significant question that led to such changes was the phenomenon, captured as "otherness" in the literature. While we realized that such a phenomenon was happening, it went beyond the use of a humanitarian gaze and the depiction of walls, as captured by previous studies. There was a major co-production process between users' intentions and platform affordances that also produced an aesthetics of otherness embedded in the posts, as we will soon discuss in the "migrant as other" category. As a result, we created a qualitative codebook of twenty-eight codes, available in appendix 1, with the definition of each code present. Separately, we went through all the posts again, focusing on filling the new codes, then realigned our answers to generate table 1, to be analyzed in the next section.

During the rounds of coding and until the final calculation of embedded frequencies, some posts were deleted from Instagram, and as a result they were excluded from our data set. While it is not possible to know whether removal was a result of Instagram policies or users' decisions, we understand that such posts should not be included in our sample. When four removals happened in the first rounds of coding (one in the English hashtag and three in the Spanish), we replaced the posts with the next posts in line within our bigger sample. As removals continued to happen during the course of the project, we noticed it became counterproductive to replace them. We were aiming to keep intact the number of posts to be analyzed (n=100), but our collection of manual posts transformed our sample into a dynamic object, which was last checked on June 29, 2020. The final number of posts that we analyzed was ninety-two, comprising forty-four in Spanish and forty-eight in English.

An Aesthetics of Otherness

The representation of the migrant caravan on Instagram is shaped by stories that transmit sympathy to the movement while also creating a substantial distance from its protagonists. Migrants are rarely heard and only partially seen—in part because of their absence, and in part because of aesthetic choices. Their journey is consistently mediated by others. Photojournalists, amateur photographers, advocates, companies, and nongovernmental organizations (NGOs) constitute the mediators of the #caravanamigrante and #migrantcaravan communicative spaces. Their posts demonstrate a variety of goals that, while matching the platform's purposes, do not always focus on the caravan. As a result, the representation of the migrant caravan on Instagram is connected to numerous other issues and groups, as our codes show (see table 1).

TABLE 1. Frequency of Subthemes in Instagram Posts

CATEGORY	CODES	#MC	#CM	TOTAL
Immigration Politics	The humanitarian gaze	18	22	40
	Art and migration	22	35	57
	Migrant as threat to nation	1	3	4
	COVID-19 and migration	21	13	19
	Economics of migration	6	8	29
	Violence as a reason to migrate	6	4	10
	Electoral politics and migration	6	15	21
	Migrant men	21	24	46
	Migrant women	12	11	23
Migrant as Other	Violence towards migrants	9	7	16
	Migrant voices	7	4	11
	Migrant biography	4	7	11
	Obscuring of migrant face	11	18	29
	Migrants as a group of people	11	12	23
	Privileged migrant	5	8	13
	Tenebrous photo	4	7	11
Borders	Border as man-made physical barrier	15	14	29
	Border as water barrier	5	6	11
	Border as human barrier	8	9	17
	Border as information technology barrier	3	5	8
	Metaphorical border	25	28	53
Place	Globalized	4	14	18
	Exportation of borders	6	6	12
	Temporary place	18	28	46
Contested Platform	Promotion of own work	32	39	71
	Hashtag hijacking	15	18	33
	Connection to other publics using hashtags	31	47	78
	Repost of another social media content	8	10	18

Immigration Politics

Benson describes the humanitarian frame in immigration news coverage as when immigrants are described as "victims of unjust government policies" (2013, p. 88). Our coding scheme adapted Benson's frame as the "humanitarian gaze." These posts (n=40) use liberal language to sympathize with migrants and their reasons to immigrate based on universal human rights discourses. For example, one post details the story of Octavio. He is quoted as saying, "We seek refuge because 'in Honduras they kill us' is the slogan with which new caravans of Honduran immigrants met in January 2020, to leave their country in search of a better life" (our translation). Most posts coded with the humanitarian gaze generally refer to macro reasons for migrating, such as violence and corruption, rather than micro and personal reasons. As a result, the humanitarian gaze represents the migrant as a product of social forces rather than their shaper. Fewer posts (n=4) present the "migrant as a threat to the nation." Posts with this representation use language to depict migrants as being dangerous to the nation's way of life or as destabilizing (Chavez, 2013). Almost all posts using this frame did appear with the English hashtag (n=3). In a post on March 8, 2020, the user @latinosforamerica, for example, expressed excitement about future U.S. Immigration and Customs Enforcement (ICE) raids and used hashtags about sanctuary cities and illegal immigration.

The humanitarian gaze is closely associated with the presentation of migrant struggle "as art" (n=57). This is especially and overwhelmingly present in posts tagged with #migrantcaravan (n=35). In other words, the migrant journey became an object of artistic expression, especially in English. Most of the English-hashtag posts were from professional and amateur photographers, usually showcasing their work from their personal or institutional profiles. This may be a function of time, since the first prominent migrant caravan occurred in late 2018. The news professional photos taken at that time were winning awards and being submitted to fine art galleries in early 2020. A post featuring a young migrant girl has a caption that even acknowledges this position, saying, "While much of the art concerning the U.S.-Mexican border focuses on the imagery and symbolism of visual barriers and border technologies, Trillo shifts our attention from infrastructure to human crisis." It then shifts to promote the gallery exhibition in New York City and uses hashtags like #fineartphotography. The disjuncture between image and text is discussed by Fernández and Lirola (2012) in their study of Spanish-newspaper images of African immigrants, warning that discrimination may be subtle, through images or words used inadvertently. Just as in photojournalism, and perhaps even more so, Instagram provides space for a complex multiplicity of positive and negative representations. Captions may advocate for migrants, while the imagery commodifies "beautiful" suffering.

The multiplicity of representation is captured in the six other codes associated with immigration: "electoral politics and migration," "COVID-19 and migration," "economics of migration," "violence as a reason to migrate," "migrant men," and "migrant women." Electoral politics was sometimes related to discussions of immigration, often tying decisions by politicians to the issue (n=21). There were several posts, usually in English, that negatively referred to the Trump administration. A few referred to decisions by the Obama administration as well. Posts relating COVID-19 to migration also are present (n=19), especially after March 2020. For instance, one post from April 19 by the NGO @xxtap_sol, a mutual aid collective operating in Tapachula, Chiapas, Mexico, states, "If anyone breaks the barricades for Central Park, a park that just weeks ago served as an all day and night space for migrants to sleep, socialize and make money, they are arrested or ticketed." It is clear that COVID-19 does not affect people equally, and that vulnerable social conditions and displacement require immediate answers and support wherever people are.

The "economics of migration" code includes the labor of migrants and the economic effects of migration in addition to economic reasons for migrating. Posts (n=29) often referred to many of these elements in their images and captions. One post says, "The hollowing of their communities was well under way for years prior; the caravan being the avalanche that follows the tumbling of a pebble." Further, a majority of posts emphasizing the economics of migration came from Spanish-hashtag posts (n=21), suggesting an emphasis on contextualizing the insecurity that migrants face in their countries. Some posts also discussed migrants fleeing violence in their home (n=10), which was captured during code realignment as "violence as a reason to migrate." As previous works have found an overrepresentation of men, in our study over half of the posts using the English and Spanish hashtags depicted men (n=46), and many fewer posts featured women as compared to men (n=23). While very few men were depicted as caretakers of children, they were often represented as solitary or in large groups, a finding discussed later in more detail. Women were often presented as caretakers of children or as part of a family unit. As an exception, there is the appearance of a journalist being interviewed about her TV coverage of the caravan. Gender also appeared in the contrast between women photographers and men migrants, when the image of migrants as a threat was reinforced.

Migrant as Other

In Instagram posts using both hashtags, migrants are commonly seen but not heard. While their journey, struggles, and confrontations with border security are presented, migrant voices are present only in limited circumstances (n=11), usually in videos. The majority of captions explain the image of the migrant in the post, using the third-person point of view. The caption is written from the perspective of the poster, not the actual migrant, echoing the findings of previous research (Thorbjørnsrud & Figenschou, 2016) and suggesting a poster's gaze. In most cases, the migrant depicted in the image is also deidentified, with terms like "a migrant" or "young man" used instead. Posts rarely tell the stories of migrants using names, and when they do (n=11), it is usually from the third-person perspective. This may be an attempt to preserve privacy and prevent government surveillance. In one rare example, a post in Spanish from February 1 details an attempt by two women in Honduras to join the caravan to reconnect with family members in the United States. Their depiction communicates a mix of sadness and resilience. The photograph captures an ambivalent expression by the women, while the caption tells a story of pain, movement, and reconciliation.

Further, we found that migrant men were often depicted in large groups. The "migrants as a group of people" code accounts for this phenomenon and is embedded in twenty-three posts. Numerous posters from our analysis note that migrants from Central America travel in large groups as a means of security and protection from attacks and financial extortion. Once the caravan gained the spotlight in the media, the mass of the caravan was portrayed as a threat to the nation in U.S. right-wing and mainstream media, following the "Latino threat" narrative (Chavez, 2013; Cisneros, 2016). In such a context we noticed two trends. One is that as most of the posts analyzed were sympathetic to the migrant caravan, the Instagram posts featuring men in groups may also reassert the security frame of the caravan as protection from harm. For example, a caption from March 13 said, "Traveling in what was becoming known as the migrant caravans, they could travel safer and more families with small children dared to take on the dangerous journey." The second trend shows that despite this intention, the presentation of migrants as a group can also contribute to the othering of migrants.

While the representation of groups was common, often referencing safety and protection, it is through this lens that the sixteen posts depicting violence against migrants by border guards can be understood. Richardson (2017) notes the balance between bearing witness to the often-fatal violence inflicted by the police onto Black men in the United States and the hesitancy to turn the visualized suffering into spectacle. When few posts seem to come from migrants themselves, the choice to depict violence done to them by border guards must be complicated. The desire to make visible the harm that states inflict upon migrants as they move conflicts with the danger in using violent imagery to attract attention, similar to the tension Richardson describes. When a photo depicting Óscar Alberto Martínez and his daughter drowned in the Rio Grande on the border of the United States and Mexico emerged in 2019, it was shared by many pro-immigration organizations and activists and was prominent in news coverage. RAICES, an immigrant rights group, chose not to share the image, as they and others argued it dehumanized the subjects (Da Silva, 2019).

The tension of representation of the migrant caravan on Instagram is one between invisibility and visibility. Nevertheless, visibility can still produce an aesthetics of otherness. The journeys and stories of migrants are presented, but in limited and limiting ways that often reflect dominant frames in the news media. Depicting harm done to migrants can expose oppressive state violence but also reinforce threat narratives. Migrants on Instagram are othered with pictures often concealing their faces (though this may be for security purposes) or as obscured figures in the background (n=29). In captions, migrants are othered by not being identified by their names; they are simply called the "migrant," an oversimplified and stigmatized totality. They are further othered by the co-presence, and often centering, of "privileged travelers" in the caravan.

We define "privileged travelers" as the (photo)journalists, activists, and academics who embed themselves with the caravans and include themselves in the stories they are telling. We found these present in thirteen posts, slightly more in English (n=8). While this does not account for all posts published by professionals, with this code our intent is to identify when they make, explicit their roles as mediators between the migrants and the platform. They create proximity as characters of the stories, speaking out from the position of "travelling professional workers" who can ultimately be considered tourists with work purposes (Uriely, 2001). We find this characterization important to demarcate the distance of this group of travelers in relation to the migrants themselves in terms of the reasons to join the movement. Such distance occurs despite the apparent intention of some posters to have a sense of belonging, as can be seen in an April 4 post of a photographer, who published a photo of the undergrowth with small flowers and the caption "A sunny day, thirst, cubes of watermelon given by a stranger, juice dripping down *our* faces" (emphasis added), or a post of an academic on that same date saying "5 years ago I marched in *my* first migrant caravan" (emphasis added). What the privileged travelers illustrate is a segment of a common Instagram use, the reporting of travels. On the one hand, privileged travelers publicize dimensions of a reality otherwise not easily seen; on the other hand, they also reproduce colonial travel discourses, embedded in the search for an "authentic experience" and the production of "others" (Smith, 2018).

In fact, Instagram's incentives contribute to such processes of othering, which cannot be detached from the commodifying processes of posts and experiences—which are then given value through likes and engagement. Highly associated with the posts of privileged travelers are posts (n=11) that used a color palette and aesthetic that could be best described as "tenebrous." "Tenebrousness" is defined as the aesthetic of dark, shadowy, and obscure lighting and tone when applied to migrant representation. "Tenebrousness" does not fit the Instagram aesthetic. Manovich (2017) uses "the term Insta-gramism to refer to the aesthetics of designed photos on Instagram and other platforms" (n.p.), which he primarily argues convey mood and atmosphere over representation and emotion. Further, designed photos on Instagram also have qualities of coolness, hipness, and flatness, with a common use of pastel colors and gray neutrals. In our analysis, the migrant journey is portrayed with sadness, resilience, and tenebrous conditions. A series of images from March 4 that could be described as cheery depicts migrant children smiling at the camera. Yet the images were taken in a border encampment in Matamoros, Mexico, constantly reminding the user of the precariousness of the situation that migrants face.

Borders

Borders loom in the background of Instagram posts, often more than merely physical barriers. We conceptualized five types of mediated borders: man-made physical barriers, such as fences and walls; water barriers, such as rivers and lakes; human barriers, such as border patrol agents; information-generating technological barriers, such as visas and databases; and the metaphorical border. While national borders are national-legal boundaries, in the practical sense they take the form of the aforementioned barriers in popular spectacle (Flores, 2019). Instagram posts visualize some of these border types clearly while obfuscating and mystifying others.

Man-made physical barriers appeared in almost one-third of the posts (n=29), mostly taking the form of fencing. For example, one post by a U.S. photographer features a striking image of migrants taken from outside the fence. A group of migrant men are pressed up against the fence. The post shows a darkly hued black-and-white photo, evoking a gothic and horrific visage. In this case, the fencing acts as a separation between the viewer and the migrant, producing an object distant to the figure of the migrant. In another case, the artificial barrier appears in the background, less ominous but ever present, as a migrant family returns from the Greek-Turkish border, present in our sample due to the use of the #migrantcaravan hashtag, as will be further discussed. Both kinds of barriers are visualized as objects in the migrant's journey, made visible by the tying of migration to borders and artificial barriers.

Water barriers, such as rivers and lakes, also appeared in posts (n=11). Current borders are often formalizations of geographic separations between states. Further, border control also strategically uses natural geography to deter border crossings and the visibility of crossings in urban areas. The U.S. Border Patrol implemented Operation Hold the Line in the 1990s, which redirected unauthorized crossings through dangerous areas instead of cities (Cornelius, 2004). A video posted on Instagram using the Spanish hashtag shows the Mexican border guards refusing entry to a migrant caravan in January 2020. The video then cuts to a large group of migrants walking through the Suchiate River, with a caption stating, "without a clear response, they decided to cross the river" on the border between Mexico and Guatemala. Once the migrants in the aforementioned video cross, they are then met with resistance and violence by Mexican border guards. This is emblematic of the code "human barriers," given to seventeen of the collected posts. One post from February 14 shows a young couple and their child fleeing a phalanx of Mexican border guards. The post is also tagged with the hashtag #abolishICE, referring to U.S. ICE. Border guards along with natural and artificial barriers represent the most visibilized elements of border control in Instagram posts.

Less visibilized, but often hinted at, are advanced information generating technological barriers. These are control technologies such as databases, sensors, drones, and other means of surveillance. The digital and technical architecture makes them largely invisible in Instagram posts, yet they were hinted at in a few posts, especially mentioning visa and legal barriers to entry (n=8), while drones and sensors were not mentioned. The mystification and inaccessibility of technological barriers in regard to the public also make them more potent, especially in controlling movement (Lechuga, 2017). Databases like the Schengen Information System (sis) in Europe allow for coordinated and pervasive border control, so that a refugee denied entry at one checkpoint may not try their luck again at a different entry point in another country, as they have already been marked and flagged by the system (Broeders, 2007).

To account for borders also functioning symbolically and affectively in addition to materially (DeChaine, 2012), we developed the code of the metaphorical border, tied to the depiction of migrants' hardiness and resilience. More than half of the posts were tagged this way (n=53), making it the most prominent kind of mediated border we observed. For example, a black-and-white photograph of a migrant woman, posed in a similar fashion to the *Migrant Mother* photograph from the Great Depression, included the caption, "Minute by minute I lose hope" (our translation). The woman in the photo holds a sleeping child in her lap, while she rests her head in her hand and gazes into the distance. Other posts coded with "metaphorical border" also imply an empathetic barrier between those in Europe and the United States and those attempting to migrate, very often expressing a humanitarian gaze—another way in which bordering produces otherness and difference among migrants.

Place

Given platform affordances such as geotagging, Instagram is unique among social media platforms as a medium where place experience can be mediated and reinterpreted (Soto-Vásquez, 2021). This is evident in the globalized mediated flow of the migrant caravan from the Americas to Europe and Asia. In eighteen posts, predominantly using the English hashtag (n=14), the phenomenon of the migrant caravan was used to depict the experiences of migrants around the world. This included Syrian migrants waiting to cross into Turkey and Greece, and Indian migrants living under COVID-19 lockdown. In other words, the hashtag became a communicative space where the journeys of migrants could be connected across different geographic and political contexts. As is discussed in the next section in more detail, Instagram allows for anyone to use a hashtag to represent the migrant experience. This opens up the possibility of immigration movement connections in the digital space of the hashtag.

In a similar sense, Instagram posts also showed a recent phenomenon in geopolitical immigration control, the "exportation of borders," which appeared in twelve posts. For instance, recent agreements between the United States, Mexico, and Guatemala have resulted in the increased militarization and securitization of the Mexico-Guatemala border. A CNN article covering a violent clash between border guards and a smaller migrant caravan in January 2020 states that "Mexico, in effect, has already built Trump's border wall by increasingly cracking down on immigrants" (Shoichet, 2020). Similarly, a video posted on April 13 states, "The wall that Donald Trump promised to build is nothing more than Mexico, his security border." The account who posted it, @ xxtap_sol, is very active in using the English and Spanish hashtags, specifically to call attention to the exporting of immigration control to the southern Mexican border. On their GoFundMe page, they state, "After a grueling and dangerous passage, Indigenous, African, Caribbean and Central American refugees arriving at Mexico's southern border were now being denied humanitarian visas and travel visas needed to transit the country to get to the U.S. border." In a similar fashion, several posts from @emrahozesen, a Turkish journalist, document the exportation of the EU border and what has been called EU "migration management" (İçduygu & Demiryontar, 2019) to the Greece-Turkey border.

Finally, the liminal and temporary place that migrants occupy as they journey is highly embedded, appearing in forty-six posts. Government asylum policies in the United States, especially the Remain in Mexico policy, are designed to limit the mobility of migrants into the United States and have resulted in temporary encampments on the Mexican side of the border. The United Nations High Commissioner for Refugees (UNHCR) has emerged as an international broker of geopolitical migration management in Mexico and Turkey, which ultimately disciplines migrant mobility (Basok & Candiz, 2020). The camps as they emerge on Instagram represent both the intervention of the UNHCR to manage migrant populations through health and safety as well as liminal spaces where migrants are prevented from moving further. Additionally, the COVID-19 pandemic and its public health concerns were used to clear some encampments, as seen in a @xxtap_sol post from April 17 that states, "All migration processes have been stopped for the indefinite future and anyone who was living in Tapachula on the street has been pushed into shelters or deported." The large number of posts showing camps and liminal spaces bring the reality of migrants' conditions to the public in a vivid way, while also showing the limits of the mediation of this reality via Instagram. In a post from February 12 in which a TV reporter is interviewed, and her experience covering the migrant caravan is presented as rewarding, scenes from the interview depict her in a camp with clothes and a microphone that distinguish her as a class apart from the others. The process of otherness broadcasted on TV, in this case, is reiterated on Instagram through the interview. The assumed horizontality that Instagram affords by enabling content distribution without the apparatus and aesthetics of mainstream media has not been enough to break barriers of migrants' representation. On the contrary, affordances on Instagram have contributed to expanding the otherness.

Contested Platform

The call to conduct medium-specific analysis informs the final category of codes, which focuses on the affordances of Instagram as a platform. These codes are "promotion of own work," "hashtag hijacking," "connection to other publics using hashtags," and "reposting" of other social media content. As mentioned before, many of the images depicting migrants were posted by professional photojournalists and amateur photographers. In seventy-one cases, we coded their posts as "promotion of own work" when the caption of the image mentioned the subjectivity of the photographer or used hashtags that indicated the poster intended for the image to be viewed as a part of a photographer Instagram public hashtag, such as #everydaylafrontera or #reportagespotlight. In addition, we found many migrant-focused NGOs using the platform of Instagram to promote their own advocacy on behalf of migrants, usually calling for financial support. The high number of posts coded this way strongly suggests that the platform is being used by actors surrounding the migrant caravan and not by migrants themselves. As the majority of the posts are sympathetic to the movement, they work as a way to bring public attention to the causes at the same time that they engender self-promotion of their work.

The open nature of a hashtag also allows for the practice of hashtag hijacking. We found this concept inspiring to reflect on what we have seen in the use of #migrantcaravan and #caravanamigrante publics. More than one-third of the posts clearly hijacked the intent of the hashtag to intervene in the public with other migrant movements, opposite opinions, or promote works and businesses (n=33). Opinions opposing sympathetic views of the migrant caravan appeared in very few posts, all of which were in English. These included the already mentioned post from @latinosforamerica praising the U.S. border patrol with the hashtag #buildthewall, and a post from @losmiamimemes on April 12 promoting conspiracy theories about global elites. The low right-wing interventions found in this study may have occurred because of the period of our data collection. In fact, the migrant caravan was not in the spotlight of the mainstream media from February to April 2020, which may have attracted fewer people interested in reframing the discussion on the platform. On the other side, when it comes to the promotion of their own works, one account posted several times using the English hashtag about the migrant caravan and the COVID-19 pandemic to promote their music—a result of two other Instagram affordances, the use of multiple hashtags and the repost of other social media content. Other posts coded as "economics of migration" construct the United States as a place with jobs for migrants. In the Spanish hashtag, many posts are from @sunset_tech_center, a professionalizing school in New York that offers migrants the chance to learn new skills toward a career as a "#tecnicoelectricista." They use the hashtag #caravanamigrante as a way to advertise their coursework, imagining an audience of migrants looking for professionalization courses in Spanish. They also reinterpret the mythology of the American dream to attract students to their school.

Using hashtags on Instagram also can connect one post to multiple other publics, a fact that generates numerous hashtag citations on the platform. Connection to other publics using hashtags was very common in the posts (n=78) using both the original English and Spanish hashtag. For example, a post with

#migrantcaravan may also use #daca and #fineartphotography to connect the post to the publics of the Deferred Action for Childhood Arrivals (DACA) law and users interested in specific types of photographs. The average of hashtags in both languages is quite high: 18.6 in Spanish and 17.9 in English, generating connections with other publics that differ considerably among them. In Spanish, the hijacking of the professionalizing school shapes the hashtag connections. Words like #electricity, #electricianlife, and #lightbulb dominate the cloud, while #defendthesacred, #humanrights, and #blacklivesmatter also call attention to connecting the movement to Indigenous and anti-racist agendas. In English, beyond #migrant, #mexico, #border, and #refugee, the connection with arts and photography publics stands out with hashtags like #documentary and #photojournalism, while #music and related hashtags result from the most recurrent hijacking in English.

The use of multiple hashtags poses questions of accuracy and ethics for qualitative research on Instagram. While we defined codes analyzing posts holistically, a hashtag citation did not carry the same weight as the presence of an element in a photo. For example, we found twelve posts with hashtags mentioning the border wall, but only six of them were coded as border as "man-made physical barrier." In one post from March 4 not coded as such, the photographer uses the hashtag #instawall to connect a slideshow of migrants' photos to a public that depicts walls with the cool and hip aesthetics characteristic of Instagram. In another example, posts of the aforementioned professionalizing school that depicted only migrant men in its photos cited the hashtag #strongwomen in all posts, but that was not enough for us to code it as "migrant woman." Actually, it stands out that once posters who use Instagram to promote their work determine which hashtags are important to distribute their content, they may just copy and paste hashtags from one post to another, showing that interoperability is an important feature on the platform.

Finally, since Instagram only allows for posts to be uploaded from its mobile phone application, it also affords users the ability to post screenshots and images of other social media content. Further, the reposting as it exists in our sample (n=18) also layers new meaning onto the original social media content. For example, the account @themexicancommunity primarily reposts screenshots and memes from other social media accounts on their page. They then take the original social media post and remix new meaning onto it, contextualizing the information for their audience or reinterpreting the post. In the hijacking context, two reposts of the user seeking to promote their music on March 30, 2020, showed videos supposedly taken in New York at the peak of the pandemic with dead bodies being placed in trucks. In this COVID-19 spectacle, an aesthetics of death is used to promote a song, adding such intention to the representation of the migrant caravan on Instagram while purposely hijacking the #migrantcaravan hashtag. Thus, the citation of hashtags means more than the interaction with Instagram algorithms to attract a certain audience to a post. It connects communicative spaces to each other, altering the hashtags publics, and, in consequence, the representation of social phenomena mediated by them.

Conclusion

The representation of the migrant caravan on Instagram is a result of a process where users' intentions and the platform's affordances interact, which we term "the aesthetics of otherness." While this is somewhat medium-specific to Instagram, we also argue that the concept is flexible enough to other mediums where migrants are represented. The creation of the migrant as "other" on Instagram by users is accomplished through the use of dark coloring, obscuring of faces, presenting the migrant in groups, hashtag citations, and connection with other publics via hashtag hijacking. Opposing the aesthetics of otherness that has emerged from this relation is possible, as some differences between the English and Spanish versions show. The hashtag #caravanamigrante was much more receptive as a communicative space to contextualize the reasons for the movement, and it was more inclined to show migrants' voices and less inclined to frame them as a threat. It also consistently used fewer frames that commodify the suffering with art, the obscuring of faces, the tenebrous photos, the privileged traveler, the promotion of the user's own work, and the connection to other publics. The differences between the English and Spanish hashtags also shows how different publics domesticate the affordances of a platform according to their cultural ideologies and political agendas. Further research should take this into account.

There are limitations to our approach. Our glimpse into migrant representation was highly influenced by the time period we chose to focus on, including the unexpected emergence of COVID-19 at the midpoint of data collection. This is a context to take into consideration. Also, we hope to inspire other researchers to apply the codebook created to other migration data in order to expand the reflections obtained here. Our work joins scholarship positing the limits of homogenizing representations and the mediation that prevents voices from being heard. It should caution researchers, designers, and users against ignoring the platform's role in shaping representations of vulnerable demographics while also motivating them to continuously and actively shape social media platforms. As these platforms are profit- and performance-centric, their utility will always be limited by the logic of late capitalism. In other words, it is unlikely that new migrant epistemologies will emerge through social media platforms, no matter how revolutionary the hype during their rise is.

Appendix 1. Aesthetics of Otherness Codebook

CATEGORY	CODES
IMMIGRATION POLITICS	1. Humanitarian gaze: Post uses language to sympathize with migrant and reasons to immigrate (security, survival) based on universal human rights discourses, hope, and compassion.
	2. Art and migration: Post of fine art photography, photojournalism, or amateur photography that uses art as protest against anti-immigrant sentiment. Also turns suffering into art using aesthetics of migration and through commodification.
	3. Migrant as threat to nation: Post uses language to present migrant as dangerous to nation's way of life or as destabilizing.
	4. COVID-19 and immigration: Post illustrates the effects of COVID-19 on immigration and the relationship between the two.
	5. Economics of migration: Post explicitly discusses labor of migrants and/or economic causes and effects of migration.
	6. Violence as a reason to migrate: Post explicitly references violence in home country as reason to migrate.
	7. Electoral politics and migration: Post connects migration with government, elections, political figures, and voting.
	8. Migrant man: Post features someone presenting as a man and also as a migrant (migrant caravan participants, immigrants, and travelers). Children were not coded.
	9. Migrant woman: Post features someone presenting as a woman and also as a migrant (migrant caravan participants, immigrants, and travelers). Children were not coded.

CATEGORY	CODES
MIGRANT AS OTHER	10. Violence towards migrants: Post depicts or references violence inflicted on migrants, such as crowd control, mistreatment, family separation, and disappearance, by border security and/or gangs during the journey.
	11. Migrant voices: Post uses migrants' own words. Posts are uploaded by migrants.
	12. Migrant biography: Post uses migrant's story and/or presents migrant as an individual using name and/or age.
	13. Obscuring of migrant face: When a migrant is depicted, their face is turned away from the camera and/or blocked or blurred from view.
	14. Migrants as a group of people: Post depicts a group of migrants, without a main migrant as the subject of the picture.
	15. Privileged migrant: Post centers concurrent travel with a migrant caravan as part of job (journalist, student, artist) or as work of an advocate (activist)
	16. Tenebrous photo: Post is dark or in black and white.
BORDERS	17. Border as man-made physical barrier: Post depicts a fence or wall that serves as a barrier.
	18. Border as water barrier: Post depicts a body of water (river, lake) that serves as a barrier.
	19. Border as human barrier: Post depicts or references border security agents or officers.
	20. Border as information technology barrier: Post depicts or discusses borders built with digital and information technology (databases, drones, visas).
	21. Metaphorical border: Post implies difficulty, hardness, or resilience.
PLACE	22. Globalized: Post uses hashtag outside Americas.
	23. Exportation of borders: Post shows border security away from global north nations toward Global South (Mexico, Turkey).
	24. Temporary place: Liminal space, camp, border zone.
CONTESTED PLATFORM	25. Promotion of own work: Post is used to promote work of individuals, companies, or NGOs.
	26. Hashtag hijacking: Post does not address phenomenon of migrant caravan while still using hashtags.
	27. Connection to other issues using hashtags: Post uses hashtags not related to the migrant caravan to connect publics.
	28. Repost of other social media content: Post uses other social media content to remix and/or add new meaning to original post.

NOTE

A condensed version of this chapter was published with the title "Aesthetics of Otherness: Representation of #migrantcaravan and #caravanamigrante on Instagram" at *Social Media + Society*.

REFERENCES

Aynsley, M. (2018, August 9). "How to Write Good Instagram Captions: Tips, Ideas, and Tools." *Hootsuite Social Media Management*. https://blog.hootsuite.com/social-media-definitions/caption/.

Basok, T., & Candiz, G. (2020). "Containing Mobile Citizenship: Changing Geopolitics and Its Impact on Solidarity Activism in Mexico." *Citizenship Studies*, *24*(4), 474–492.

Benson, R. (2013). *Shaping Immigration News*. Cambridge: Cambridge University Press.

Bleiker, R., Campbell, D., Hutchison, E., & Nicholson, X. (2013). "The Visual Dehumanisation of Refugees." *Australian Journal of Political Science*, *48*(4), 398–416.

Boczkowski, P. J., & Lievrouw, L. A. (2008). "Bridging STS and Communication Studies: Scholarship on Media and Information Technologies." In *The Handbook of Science and Technology Studies*, 3rd ed., edited by E. J. Hackett, O. Amsterdamska, M. E. Lynch & J. Wajcman (pp. 949–977). Cambridge: MIT Press.

Broeders, D. (2007). "The New Digital Borders of Europe: EU Databases and the Surveillance of Irregular Migrants." *International Sociology*, *22*(1), 71–92.

Charmaz, K. (2008). "Grounded Theory As an Emergent Method." In *Handbook of Emergent Methods*, edited by S. N. Heese-Biber & P. Leavy (pp. 155–172). New York: The Guilford Press.

Chavez, L. (2013). *The Latino Threat: Constructing Immigrants, Citizens, and the Nation*. Stanford: Stanford University Press.

Chowdhry, A. (2018, May 16). "Instagram Is Testing a Feature That Shows How Much Time You Spend Using It." *Forbes*. https://www.forbes.com/sites/amitchowdhry/2018/05/16/instagram-usage-insights/?sh=6809658e41f7.

Cisneros, J. D. (2016). "Racial Presidentialities: Narratives of Latinxs in the 2016 Campaign." *Rhetoric & Public Affairs*, *20*(3), 511–524.

Clement, J. (2020, April 24). "Leading Countries Based on Instagram Audience Size as of April 2020." *Statista*. https://www.statista.com/statistics/578364/

countries-with-most-instagram-users/.

Cornelius, W. A. (2004). "Death at the Border: Efficacy and Unintended Consequences of US Immigration Control Policy." *Population and Development Review, 27*(4), 661–685.

Da Silva, C. (2019, June 27). "Stop Sharing 'Dehumanizing' Photo of Drowned Migrant Father and Daughter, Immigration Groups Say: 'Before They Were Migrants, They Were a Family.'" *Newsweek*. https://www.newsweek.com/father-child-rio-grande-deaths-photo-oscar-alberto-martinez-ramirez-valeria-1446238.

DeChaine D. R. (2012). *Border Rhetorics: Citizenship and Identity on the US-Mexico Frontier*. Tuscaloosa: University of Alabama Press.

DeNardis, L., & Hackl, A. M. (2015). "Internet Governance by Social Media Platforms." *Telecommunications Policy, 39*(9), 761–770.

Dixon, S. (2022, May 4). "Instagram Posts Impression Rate 2021–2022, by Number of Hashtags." *Statista*. https://www.statista.com/statistics/1305917/instagram-post-engagement-by-number-of-hashtags/.

Duggan, M. (2015, August 19). "Demographics of Social Media Users in 2015." *Pew Research Center*. https://www.pewresearch.org/internet/2015/08/19/the-demographics-of-social-media-users/.

Fernández, E. C., & Lirola, M. M. (2012). "Lexical and Visual Choices in the Representation of Immigration in the Spanish Press." *Spanish in Context, 9*(1), 27–57.

Ferrara, E., Interdonato, R., & Tagarelli, A. (2014, September). "Online Popularity and Topical Interests through the Lens of Instagram." In *Proceedings of the 25th ACM Conference on Hypertext and Social Media* (pp. 24–34).

Fitzmaurice, R. (2017, November 5). "The 30 Most Stunning and Influential Instagram Travel Accounts on the Planet." *Insider*. https://www.insider.com/the-most-followed-instagram-travel-accounts-2017-11.

Flores, L. A. (2019). "At the Intersections: Feminist Border Theory." *Women's Studies in Communication, 42*(2), 113–115.

Freelon, D. (2010). "ReCal: Intercoder Reliability Calculation as a Web Service." *International Journal of Internet Science, 5*(1), 20–33.

Gibbs, M., Meese, J., Arnold, M., Nansen, B., & Carter, M. (2014). "#Funeral and Instagram: Death, Social Media, and Platform Vernacular." *Information, Communication & Society, 18*(3), 255–268.

Gillespie, T. (2010). "The Politics of 'Platforms.'" *New Media & Society, 12*(3), 347–364.

Gillespie, T. (2014). "The Relevance of Algorithms." In *Media Technologies: Essays on Communication, Materiality, and Society*, 1st ed., edited by T. Gillespie, P. J.

Boczkowski & K. A. Foot (pp. 167–194). Cambridge: MIT Press.

Griffin, A. (2020, June 2). "Why People Are Posting Black Squares to Their Instagram." *Independent*. https://www.independent.co.uk/tech/blackout-tuesday-instagram-black-squares-how-to-post-box-a9543896.html.

Guidry, J. P., Austin, L. L., Carlyle, K. E., Freberg, K., Cacciatore, M., Meganck, S., Jin, Y., & Messner, M. (2018). "Welcome or Not: Comparing #Refugee Posts on Instagram and Pinterest." *American Behavioral Scientist*, 62(4), 512–531.

Guo, L., & Harlow, S. (2014). "User-Generated Racism: An Analysis of Stereotypes of African Americans, Latinos, and Asians in YouTube Videos." *Howard Journal of Communications*, 25(3), 281–302.

Gupta, A. (2013, July 2). "The Shift from Words to Pictures and Implications for Digital Marketers." *Forbes*. https://www.forbes.com/sites/onmarketing/2013/07/02/the-shift-from-words-to-pictures-and-implications-for-digital-marketers/?sh=441b37f5405a.

Hayles N. K. (2004). "Print Is Flat, Code Is Deep: The Importance of Media-Specific Analysis." *Poetics Today*, 25(1), 67–90.

İçduygu, A., & Demiryontar, B. (2019). "Mediterranean's Migration Dilemma and the EU's Readmission Agreements: Reinforcing a Centre-Periphery Relation." *EuroMedMig Working Paper Series*, no. 1 (December).

Immigration Nation (Rep.). (2018, October). "USC Annenberg Norman Lear Center's Media Impact Project and Define America." *Norman Lear Center*. https://learcenter.org/wp-content/uploads/2018/10/Immigration-Nation.pdf.

Instagram. (2018). "Instagram Year in Review 2018." Instagram Blog. https://about.instagram.com/blog/announcements/instagram-year-in-review-2018.

Jackson, S. J., & Foucault Welles, B. (2015). "Hijacking #myNYPD: Social Media Dissent and Networked Counterpublics." *Journal of Communication*, 65(6), 932–952.

Jang, J. Y., Han, K., & Lee, D. (2015, August). "No Reciprocity in 'Liking' Photos: Analyzing Like Activities in Instagram." In *Proceedings of the 26th ACM Conference on Hypertext & Social Media*, 273–282.

Jaramillo-Dent, D., & Pérez-Rodríguez, M. A. (2019). "#MigrantCaravan: The Border Wall and the Establishment of Otherness on Instagram." *New Media & Society*, 23(1), pp. 121–141.

Jasanoff, S. (Ed.). (2004). *States of Knowledge: The Co-production of Science and Social Order*. Routledge.

Kitchin, R., & Lauriault, T. P. (2015). "Small Data in the Era of Big Data." *GeoJournal*, 80(4), 463–475.

Laestadius, L. (2017). "Instagram." In *The SAGE Handbook of Social Media Research*

Methods, edited by A. Quan-Haase & L. Sloan (pp. 573–592). Thousand Oaks: Sage Publications.

Lamont, M., & S. Ross, A. (2019). "Deconstructing Embedded Meaning within Cyclists' Instagram Discourse: #fromwhereiride." *Annals of Leisure Research, 23*(3), 339–363.

Leaver, T., Highfield, T., & Abidin, C. (2020). *Instagram: Visual Social Media Cultures.* London: John Wiley & Sons.

Lechuga, M. (2017). "Coding Intensive Movement with Technologies of Visibility: Alien Affect." *Capacious: A Journal for Emerging Affect Inquiry, 1*(1), 83–97.

Lind, F., & Meltzer, C. E. (2020). "Now You See Me, Now You Don't: Applying Automated Content Analysis to Track Migrant Women's Salience in German News." *Feminist Media Studies*, 1–18.

Losh, E. (2015). "Feminism Reads Big Data: 'Social Physics,' Atomism, and Selfiecity." *International Journal of Communication, 9*(3), 1647–1659.

Manovich, L. (2017). *Instagram and Contemporary Image* (Self-published).

Massanari, A. (2017). "#Gamergate and The Fappening: How Reddit's Algorithm, Governance, and Culture Support Toxic Technocultures." *New Media & Society, 19*(3), 329–346.

Mozilla (2021). "YouTube Regrets: A Crowdsourced Investigation into YouTube's Recommendation Algorithm." https://foundation.mozilla.org/campaigns/regrets-reporter/findings/.

Muñoz, C. L., & Towner, T. L. (2017). "The Image Is the Message: Instagram Marketing and the 2016 Presidential Primary Season." *Journal of Political Marketing, 16*(3–4), 290–318.

Naguib, S.-A. (2004). "The Aesthetics of Otherness in Museums of Cultural History." *Tidsskrift for Kulturforskning, 3*(4), 5–21.

Navarro, J. G. (2020, May 14). "Countries with the Most Instagram Users in Latin America as of April 2020." *Statista.* https://www.statista.com/statistics/950923/countries-with-most-instagram-users-latin-america/.

Newberry, C. (2019, October 22). "37 Instagram Statistics That Matter to Marketers in 2020." *Hootsuite Social Media Management.* https://blog.hootsuite.com/instagram-statistics/.

Newberry, C. (2020, June 23). "The 2020 Instagram Hashtag Guide—How to Use Them and Get Results." *Hootsuite Social Media Management.* https://blog.hootsuite.com/instagram-hashtags/.

Ono, K. A. (2012). "Borders That Travel: Matters of the Figural Border." In *Border Rhetorics: Citizenship and Identity on the US-Mexico Frontier*, edited by D. R.

DeChaine (pp. 19–32). Tuscaloosa. University of Alabama Press.

Richardson, A. V. (2017). "Bearing Witness While Black: Theorizing African American Mobile Journalism after Ferguson." *Digital Journalism, 5*(6), 673–698.

Semple K. (2018, April 2). "Trump Transforms Immigrant Caravans in Mexico Into Cause Célèbre." *New York Times*. https://www.nytimes.com/2018/04/02/world/americas/caravans-migrants-mexico-trump.html.

Shoichet, C. E. (2020, January 21). "Migrants Clash with Mexican Troops at the Guatemala Border." *CNN*. https://www.cnn.com/2020/01/21/americas/mexico-guatemala-border-caravan/index.html.

Smith, S. P. (2018). "Instagram Abroad: Performance, Consumption and Colonial Narrative in Tourism." *Postcolonial Studies, 21*(2), 172–191.

Soto-Vásquez, A. D. (2021). "Mediating the Magic Kingdom: Instagram, Fantasy, and Identity." *Western Journal of Communication, 84*(5), 588–608.

Thorbjørnsrud, K., & Figenschou, T. U. (2016). "Do Marginalized Sources Matter? A Comparative Analysis of Irregular Migrant Voice in Western Media." *Journalism Studies, 17*(3), 337–355.

Uriely, N. (2001). "'Travelling Workers' and 'Working Tourists': Variations across the Interaction between Work and Tourism." *International Journal of Tourism Research, 3*(1), 1–8.

South Asian American Subjectivities

Searching for Agency among "Forever Foreigners"

Anjana Mudambi

he colonization of South Asia was in part rooted in an Orientalist master narrative premised on the Eurocentric exoticization of South Asian cultures, including food, religion, clothing, and even political structures, as fundamentally strange.[1] Because these cultural facets were deemed backward and unamenable to change, colonial powers claimed that the region required their benevolent assistance to help its cultures advance toward the "superior" Western civilization (see Mehta, 1999; Narayan, 1997; Said, 1979; Shome, 1996).

In the United States, this exoticization was fueled in the 1800s by a fetishization of India's spirituality that was contrasted with the materialism of the West (Prashad, 2000)—ideas later embraced, for example, by hippies and Hare Krishnas in the 1960s, Deepak Chopra in the 1990s, and Elizabeth Gilbert's book *Eat, Pray, Love* in 2007, which was adapted into a film in 2010. That same year, *Time* magazine published an ostensibly satirical column entitled "My Own Private India" in which Joel Stein wrote about the many changes that had occurred in his hometown of Edison, New Jersey, due to the influx of South Asians, making the town "unfamiliar" to him.[2] He mentioned, among other things, "dot heads,"[3] a slur alluding to bindis that many Hindu women traditionally wear on their foreheads for both religious and ornamental purposes; and gods with "multiple hands and an elephant nose," in reference to the Hindu deity Ganesha worshipped for his intellect. In addition to derogatively minimizing a complex nearly five-thousand-year-old civilization into a few stereotypical nuggets, such references reproduced the idea that South Asian Americans remain tied to a backward and static culture.

This enduring exoticization has real consequences for South Asian Americans because it positions them as "forever foreigners"—a racialized representation that constrains the identities of certain non-white immigrant groups by implying that, regardless of the number of generations present in the United States or their degree of cultural adaptation, they can never be considered sufficiently "American" (Shim, 1998, Tuan, 2005; Zhang, 2010). This representation then pivots into and justifies anti-immigrant sentiment toward them, such as the June 2020 vandalism of an Indian restaurant in Santa Fe, New Mexico, with graffiti telling the owners to "go home" and "go back to your country" (Martinez, 2020). Stein (2010) followed his own exoticized description of an "Indianized" Edison with a comparison to the anti-immigrant bill that had recently passed in Arizona known as SB 1070:[4] "Whenever I go back [to Edison], I feel what people in Arizona talk about—a sense of loss and anomie."

I learned about the column through a South Asian American blog that I had been following as a member of that community; that led me to read the original text, which I found to be racist and problematic. As a reproduction of Orientalist discourse, Stein's content was not particularly surprising—but its publication in a world-renowned news magazine to which many South Asians subscribed was. As Samhita (#2), a South Asian blogger, wrote, "This type of writing is totally unacceptable for a magazine that is patronized by South Asians and considered an industry standard for weekly news."[5] With over two million paid subscribers for the magazine's print version (Chozick & Gelles, 2018), this placement and publication granted the column wide readership and conferred upon it a degree of legitimacy. Lacking the same media access, the South Asian American community had turned to blogs as a space for engaging, responding to, and countering the ideas in the column. These blogs became a space where I could read more about other South Asians' varied reactions to the article, and I became enthralled by the online discourse that ensued. Stein initially responded to outrage from within the community with a problematic non-apology on Twitter that incorporated yet another stereotype: "Didn't meant [sic] to insult Indians with my column this week. Also stupidly assumed their emails would follow that Gandhi non-violence thing" (Stein, 2010, as cited in Weiner, 2010). *Time* magazine also appended the following non-apology to the column: "We sincerely regret that any of our readers were upset by this humor column of Joel Stein's. It was in no way intended to cause offense" (Stein, 2010, para. 10). I have previously explained that these statements blamed the reader for misreading Stein's satirical intent by relying on a form of race talk known as "intention-denial" (see van Dijk, 1992) and maintaining his privilege to discursively construct another cultural group (Mudambi, 2019b).

Although the effects of the bloggers' discourses are therefore not readily apparent, the relationship between discursive engagement and agency should not necessarily be evaluated in terms of concrete and immediate change. As Wanzer-Serrano writes, "While the practical goal of any rhetoric may be to persuade people to act in one way or another, instrumental success is but one rather shortsighted criterion on which to base our critical judgments" (2015, p. 136). After all, discursive change is a process, not an event (Hall, 1985, 1988). I draw on multiple scholars (Anguiano & Chávez, 2011; Calafell & Delgado, 2004; Chávez, 2015; Cisneros, 2012, 2013; Enck-Wanzer, 2011a; Flores, 1996; Hasian & Delgado, 1998; Holling, 2006; Holling & Calafell, 2011; Lechuga, 2020; Mudambi, 2015; Ono & Sloop, 1995, 2002; Sowards, 2010; Wanzer-Serrano, 2015) who have established the need to understand nondominant subjectivities and different forms of agency by examining the vernacular rhetorics of marginalized groups. As I have argued elsewhere (Mudambi, 2015), this body of research largely focuses on the development of Latina/o/x vernacular studies with scope for expanding its application to other nondominant groups.

As a diasporic community, South Asian Americans turned to online spaces to create a collective subject and enact strategies for performing agency. In this study, I critically analyze a set of blogs as a form of vernacular rhetoric to explore the discursive strategies employed in response to Stein (2010) and to demonstrate the complexities of discursive agency. First, I explore how the history of South Asian immigration to the United States has discursively positioned us as culturally unassimilable Others within the racist trope of "forever foreigners." Then, I explain how the development of a collective subject can facilitate alternate subject positions and the use of mimicry to disrupt colonialist authority, forging avenues for discursive agency within the framework of vernacular discourse. After a review of my methodology, I present my analysis of the bloggers' discourses. Finally, I argue that South Asian Americans' use of vernacular rhetorics online was an important move because it created opportunities to challenge exoticized representations as "forever foreigners" through a collective sense of agency.

A Historical Overview of Representations of South Asian Americans

The immigration of South Asians to the United States can be divided into two periods, both marked by ambiguity in their representation. The first period in the early 1900s established the struggles around their categorization within a racial classification system founded on a Black/white binary, particularly given the range of skin colors among South Asians (Mudambi, 2015). Although they came from the Asian continent, they were distinct from other Asians because they were considered "Aryan"—a label tied to colonialist and caste-based logics—and therefore belonging to the Caucasian race, a seemingly advantageous positioning (see Mudambi, 2023). Court cases in 1910 and 1913 confirmed this status, and South Asians were considered eligible for citizenship and property ownership. However, their white labor competitors saw them as an economic threat. That fact, combined with their darker skin, led to South Asians occasionally being called the N-word, a derogatory term that not only compares them to African Americans but makes clear that this comparison is undesirable.[6] This struggle played out before the Supreme Court in the 1923 *Bhagat Singh Thind* case after the 1917 Immigration Act effectively ended this period of immigration by South Asians to the United States, leaving uncertain the status of several hundred South Asian naturalized U.S. citizens. Although the plaintiff tried to claim whiteness, the Supreme Court pronounced that "Hindus" could not be considered "white" because it was a reference to skin color and not race, rendering stateless South Asians who had previously acquired U.S. citizenship (Ngai, 2004; Takaki, 1989).

The 1965 Hart-Celler Act heralded the contemporary period of South Asian immigration, which shifted to a national quota system for immigration and made twenty thousand immigrant slots available for *each* South Asian nation (Ngai, 2004; Takaki, 1989). In this period, the difficulties with racial classification became interlaced with the model minority discourse, which ignores history and structural racism to establish certain non-white immigrant groups as a standard to which other racial groups should aspire. Because the act prioritized skilled technical labor, South Asians originally admitted under this act were predominantly highly educated medical, engineering, and managerial professionals from upper-caste, urban backgrounds. They were therefore easily subsumed within the model minority discourse, again positioning them closer to whiteness than blackness within the racial hierarchy (Mudambi, 2015, 2019a, 2023). However, the Hart-Celler Act also included family reunification provisions, which was intended for European families but inadvertently led to the arrival of a "second wave" of South Asian immigrants who tended to be less educated and of a working class. Stein alludes to this history when he writes, "For a while, we assumed all Indians were geniuses. Then, in the 1980s, the doctors and engineers brought over their merchant cousins, and we were no longer so sure about the genius thing" (2010, para. 5). Because this wave of working-class South Asians helped propel the community into one of the fastest growing immigrant populations in the United States, our representation shifted somewhat to a "yellow peril" discourse in which we were again seen as an economic and cultural threat (Kawai, 2005; Kurien, 2003; Li & Skop, 2010; Mudambi, 2019a).

Orientalist master narratives "that reinforce South Asians as alien and foreign to America" (Davé, 2013, p. 7) have underscored this complicated history. The initial denial of a "white" classification stemmed from the notion that Asian Indians were a part of the "white man's burden." Because European colonizers needed to "civilize" them, they could not be considered "white" (Ngai, 2004). The United States' obsession with spirituality had given way to the protection of the white civilization "when confronted by real, living Indians" (Prashad, 2000, p. 42). As Ngai writes, "For Europeans, assimilation was a matter of socialization and citizenship its ultimate reward. Asians, no matter how committed to American ideals or practiced in American customs, remained racially unassimilable and, therefore, forever ineligible to citizenship" (2004, p. 46). South Asian Americans had consequently met with the reality of U.S. immigration and citizenship policies defined by Eurocentric racial and class-based exclusions rather than multicultural ideals (Luibhéid, 2002).

Given the ambiguity in our racial classification within the dominant Black/white racial structure, "model minority" became an easy way to "know" South Asian Americans. Although this representation seemingly affords us access to certain privileges, it inherently marks us as a racialized Other—antithetical to the white U.S. body politic both culturally and racially. As such, we remain "forever foreign" to the full privileges of white America (Prashad, 2000; Skop, 2017). Our primary allegiance as "foreigners" must remain with our "homelands," reinforcing our threat to the United States under the "yellow peril" discourse (Pham, 2015). Prashad (2000) repeatedly states that South Asians were wanted for our labor, not our lives. South Asians were never supposed to stay in this country, much less bring our families and cultural traditions; our commitment to doing so paradoxically works against us. Although at times we have contested our "white" classification to facilitate challenging our discrimination, we have also reproduced our model minority status to distance ourselves from the "yellow peril" representation (Das Gupta, 2006; Mudambi, 2019a).

South Asian Americans are consequently always necessarily tied to our geographical past, which is grounded in an Orientalist legacy. Cities like Edison, New Jersey, "are places of exoticism (where nondesis can go to taste the culture of the subcontinent without leaving the United States) . . . that represent the loss of *native* control over the cities" (Prashad, 2000, p. 106). Despite the multiple generations of South Asians now living in the United States and the cultural, linguistic, and religious diversity among us, exoticized media representations that reinforce our foreignness construct South Asian Americans for a white audience (Lopez, 2016; McWan & Cramer, 2022). Contemporary popular culture remains littered with stereotypical Indian accents (Davé, 2013) and "consumable icons of 'Indian-ness' . . . such as the presence of an elephant, representations of Indian gods, Hindi pop music, and extravagant Indian clothing" (Davé, 2012, p. 170). The persistence of these representations raises the important question of how South Asian Americans can exercise discursive agency to challenge them. In the following section, I situate this question within literature that explores how vernacular discourses can theoretically operate to counter dominant discourses through the construction of a collective subject to create alternative subject positions and disrupt the colonialist authority.

Vernacular Discourses and Rhetorical Agency

The critical study of discourse has undergone a crucial development within communication studies to analyze how subjects and subject positions are (re) produced, challenged, and rearticulated. Foucauldian (1978) subjects are sociologically, ideologically, and politically disciplined from birth by the ideological systems that precede and produce them. Hence, the dominant ideological framework of Orientalism produces and disciplines the South Asian American as an Oriental subject (Said, 1979)—a "forever foreigner" who can never fully be "American." However, because the discourses that produce and reproduce identities are not static, these positions are not fixed or stable but subject to production, reproduction, and contestation. This unrelenting process allows for changes in one's subjectivity (Butler, 1993), raising important questions about human agency, a term that has been contested in literature.

Traditionally, definitions of agency have tended toward an approach that is vested in Western, masculine notions of rhetoric as persuasion. For example, Campbell defines rhetorical agency as "the capacity to act, that is to have the competence to speak or write in a way that will be recognized or heeded by others in one's community" (2005, p. 3). However, faced with inherent challenges to "be[ing] recognized or heeded by others," marginalized groups have sought out other forms of agency that are more performative in nature and that are usually tied to the negotiation and affirmation of their identities (see Chávez, 2015; Cisneros, 2012). For instance, although the Young Lords garbage offensive did not accomplish their main goal of cleaning up their barrio, by constructing "a revolutionary, decolonial discursive space and defin[ing] a radical ethos" (Wanzer-Serrano, 2015, p. 136), their movement successfully enacted agency because it awakened its people's consciousness. Identifying nondominant forms of agency responds to scholars' calls for the communication discipline to engage in nondominant ways of knowing (Chávez, 2015; Flores, 2016; Shome, 1996).

The critical analysis of vernacular discourse (Ono & Sloop, 1995) has been a crucial development in this regard because it centers "communities of color as authors and creators of cultural practices and discourses that have been constitutive of their identities" (Flores, 2016, p. 11). Because vernacular discourses are not necessarily counterhegemonic in nature (Calafell & Delgado, 2004; Cisneros, 2013; Holling & Calafell, 2011; Mudambi, 2015; Ono & Sloop,

1995), they produce impure spaces in which community members may negotiate their identities and sense of belonging (Flores, 2016). By focusing on these spaces of rhetorical activity, the critique of vernacular rhetoric allows scholars to recognize new forms of agency operating in contrast to the dominant voices (Ono & Sloop, 1995). Various critiques of vernacular discourses have identified agentic strategies among marginalized groups, such as *"haciendo caras"* (Sowards, 2010), border rhetorics (Cisneros, 2012), mestizaje/nomadic thinking (Lechuga, 2020), border thinking (Enck-Wanzer, 2011a), collective agency (Wanzer-Serrano, 2015), and using visual rhetoric to "[constitute] a united Latina/o front" (Calafell & Delgado, 2004, p. 18). These examples illustrate the need to look beyond traditional forms of agency to understand the strategies employed by marginalized groups.

There are two defining facets of vernacular rhetorics. The first, syncretism, relates to the articulation of community that affirms cultural expression while potentially protesting "against the dominant cultural ideology" (Ono & Sloop, 1995, p. 21). Cultural syncretism may be seen in the construction of *collective subjects*. This process, drawing from the notion of constitutive rhetorics (Charland, 1987), rearticulates fragments of discourse to produce an identity through which subjects become linked as a community (Drzewiecka, 2002; Hasian & Flores, 1997). For a diasporic community, the formation of a collective subject allows them to develop strength in numbers and in terms of an affective connection to each other and to the issue at hand (Lopez, 2016). Crucial to this process is the construction of discursive spaces that afford marginalized groups the opportunity to "name themselves" (Flores, 1996, p. 146), affirm their community, and enable social organizing in a struggle against the dominant culture.

This process then facilitates their engagement in social and performative avenues of agency by which they shift and destabilize subject positions, challenging the existing ideological systems (Wanzer-Serrano, 2015; Sowards, 2010). When collective subjects (re)position themselves within the preexisting discursive structures, they challenge how discourses produce people as subjects and objects. Subjects are entitled to understand and interpret the subjectivities of objects, as in the case of colonizers (subjects) who could interpret the experiences of their colonized objects based on Orientalist discourse (Said, 1979). Shome, referencing Edward Said, states, "To do so is to have 'knowledge' of such subjects—who in the process become objects—and such 'knowledge' then provides the intellectual power 'to dominate it, to have authority over it,' and in the process 'deny autonomy to it'" (1996, p. 43). Therefore, for the object to become a subject and "become an active agent in the construction of [their] identity" (Flores, 1996, p. 147) facilitates empowerment.

The second aspect of vernacular discourse is pastiche, a process of "constructing a unique discursive form out of cultural fragments . . . [that] emphasizes invention and organization and reconstitutes discourses within specific racial, cultural, gendered, and ethnic communities" (Ono & Sloop, 1995, p. 23). Despite Ono and Sloop's exclusion of mimicry from pastiche, I argue that mimicry functions as such specifically by destabilizing identity positions and disrupting the Orientalist framework that maintains colonialist authority. In making this claim, I diverge from Ono and Sloop's reliance on Jameson's (1992) notion of postmodern mimicry, which they assert has become lifeless and devoid of ulterior political motives, and turn instead to Bhabha's (1994) conception of mimicry as an alternative, incomplete repetition of the traits and discourse of colonizers. With this understanding, destabilization occurs precisely because marginalized communities use mimicry to reconstitute colonialist discourses in new and unimagined ways, constructing a culturally syncretic pastiche that is politically disruptive and shifts the gaze.

My focus on how South Asian American bloggers form a collective subject to construct alternative subjectivities and use mimicry to disrupt colonial authority offers a critical paradigm from which to examine the rhetorical agency of diasporic communities in the United States and contributes to an understanding of how online discursive spaces are used in the context of rhetorical agency (Lechuga, 2020; Yueh, 2020). In what follows, after reviewing my methodology, I present my analysis of the bloggers' responses to Stein (2010) to elucidate how they use culturally syncretic discourse to exercise agency in challenging their representation as exoticized "forever foreigners."

Data Collection and Methods

Data consisted of blogs written by South Asian Americans in response to Stein (2010) and was gathered as part of a larger project. Several characteristics make blogs an appropriate choice of data for this project. First, they are significant sites of vernacular discourse—a form of participatory media that provides wider networks with greater access to discourse and creates new avenues for vernacular expression (Howard, 2008a, 2008b; see also Rome, 2021). As such, they provide spaces wherein migrant communities may construct their own subjectivities, agency, and ways of knowing (see also Mudambi, 2015). Second, blogs are not confined by the geographic locations where the texts are produced (Howard, 2008b), enabling syncretism among diasporic communities. Third, by "creating an arena of public discourse in which audiences can interact directly with the bloggers" (Mudambi, 2015, p. 49), the texts emerge from destabilized locations and intersections of network communications. These locations may then shape the discourse in unpredictable and uncontrollable ways, increasing the potential for agents to exert a "transformative influence" (Howard, 2008b, p. 508).

In qualitative research, one must consider the point at which data becomes saturated, or so repetitive that no new information or insights can be obtained (Mason, 2002). When blogs are the unit of analysis, data saturation may occur earlier than in more traditional forms of qualitative research because the "network" nature of blog discourses leads to the "distinct possibility of a self-limiting 'echo-chamber'" (Kenix, 2009, p. 793). This characteristic must be balanced with the need for breadth of data. I began by using *Google Blogs* search, including but not limited to terms such as "Joel Stein" and "New Jersey Indians," and then scanning those results for links to additional posts that addressed the same topic and constituted a blogosphere with a networked discussion (Harp & Tremayne, 2006). I reviewed each post to ensure that it and/or a substantial number of comments fit the project criteria by (a) engaging with the Stein (2010) article; and (b) being written by a South Asian American. These identities were confirmed to the extent possible by a combination of screen names, personal details revealed, and linguistic cues. Once I established the blogs that fit these criteria, I saved them to establish the date of analysis. The platforms included personal blogs, culture-specific group blog sites, and issue-oriented websites (such as Change.org).

I then located the point of data saturation in several ways. First, I observed that after two months following the column's publication, further responses were either repetitive or less directly responsive to the discourse. Because websites hosted multiple blog posts with many comments by the same general group of bloggers within days of each other and the publication of the column, I selected only one main post per site. In addition, the blog on one site, Sepia Mutiny, had 395 comments within two days, making repetition inevitable; therefore, I stopped analysis once it reached saturation. This process resulted in ten blogs that were used in the larger project; for this study, data relevant to this study emerged from seven of the ten blog posts, with two hundred comments, and I have used screen names throughout (see appendix). I begin by analyzing how bloggers constitute a collective subject through their blogs.

Affirming Community as a Collective Subject

Bloggers use specific language to construct a collective subject and affirm their sense of community, expanding from an Asian Indian heritage to identification across the subcontinent, raising complex questions of labeling. For example, Curry Bear (#4) uses the phrase "my fellow" and the word "we" to construct a relationship within the Indian community: "Finally, to all my fellow Indians . . . how should we react to all this?" He then references "my fellow Pakistanis, Sri Lankans & Bangladeshis who are like collateral damage in Joel's article" to purposefully expand this collective. In the following instance, Samhita (#2) shifts seamlessly between "Desis" and "South Asians":

> There is no "best practice" in talking about South Asians and it is OK to say horrendously offensive and uncomplicated stories about us with little to no accountability. . . . Desis have thus far been the butt of jokes or a cultural oasis of things to point at and gush or a target for racism both institutional and in foul attempts at comedy.

Notably, the term "Desi," commonly used among Indians to refer to themselves, has been criticized for its exclusivity and its origins in hegemonic North Indian linguistic traditions. Similarly, the broader "South Asian" label has been criticized for its India-centric origins (see Singh, 2007). However, the interchangeable, if unreflexive, usage of the labels "Desi," "Indian," and "South Asian" also functions to produce a broad, collective subjectivity that is inchoate and contextually contingent. The term "South Asian" bears historical significance, particularly following the events of 9/11, in terms of recognizing the shared experiences from our brown racialization, much like "Black" or "Latina/o/x" communities (Kurien, 2003; see also Mudambi, 2015).

It may also be noted that insofar as the "South Asian" label follows from our racial naturalization (see Carbado, 2005) within the United States, it constructs and names ourselves as a U.S.-based community, belying our foreignness and connoting a common pan-ethnic and racial identity we can strategically use to mobilize for social justice. The role these blogs play in such mobilization is evident in two ways. First, the very act of engaging in these blog spaces indicates a strategic interpellation into a particular subjectivity, suggesting a dominant, collective response to the article around which South Asian bloggers unite. In response to Samhita, DeafBrownTrash (#2) comments, "Thanks, Samhita, for writing this. I read this article last night and was enraged. I was waiting for one of my fave blogs (Feministing, Racialicious, Sepia Mutiny, Angry Asian Man, etc) to comment on this." He refers to specific blog sites that center around a South Asian identification, a blogosphere that "has emerged primarily in connection with a drive for social activism" (Mudambi, 2019b, p. 249). These spaces therefore facilitate the formation of a collective subject by allowing for connection, appreciation, and validation among the bloggers, thereby fulfilling a purpose of vernacular discourse to affirm community.

Second, the blog spaces establish an action orientation among the bloggers based in the establishment of their collective identities, which has been a key feature in the social movements of racial minorities since the 1950s and 1960s. For example, EmeraldJade (#3) proclaims within a comment:

> Due to troubl[ing] new developments against Indian-origin people, it's time to stand united for ALL PEOPLE FOR PEACE:
>
> Joel Stein of Time magazine has written a scathing openly racist "humorous" article against "dothead" Indians (discussing his hometown Edison and the growing Indian population & his discomfort of it), which is uniting Indians all over the world to have a peaceful resistance against any form of negativity on any group. If people may recall, the dothead name was derived from the dot-buster movement, designed to promote violence against Indian-origin people. THIS IS NOT ACCEPTABLE TO US.
>
> Please take a moment to join the petition and please take a moment to write to Time magazine (letters@time.com), if you believe that all groups, including Indians, deserve positive treatment: http://org2.democracyinaction. org/o/6237/p/dia/act.

Ram Ramaswami (#5) also asserts in a comment:

> Time has a big business in India. You and many others may want to teach Time that if they want our money, they need to show due courtesy and sensitivity, if not love and respect. If you do, please join me in this worthwhile educational effort and pass on this mail to as many fellow Indians as you can.

His comment uses the words "our" and "fellow" to identify the collective and then incorporates a call for that community to act together. EmeraldJade, drawing upon the historical context from which the slur "dothead" emerged, appeals to the international diasporic community to "stand united." This process of uniting as a collective shifts resistance from "an emphasis on individual survival to one of collective action" (Omi & Winant, 1994, p. 101). By demonstrating collective action upon the discourse beyond the space of the blogs, these comments illustrate the syncretic function of the space. Having established themselves as subjects through naming and constructing their collective community with this action orientation, bloggers then use this space to destabilize Stein's as well as a larger colonialist authority over the South Asian American subject by disrupting subject and object positions.

Disrupting Subject and Object Positions

To shift the gaze within this space, bloggers begin by defining their own diasporic subjectivities based on their experiences that emerge from interstitial spaces. Such subjectivities recall Cisneros's (2012) theorization of border rhetoric as a type of vernacular discourse in which "the border" may serve as a metaphorical space inhabited by migrant communities. He explains that "border(land)s represent spaces of contradiction that can be embraced as a source of affirmative identity" (2012, p. 564) precisely because they are spaces from which subjects must find strategies for survival. This is particularly notable in edisongirl's (#1) ambivalence, when she writes in a comment,

> Don't get me wrong—I'm thrilled that our people have populated the place. I'm thrilled that Indian culture has become such an important part of American

culture—of Jersey culture! But I'm sad that some of the staples in the town I grew up in have been replaced.

By writing from a location that is both insider and outsider, she implicitly rejects the object position of "forever foreigner" because speaking from such border spaces disrupts the very construction of the subject/object relationship.

Considering how histories can support and challenge ideological perspectives (Westwell, 2011), it is also significant that this space allows bloggers to assume a subject position from which they define their own histories. When Stein (2010) blames India's poverty on a lack of intelligence among its people, jagr721 (#1) explains in a comment that India's economic plight "has a great deal to do with colonialism . . . [and not with] the inherent stupidity of its people." By using colonial histories otherwise hidden in the larger immigration discourse, he disrupts mainstream discourses and dislocates First World epistemic privilege. Curry Bear (#4) refers to how Manifest Destiny was used to "acquire more land and kill an entire ethnic group of, ironically, Indians. Now that Indians have taken over your childhood town, you can think of this as karma." Prerna Lal (#7) writes, "Incidentally, Stein, since whites once dubbed the U.S. as 'Indian land,' what's wrong with flooding the country with immigrants from India?" These statements employ irony to highlight the hypocrisy and illogical nature of Stein's anti-immigrant sentiment, co-opting the colonialist language of being "taken over" by "forever foreigners" and juxtaposing it with the United States' history of genocide. In this sense, vernacular rhetorics can tell a historical narrative ideologically distinct from the grand narratives of the United States as a nation-state with open doors to immigrants.

Finally, as subjects, bloggers can then interpret the experiences of an "other" that they construct as object. Yeğenoğlu explores this in her discussion of the veil, wherein "the veiled woman can see without being seen" (1998, p. 43), effectively changing the direction of the gaze. Samhita (#2) explains Stein's psyche in a feigned display of benevolent sympathy that assigns Stein an object position:

There are few things sadder than reading a writer that is so caught up in their own ego, racism and bad writing that they don't even have the foresight to see how poorly their piece has not only come across but will be received.

Several bloggers also highlight and construct Stein's Jewish identity. For example, meegan (#3) writes in a comment, "Stein appears to be oddly unaware of his Jewish ethnicity, but fancying himself as waspy as white bread." She criticizes his lack of empathy for the South Asian community as a fellow marginalized group member, calling out his apparent ability to pass for white.

Given Stein's claims to satire, turning the stereotypes toward him also effectively shifts the gaze. For example, Anna (#1) calls out Stein's blatant use of stereotypes in the following paragraph:

> Why do you have to be so Indian about everything? Why can't you be dishonest and White, and not change everything, and not take over the businesses where I learned to be a petty thief and . . . and . . . stuff? NOTHING SHOULD EVER CHANGE, DAMNIT. IT'S JOEL STEIN'S WORLD AND WE'RE ALL JUST LIVING IN IT.

She reiterates a problematic and essentializing notion of "be[ing] so Indian" and then constructs incongruous stereotypes of whites as "dishonest," bringing attention to the inadequacies of the stereotypes on which Stein relies. Her sarcastic claim that "it's Joel Stein's world" challenges the self-proclaimed right of dominant groups to construct society and define the identities of South Asians within that society. Notably, bloggers use humor to construct Stein as a "clown" who "embodies all the problems of the social order . . . [but is] not an evil person, although s/he may do evil through ignorance" (Carlson, 1988, p. 312). Curry Bear (#4) does this when he writes:

> You know Joel, I understand where you're coming from. No one likes change, whether it's for good or bad. . . .
> You can either be fearful of the changes, or you can embrace them. It is your choice. . . . People fear what they don't understand, and I feel that you Joel are a victim of this. You don't have to be scared of Indians or Indian things.

In these examples, Anna and Curry Bear invert a common trope of Orientalism by ironically labeling Stein (and white people in general) as unchanging. Humor functions as an agentic strategy to redefine the subject/object relationship.

Mimicry as Pastiche

Bloggers further use humor to mimic Stein's satire as a form of pastiche that disrupts his authority within the colonial matrix. According to Ono and Sloop, "Vernacular discourse forms a pastiche of popular culture from elements that have been torn out of context for the explicit purpose of constituting new effects" (1995, p. 23). Throughout the texts, bloggers draw from Stein's discourse, using mimicry as pastiche to reconstruct popular stereotypes and representations of South Asians in humorous and incongruous ways. For example, Prerna Lal (#7), calling the column "tasteless," suggests, "Maybe their [Stein and *Time* magazine's] tastes would have improved if they'd stuck to hot and spicy Indian foods, instead of attempting social commentary?" She humorously suggests that Stein's complaints could be resolved through consuming *more* Indian culture, not *less*. Anna (#1) borrows multiple "consumable icons of 'Indian-ness'" (Davé, 2012, p. 120) in which Stein traffics and uses amusingly exaggerated reclamations of them to demonstrate their absurdity and one-dimensionality:

> But first, to really do Mr. Stein justice, I'm going to light some incense, play a "Jai Ho" remix, and nosh on some curry—but daintily! I don't want to stain my exotic silk costume, which I bought in . . . of all places . . . Edison. What are the odds, right? Oh, wait . . . according to TIME magazine, the odds are very good that my Indian garb is from Edison. The whole place is infested with Patels. Did I mention there's a dot on my forehead? I'm a dothead! Wheee! Oh, but I am getting ahead of myself (I am waggling my head as I type that. If you're reading this, switch to an "Apu" voice, would you? Thanks, you're a doll. I mean, you're an Aishwarya!)

She engages in stereotypical representations—such as eating curry, wearing a bindi and "exotic" clothing, listening to Bollywood music, and lighting incense—with cultural pride in the South Asian dominance of Edison, even mockingly claiming the label "dothead." These are things that many South Asians might do and would necessarily recognize, but she claims to do them all simultaneously while she blogs in the middle of night, referencing the problematic accent of the character "Apu" from *The Simpsons* (see Davé, 2012, 2013) in the process. In other words, she employs those stereotypes on her own terms, inflating them to a point where their incongruities are unmistakable.

Similarly, having positioned Stein as fearful of change and of Indian culture, Curry Bear (#4) humorously describes a similar series of consumable icons, such as in this explanation of Bollywood movies:

> Have you ever seen an Indian movie? Check out some of our women. They're hot and they seduce you with songs in the rain. Seriously, white guys get all the Indian bitches these days. If you tried your luck, you could be the chutney pimp of Edison.

Humor allows an argument to be heard "by providing a unique vantage point from which to see the inaccuracies of a situation" (Demo, 2000, p. 135). In this case, Curry Bear uses humor as "imaginative reconstructive surgery" (Ono & Sloop, 1995, p. 23) to explain Indian artifacts, de-exoticizing them to challenge the "forever foreigner" representation while satirizing Stein's own satire of the influence of Indian culture in Edison.

Bloggers also turn their attention to Jewish stereotypes. Anna (#1) writes, "What about a person with two arms and a prominent nose who lights a menorah? Because India has those, too. What thrilling invective should be hurled their way?" This statement functions at multiple levels. First, it turns Stein into the object of the discourse by highlighting his Jewish identity. Second, it engages Jewish stereotypes ironically; given the well-known dangers of antisemitic tropes, this mimicry of Stein's "humor" in fact demonstrates how his humor fails. Finally, it highlights how the stereotypes he engages minimize the cultural and religious diversity found among South Asians, a broad category that includes Jewish people.

Last, mimicking "white" traditions and stereotypes places dominant U.S. culture on par with marginalized racial and ethnic groups in terms of its subjection to ridicule and satire (see Carmack, 2011) while "claiming" to assimilate. For example, Goutam Jois (#6) mimics the "'wonderfully American' [tradition of] petitioning for redress of one's grievances" and urging his readers to sign a petition against Stein's column. He mocks the litigiousness of U.S. society, as he recognizes his nonlegal appropriation of the verb "petition." By naming petitioning as an "American" act in which South Asians can engage, he participates in a Bhabha-esque (1994) form of mimicry that locates the Other within the subject. Anna (#1) uses this form of mimicry when she challenges the typical silence of Indian Americans in the face of insult:

No more. I'm an American. The residents of Edison have been Americans for longer than Stein's had a column. They don't need this. Fuck you if you CAN take a "joke." Word. This born-American citizen is over and out. Let the wild rumpus begin.

Claiming her "American" identity via the stereotype of the obnoxious American, she mimics American culture and, in so doing, creates space for South Asians to speak against the mainstream discourse. These statements also mock the expectation of assimilation that relegates South Asians to be "forever foreigners."

Through these instances of mimicry, bloggers appropriate common stereotypical elements from hegemonic culture in ways that are exaggerated, humorous, or incongruous. It is important to note how this blog space and the collective subject that they have constructed within it enable this culturally syncretic pastiche. Specifically, the collective provides an "[audience] well-versed enough in the vernacular to understand the messages" (Ono & Sloop, 1995, p. 25) because they have created this community of understanding wherein they utilize shared references, experiences, and even stereotypes to which they can easily relate as South Asian Americans. They demonstrate nimbleness in switching from humorously employing these stereotypes to directly contesting them, enabled by the impure and hybrid spaces in which they frequently—if at times subtly and implicitly—establish themselves as Americans, to destabilize their positioning and confront their "forever foreigner" representation. In other words, their overall rhetoric ensues from the collective subject that initially forms the audience and grasps the references from an insider/outsider perspective, enabling this exercise of agency.

Conclusion

In this chapter, I have critically analyzed a set of blogs and corresponding comments by South Asian Americans written in direct response to Stein's (2010) original column in *Time* magazine as a space of vernacular discourse to contest exoticized representations that construct them as "forever foreigners." Bloggers used this space to construct and define a contextually contingent South Asian community—one perhaps dominated by Indian Americans, as is the larger population, but strategically extended to the larger South

Asian community—illustrating the culturally syncretic function of vernacular discourses. This creation of an inchoate collective subject empowers bloggers to mobilize through culturally affirming group responses. This collective then exercised agency by disrupting and destabilizing subject/object relationships, including highlighting hidden histories and shifting the gaze of humor and representations. These discursive moves are empowering because they reclaim a capacity to speak for themselves and challenge the discursive colonization imposed by Orientalism (Shome, 1996).

The use of mimicry was also apparent as a culturally syncretic pastiche that "challenges mainstream discourse, while at the same time affirm[s] and creat[es] the community and culture that produce vernacular discourse" (Ono & Sloop, 1995, pp. 23–24). This analysis has shown how Bhabha's (1994) conceptualization of mimicry is relevant to the vernacular discourses of marginalized communities. According to Bhabha, the strength of mimicry as a destabilizing force is in its reversal of the gaze that produces a "partial vision of the colonizer's presence" (1994, p. 126) through its ambivalence, questioning the colonial authority from which the problematic discourses flow. The bloggers' use of mimicry continued to construct a culturally affirming community that identified with fragments of hegemonic culture but also redefined them on their own terms, de-exoticizing their cultural identities and practices. They still functioned to affirm the South Asian community and our collective experiences and subjectivities while disrupting Stein's colonialist authority.

The use of humor, sarcasm, and irony as vernacular agentic strategies, particularly within online spaces, merits further research and exploration. It should also be considered that such strategies may be more available to certain marginalized communities than others. In this study, they may come from a subjective standpoint in which "Desis realize they are not 'white,'" (Prashad, 2000, p. 94), but we also know that we are not Black. In other words, as a model minority with some access to privilege, most of the South Asians participating in these blogs are not likely facing the same levels of violence and threat to our existence as, for instance, the Black American community or transgender community (Mudambi, 2023). Therefore, the bloggers recognize and rightfully challenge the discriminatory treatment we endure as a marginalized group, but our relative privilege may also enable us to employ more humorous strategies. For example, the sardonic use of the term "dothead" (and my choice to reproduce it here) is perhaps not constrained by the same historical and emotional weight that the N-word holds for the African American community. Consequently, examining the vernacular rhetorics of different racial and ethnic groups can help differentiate between the strategies they use to engage and challenge discourses, contextualize those strategies within their unique histories, and lead to a more nuanced understanding of agency.

This analysis has also illustrated the role that online spaces may play as sites of vernacular discourses for South Asian Americans. Flores (1996) asserts the importance, particularly for diasporic communities, of creating discursive spaces from which they can reach out to mainstream audiences. Although she does not specifically discuss this in relation to agency, she appears to suggest that the space itself is a step toward it, a proposition further bolstered in terms of the spaces that the internet offers (see Mitra, 2005; Mitra & Watts, 2002). Scholars have since referenced the significance of creating spaces for marginalized speakers "to craft their own agency and subjectivity" (Wanzer-Serrano, 2015, p. 127; see also Cisneros, 2012, 2013). Locating such spaces appears especially important for a geographically dispersed community to enact agency given their inherent challenges "to creat[ing] meaningful collective activities" (Prashad, 2000, p. 195). These challenges are further amplified for the South Asian American community whose collective commitment to racial justice has been, at best, inconsistent due to our interpellation into the model minority discourse, which urges people to follow the rules and not challenge a system that has offered them certain privileges. Digital spaces may help overcome these challenges, as South Asian Americans use them to develop alternate subjectivities (Mudambi, 2023).

The discourse can then also inform conversations beyond the space of the online community—that is, they have the "potential of being heard" (Mitra, 2005, p. 379). Recognizing that agency and its related actions are learned, performed, and practiced (Campbell, 2005; Enck-Wanzer, 2011b), these spaces may "activate performative repertoires, craft spaces of resistance to the established order, and alter the capacity for others to act" (Enck-Wanzer, 2011b, p. 351). As such, they may operate as a preliminary testing ground to try out civil discourse, mobilize and validate arguments, and thus increase opportunities for interaction, thereby offering unforeseen potential. Marginalized communities must continue to explore and exploit this potential by constructing and utilizing online spaces wherein they can explore, enhance, and exercise their collective sense of agency.

Appendix. List of Blog Posts in Response to Joel Stein

NUMBER	BLOG TITLE	BLOGGER	BLOG SITE	ORIGINAL POST DATE	NUMBER OF COMMENTS
1	"An Unfunny Joel Stein Walks Into Some Cow Cung"	Anna	Sepia Mutiny	June 29, 2010	104
2	"No HeeHee, Ha Ha, for Me Joel Stein"	Samhita	Feministing	June 29, 2010	23
3	"Wondrously, Indians Do Not Find Joel Stein's Droll Humor About their Poverty, Cologne to be Charming"	Chris Rovzar	New York Magazine	June 30, 2010	15
4	"Curry Bear's Thoughts on Joel Stein's Article about Indians in Edison"	Curry Bear	Curry Bear	June 28, 2010	32
5	"TIME Columnist Dislikes Indians; Indians Not a Fan of Joel Stein Either"	Sanjay	8asians	June 29, 2010	17
6	"What's Joel Stein Got Against Indians?"	Goutam Jois	Blackbooklegal	June 30, 2010	6
7	"TIME Magazine Thinks Insulting South Asians is Funny"	Prerna Lal	Change.org	June 30, 2010	3

NOTES

1. In the context of this chapter, the term "South Asia" refers to the southern region of Asia, including Bangladesh, Bhutan, India, Maldives, Nepal, Pakistan, and Sri Lanka (see Kurien, 2003). The term "South Asian" then refers to people whose ancestry can be traced to this region, while the majority of South Asian Americans are of Indian origin. Despite conflations with Hindus as a religious group, South Asians commonly include Muslims, Sikhs, Jains, and Christians, among others.

2. According to the U.S. Census (2010), Edison's Asian Indian population is almost 30 percent of its total population. There is no broader category for the South Asian population.

3. Although it is a slur, I present this word in its entirety insofar as it reproduces the discourses I am analyzing, including by members of the targeted community (of which I am a member). While this term has had violent consequences and generally should not be used, censoring members of the community who are challenging its deployment would undermine my analysis of their discourses.

4. This bill, later signed into law, permitted police officers to stop anyone they reasonably suspected of illegal status and request proof of lawful presence.

5. Blog numbers provided throughout this essay correspond to the blog numbers listed in the appendix. However, in some cases, I reference a person who posted a comment along with the blog number but do not reference the original blogger who is specified in the table.

6. See Mudambi (2015) for a detailed discussion of the positioning of South Asian Americans within the U.S. racial hierarchy.

REFERENCES

Anguiano, C. A., & Chávez, K. R. (2011). "DREAMers' Discourse: Young Latino/a Immigrants and the Naturalization of the American Dream." In *Latino/a Discourses in Vernacular Spaces: Somos de una voz*, edited by M. A. Holling & B. M. Calafell (pp. 81–99). Lanham, MD: Lexington Books.

Bhabha, H. (1994). *The Location of Culture*. London: Routledge.

Butler, J. (1993). *Bodies That Matter: On the Discursive Limits of "Sex."* New York: Routledge.

Calafell, B. M., & Delgado, F. P. (2004). "Reading Latina/o Images: Interrogating *Americanos*." *Critical Studies in Media Communication, 21*(1), 1–21.

Campbell, K. K. (2005). "Agency: Promiscuous and Protean." *Communication and Critical/Cultural Studies, 2*(1), 1–19.

Carbado, D. W. (2005). "Racial Naturalization." *American Quarterly, 57*(3), 633–658.

Carlson, A. C. (1988). "Limitations on the Comic Frame: Some Witty American Women of the Nineteenth Century." *Quarterly Journal of Speech, 74*(3), 310–322.

Carmack, H. J. (2011). "Everythang's Gonna Be All White: The Fightin' Whities' Use of Parody and Incongruity for Social Change." *Florida Communication Journal, 35*, 35–44.

Charland, M. (1987). "Constitutive Rhetoric: The Case of the *Peuple Québécois*." *Quarterly Journal of Speech, 73*(2), 133–150.

Chávez, K. R. (2015). "Beyond Inclusion: Rethinking Rhetoric's Historical Narrative." *Quarterly Journal of Speech, 101*(1), 162–172.

Chozick, A., & Gelles, D. (2018, September 16). "Time Magazine Is Bought by Marc Benioff, Salesforce Billionaire." *New York Times.* https://www.nytimes.com/2018/09/16/business/dealbook/time-magazine-salesforce-marc-benioff.html.

Cisneros, J. D. (2012). "Reclaiming the Rhetoric of Reies López Tijerina: Border Identity and Agency in 'the Land Grant Question.'" *Communication Quarterly, 60*(5), 561–587.

Cisneros, J. D. (2013). *The Border Crossed Us: Rhetorics of Borders, Citizenship, and Latina/o Identity.* Tuscaloosa: University of Alabama Press.

Das Gupta, M. (2006). *Unruly Immigrants: Rights, Activism, and Transnational South Asian Politics.* Durham: Duke University Press.

Davé, S. (2012). "Matchmakers and Cultural Compatibility: Arranged Marriage, South Asians, and American Television." *South Asian Popular Culture, 10*(2), 167–183.

Davé, S. (2013). *Indian Accents: Brown Voice and Racial Performance in American Television and Film.* Urbana: University of Illinois Press.

Demo, A. T. (2000). "The Guerrilla Girls' Comic Politics of Subversion." *Women's Studies in Communication, 23*(2), 133–156.

Drzewiecka, J. A. (2002). "Reinventing and Contesting Identities in Constitutive Discourses: Between Diaspora and Its Others." *Communication Quarterly, 50*(1), 1–23.

Enck-Wanzer, D. (2011a). "Race, Coloniality, and Geo-Body Politics: *The Garden* as Latin@ Vernacular Discourse." *Environmental Communication, 5*(3), 363–371.

Enck-Wanzer, D. (2011b). "Tropicalizing East Harlem: Rhetorical Agency, Cultural Citizenship, and Nuyorican Cultural Production." *Communication Theory, 21*(4), 344–367.

Flores, L. A. (1996). "Creating Discursive Space through a Rhetoric of Difference: Chicana Feminists Craft a Homeland." *Quarterly Journal of Speech, 82*(2), 142–156.

Flores, L. A. (2016). "Between Abundance and Marginalization: The Imperative of Racial Rhetorical Criticism." *Review of Communication, 16*(1), 4–24.

Foucault, M. (1978). *The History of Sexuality: An Introduction.* Translated by R. Hurley. New York: Random House.

Hall, S. (1985). "Signification, Representation, Ideology: Althusser and the Post-Structuralist Debates." *Critical Studies in Mass Communication, 2*(2), 91–114.

Hall, S. (1988). "The Rediscovery of 'Ideology': Return of the Repressed in Media Studies." In *Culture, Society, and the Media,* edited by M. Gurevitch, T. Bennett, J. Curran & J. Woollacott (pp. 56–90). London: Routledge.

Harp, D., & Tremayne, M. (2006). "The Gendered Blogosphere: Examining Inequality Using Network and Feminist Theory." *Journalism & Mass Communication Quarterly, 83*(2), 247–264.

Hasian, M., Jr., & Delgado, F. (1998). "The Trials and Tribulations of Racialized Critical Rhetorical Theory: Understanding the Rhetorical Ambiguities Of Proposition 187." *Communication Theory, 8*(3), 245–270.

Hasian, M., Jr., & Flores, L. A. (1997). "Children of the Stones: The Intifada and the Mythic Creation of the Palestinian State." *Southern Communication Journal, 62*(2), 89–106.

Holling, M. A. (2006). "Forming Oppositional Social Concord to California's Proposition 187 and Squelching Social Discord in the Vernacular Space of CHICLE." *Communication and Critical/Cultural Studies, 3*(3), 202–222.

Holling, M. A., & Calafell, B. M. (2011). *Latino/a Discourses in Vernacular Spaces: Somos de una voz.* Lanham, MD: Lexington Books.

Howard, R. G. (2008a). "Electronic Hybridity: The Persistent Processes of the Vernacular Web." *Journal of American Folklore, 121,* 192–218.

Howard, R. G. (2008b). "The Vernacular Web of Participatory Media." *Critical Studies in Media Communication, 25*(5), 490–513.

Jameson, F. (1992). *Postmodernism, or, the Cultural Logic of Late Capitalism.* Durham: Duke University Press.

Kawai, Y. (2005). "Stereotyping Asian Americans: The Dialectic of the Model Minority and the Yellow Peril." *The Howard Journal of Communications, 16,* 109–130.

Kenix, L. J. (2009). "Blogs as Alternative." *Journal of Computer-Mediated Communication, 14,* 790–800.

Kurien, P. A. (2003). "To Be or Not To Be South Asian: Contemporary Indian American Politics." *Journal of South Asian Studies, 6*(3), 261–288.

Lechuga, M. (2020). "Mapping Migrant Vernacular Discourses: Mestiza Consciousness, Nomad Thought, and Latina/o/x Migrant Movement Politics in the United States." *Journal of International and Intercultural Communication, 13*(3), 257–273.

Li, W., & Skop, E. (2010). "Diaspora in the United States: Chinese and Indians Compared." *Journal of Chinese Overseas, 6*(2), 286–310.

Lopez, L. K. (2016). *Asian American Media Activism: Fighting for Cultural Citizenship.* New York: New York University Press.

Luibhéid, E. (2002). *Entry Denied: Controlling Sexuality at the Border.* Minneapolis: University of Minnesota Press.

Martinez, A. (2020, June 23). "Vandals Strike India Palace in Racist Attack." *Santa Fe New Mexican.*

Mason, J. (2002). *Qualitative Researching.* Thousand Oaks: Sage.

McWan, B., & Cramer, L. M. (2022). "Progressive Racial Representation or Strategic Whiteness? Raj and Priya Koothrappali in *The Big Bang Theory.*" *Southern*

Communication Journal, 87(4), 312–323.

Mehta, U.S. (1999). *Liberalism and Empire: A Study in Nineteenth-Century British Liberal Thought*. Chicago: University of Chicago Press.

Mitra, A. (2005). "Creating Immigrant Identities in Cybernetic Space: Examples from a Non-resident Indian Website." *Media, Culture & Society, 27*(3), 371–390.

Mitra, A., & Watts, E. (2002). "Theorizing Cyberspace: The Idea of Voice Applied to the Internet Discourse." *New Media & Society, 4*(4), 479–498.

Mudambi, A. (2015). "The Construction of Brownness: Latino/a and South Asian Bloggers' Responses to SB 1070." *Journal of International and Intercultural Communication, 8*(1), 44–62.

Mudambi, A. (2019a). "South Asian American Discourses: Engaging the Yellow Peril-Model Minority Dialectic." *Howard Journal of Communications, 30*(3), 284–298.

Mudambi, A. (2019b). "Racial Satire, Race Talk, and the Model Minority: South Asian Americans Speak Up." *Southern Communication Journal, 84*(4), 246–256.

Mudambi, A. (2023). "South Asian Americans and Anti-Black racism: Critically Reflexive Racialization as an Anti-Racist Vernacular Discourse." *Communication, Culture & Critique, 16*(1), 1–8.

Narayan, U. (1997). *Dislocating Cultures: Identities, Traditions, and Third-World Feminism*. New York: Routledge.

Ngai, M. (2004). *Impossible Subjects: Illegal Aliens and the Making of Modern America*. Princeton: Princeton University Press.

Omi, M., & Winant, H. (1994). *Racial Formation in the United States: From the 1960s to the 1990s*. New York: Routledge.

Ono, K. A., & Sloop, J. M. (1995). "The Critique of Vernacular Discourse." *Communication Monographs, 62*(1), 19–46.

Ono, K. A., & Sloop, J. M. (2002). *Shifting Borders: Rhetoric, Immigration, and California's Proposition 187*. Philadelphia: Temple University Press.

Pham, V. N. (2015). "Our Foreign President Barack Obama: The Racial Logics of Birther Discourses." *Journal of International and Intercultural Communication, 8*(2), 86–107.

Prashad, V. (2000). *The Karma of Brown Folk*. Minneapolis: University of Minnesota Press.

Rome, J. M. (2021). "Blogging Wounded Manhood: Negotiating Hegemonic Masculinity and the Crisis of the Male (In)fertile Body." *Women's Studies in Communication, 44*(1), 44–64.

Said, E. W. (1979). *Orientalism*. New York: Vintage Books.

Shim, D. (1998). "From Yellow Peril through Model Minority to Renewed Yellow Peril." *Journal of Communication Inquiry, 22*(4), 385–409.

Shome, R. (1996). "Postcolonial Interventions in the Rhetorical Canon: An 'Other' View." *Communication Theory, 6*(1), 40–59.

Singh, A. (2007). "'Names Can Wait': The Misnaming of the South Asian Diaspora in Theory and Practice." *South Asian Review, 28*(1), 13–28.

Skop, E. (2017). "The Model Minority Stereotype in Arizona's Anti-immigrant Climate: SB 1070 and Discordant Reactions from Asian Indian Migrant Organizations." *GeoJournal, 82*(3), 553–566.

Sowards, S. (2010). "Rhetorical Agency as *Haciendo Caras* and Differential Consciousness through Lens of Gender, Race, Ethnicity, and Class: An Examination of Dolores Huerta's Rhetoric." *Communication Theory, 20*(2), 223–247.

Stein, J. (2010, July 5). "My Own Private India." *TIME Magazine.* http://content.time.com/time/magazine/article/0,9171,1999416,00.html.

Takaki, R. (1989). *Strangers from a Different Shore: A History of Asian Americans.* Boston: Little, Brown, and Company.

Tuan, M. (2005). *Forever Foreigners or Honorary Whites? The Asian Ethnic Experience Today.* Piscataway, NJ: Rutgers University Press.

U.S. Census Bureau. (2010). "Profile of General Population and Housing Characteristics: Edison Township, Middlesex County, N.J." http://factfinder2.census.gov/faces/tableservices/jsf/pages/productview.xhtml?src=bkmk.

van Dijk, T. A. (1992). "Discourse and the Denial of Racism." *Discourse & Society, 3*(1), 87–118.

Wanzer-Serrano, D. (2015). *The New York Young Lords and the Struggle for Liberation.* Philadelphia: Temple University Press.

Weiner, J. (2010, June 30). "*Time*'s Joel Stein Tries to Fit All Known Indian Stereotypes into Single Column." *Vanity Fair.* https://www.vanityfair.com/culture/2010/06/post-17.

Westwell, G. (2011). "Accidental Napalm Attack and Hegemonic Visions of America's War in Vietnam." *Critical Studies in Media Communication, 28*(5), 407–423.

Yeğenoğlu, M. (1998). *Colonial Fantasies: Towards a Feminist Reading of Orientalism.* Cambridge: Cambridge University Press.

Yueh, H. I. S. (2020). "Theorizing Vernacular Discourse in Sinophone Transnational Space: On Namewee's YouTube Music Videos." *Critical Studies in Media Communication, 37*(2), 174–187.

Zhang, Q. (2010). "Asian Americans beyond the Model Minority Stereotype: The Nerdy and the Left Out." *Journal of International and Intercultural Communication, 3*(1), 20–37.

Transhistorical Resistance and Containment

Vernacular Discourses of Coalition at Fort Sill

Corinne Mitsuye Sugino

O n July 20, 2019, around four hundred people gathered and marched at the Fort Sill military base in Lawton, Oklahoma, to protest against the U.S. government's plans to use it as a camp to incarcerate undocumented children, primarily from Central America. These plans were part of a broader nationwide assault on immigration with U.S. Immigration and Customs Enforcement (ICE) and the Customs and Border Protection agencies harassing, detaining, and deporting immigrant communities. Dream Action Oklahoma, a local immigration justice group who had participated in the action, later recounted:

> We stood strong, demanding that the concentration camps are not OK under any circumstances. Not in Fort Sill, not anywhere; No matter where they plan the next camp, we will be there over and over again until our people are free. But we were not alone; We had the honor to be a part of an amazing coalition of local and national organizations who put their bodies on the line, their resources for the cause, and their untiring efforts and time. (Dream Action Oklahoma, 2019)

This statement named not only the violence occurring at Fort Sill but its connection to larger practices that criminalize immigrant communities. Additionally, the coalition they referred to represented another significant part of the actions taken in July 2019; that is, multiple different activist groups and individuals helped to challenge the violence at Fort Sill, including Black Lives Matter Oklahoma City, Tsuru for Solidarity, the American Indian Movement Indigenous Territory, and many others.

An important factor that motivated this coalition was the historically charged nature of Fort Sill itself. The military base was originally built in 1869 as part of federally designated "Indian territory," or territories where many Indigenous communities were forcibly relocated to as part of a larger colonial project. Later, Fort Sill was also utilized as an internment camp during World War II. In 1942, President Roosevelt instituted Executive Order 9066, ordering over 120,000 Japanese Americans to relocate to camps throughout the United States, particularly in the West. Fort Sill housed hundreds of Japanese Americans, as well as people of Japanese ancestry from Panama, Bolivia, Peru, and Nicaragua (Okihiro, 2013). The base thus represents a charged space saturated with intergenerational and transracial trauma. Indeed, it was precisely these interweaving histories of oppression at Fort Sill that protesters drew on to decry and protest plans to incarcerate immigrant children. By naming the repeated racial trauma suffered at this particular base and its continuation into the present day, the protests linked struggles between Indigenous, Latina/o/x, and Asian American people against state-sanctioned racial violence.

This chapter explores the way marginalized communities decried racial violence at Fort Sill precisely by drawing on the historically charged nature of the space. Scholars have named the way in which space and place act not as passive backdrops but as active rhetorical mediums in constituting power relations, as well as the way marginalized groups have used place-based discourses to challenge racialized violence (Endres & Senda-Cook, 2011; Shome, 2003; Wanzer-Serrano, 2006). I extend the insights of these scholars to consider how activists drew on the interwoven histories of violence at Fort Sill to connect their struggles against oppression. Consequently, in considering the discourses of these groups, my work also explores what Ono and Sloop (1995) refer to as "vernacular discourse" by examining public statements, news articles, and websites of those oppressed communities involved in resisting Fort Sill.

Ultimately, three interrelated arguments based on themes that emerged from activist discourses frame the planned designation of Fort Sill as a migrant detention center. Firstly, these groups' statements represented vernacular discourses of coalition that drew on the place of Fort Sill, as a site of repeated violence, to name interweaving histories of oppression and to stage collective struggle. As a result, Fort Sill demonstrates the interplay of dominant and vernacular discourses in the process of forming place-based coalitions. Secondly, this rhetoric surrounding Fort Sill demonstrates the way in which multiple vernacular discourses interact not only with dominant power but also with each other by using place as a conduit for linking the struggles of different oppressed communities. Finally, much of the activists' rhetoric also employed analogy in seeking to facilitate coalition, analogizing the experiences of Japanese American internees and displaced Indigenous communities with the violence at the U.S.-Mexico border. While this aspect provided a powerful organizing message at Fort Sill, I suggest that it potentially represents some of the limits of the coalitional rhetoric by confining coalitions to moments of "shared" oppression that cannot account for cross-racial solidarity outside of interest convergence or the complexity of how racialized groups might become implicated in racial violence against each other.

In what follows, I first situate my analysis within ongoing conversations about space and place and vernacular discourse. Then, I briefly explicate Fort Sill's history as an Indigenous relocation camp, Japanese American internment camp, and its recent designation as a migrant detention center. Then, having established how this repeated legacy of violence at Fort Sill has made it a historically charged site, I examine how marginalized groups drew on this history in order to build connections from their experiences of oppression. Finally, I conclude by arguing that exploring the connections between space, place, and vernacular discourse provides opportunities for scholars to consider the politics of coalition and the situated nature of vernacular discourse.

Space and Place in Vernacular Discourses

The various groups opposing Fort Sill reveal the way vernacular discourses can produce connections across racial lines by drawing on the historically charged nature of a particular place. Ono and Sloop describe vernacular discourse as that which "resonates within and from historically oppressed communities" (1995, p. 20). For them, vernacular discourses encompass, for instance, pamphlets or communications from community organizations, films by independent filmmakers, music, art, and other forms of cultural expression in marginalized communities, as well as everyday conversations (Ono & Sloop, 1995). Though Ono and Sloop focus primarily on print mediums in their article, vernacular discourses may also include online mediums. Elsewhere, scholars have also considered the ways that Asian Americans use online spaces such as YouTube to collaborate and communicate vernacular discourse (Guo & Lee, 2013; Pham, 2017), as well as the ways in which DREAMers utilize social media to produce vernacular rhetorics that disidentify with U.S. citizenship narratives (Morrissey, 2013). Similarly, I explore the forms of vernacular discourse expressed by marginalized communities decrying Fort Sill's use as a migrant detention center by examining public statements, petitions, and accounts of the protests published online by the groups involved.

Though they may often seek to oppose dominant logics of power, vernacular discourses are not entirely separated from mainstream discourse. Instead, vernacular discourses often interact with, draw on, and sometimes reimagine mainstream discourses, a process Ono and Sloop (1995) refer to as "pastiche." I expand on this notion of pastiche to consider the interplay of dominant and vernacular discourses surrounding a particular place. The place of Fort Sill is not only material but also rhetorical; that is, it has functioned as a conduit for multiple dominant discourses that have criminalized Japanese American, Native American, and Central American communities across time. By drawing on this history, the activists demonstrated a form of pastiche insofar as they drew on the dominant power of the place in their vernacular discourses of coalition and resistance.

Moreover, I suggest that the protests decrying Fort Sill demonstrate the salience of space and place in the expression of vernacular discourse. Broadly speaking, scholars differentiate "space" from "place" by using "place" to refer to specific locations, and "space" to refer to the more general ways in which society is constructed in accordance with spatial thinking (Endres & Senda-Cook, 2011). De Certeau (2011) constitutes an exception to this general trend in the literature, denoting space and place to reflect particular to general, respectively. For the purposes of consistency, when referring to "place" I mean the meaning-laden, particularized history of a location, and when referring to "space" I mean the larger, abstract notions of an area—though I acknowledge these categories often overlap.

In the context of Fort Sill, we might consider "space" to be the larger logics of colonial displacement at play, while "place" would refer to the particular location of Fort Sill and its designation as a detention center. Indeed, space and place do not operate as neutral backdrops to power relations but play an active role in reproducing them (Aiello, 2011; McKittrick, 2011; Shome, 2003). In the context of the U.S.-Mexico border, for example, Shome (2003) points to the way it is in part through spatial practices at the border—including surveillance, harassment, and containment—that immigrant identities are rendered "out of place," threatening, and different.

At the same time, scholars (Chávez, 2009, 2010; Endres & Senda-Cook, 2011) have also pointed to the ways marginalized communities draw on space and place to resist conditions of violence. For instance, Chávez (2009) describes "performance cartography" as the process by which marginalized subjects employ narrative to remap hegemonic relationships between bodies and their environments, a concept that Lechuga (2019) draws on in his study of how migrant communities navigate notions of citizenship and the U.S.-Mexico border. Additionally, Endres and Senda-Cook (2011) point to how the American Indian Movement was able to temporarily reappropriate and play on the politically charged nature of Alcatraz Island to critique colonial power. Relatedly, I highlight the way in which vernacular discourses at Fort Sill capitalized on the historically charged nature of place to connect their struggles against racial violence.

Considering vernacular discourses specifically as they relate to space and place helps illuminate dynamics at Fort Sill that may not be apparent otherwise. In this regard, space and place—not only texts or speech—can operate as forms of rhetorical expression and protest in vernacular discourse (Wanzer-Serrano, 2006). Moreover, Light uses the term "emplaced vernacular" to refer to vernacular expressions that explicitly engage with the dynamics of place (2018, p. 181). Similarly, the rhetoric surrounding Fort Sill constituted forms of "emplaced vernacular" rhetoric in the sense that activists drew on the history of the site to highlight connections between various communities. This chapter considers not only the "emplaced" nature of the protests addressing Fort Sill, but also the way in which place functions as a key conduit for forming cross-racial coalition. Indeed, as Yueh (2020) contends, it is important to consider forms of "vernacular collaboration"—or the way in which multiple minority groups' discourses sometimes interplay with and collaborate with each other. As I argue, Fort Sill illustrates the operation of vernacular discourses of coalition, in which multiple vernacular discourses sought to name the connections between various racial groups in order to stage collective resistance. Importantly, I contend that place played an essential role in the formation of these vernacular discourses of coalition, insofar as groups used the historically charged nature of Fort Sill to name the interconnected nature of their oppression. In this way, I highlight how space and place, vernacular discourse, and coalitional politics operate not as discrete units but as dynamic, intimately entangled elements of the discourses protesting Fort Sill's designation as a detention center.

Overlapping Histories of Violence at Fort Sill

Before turning to a discussion of the activist discourses, I briefly explicate the history of Fort Sill to describe what different groups draw from in critiquing plans to designate Fort Sill as a migrant detention center. Fort Sill was established by Gen. Philip H. Sheridan in 1869 in present-day Oklahoma. It was built as part of the so-called Indian Territory—land that had been designated for Native Americans' forced displacement by the federal government. Those Indigenous people who roamed the Southern Plains—including the Comanche, Cheyenne, Kiowa, and others—were forced to reside at Fort Sill as part of a larger colonial policy (Fort Sill Indian Agency Cemetery, 2011). Additionally, in 1894 Chiricahua Apache prisoners of war were relocated to Fort Sill from prisons in Alabama and Florida. It is in part this process of displacement and incarceration that caused the Chiricahua Apache to lose their land—which stretched from southern New Mexico and Arizona to Mexico (Mithlo, 1995). Today, Fort Sill is infamously associated with Geronimo, who was among those prisoners of war incarcerated at the encampment. Considering the broader history of the United States' annexation of Mexico, we might situate President Trump administration's plans to incarcerate immigrant children as an extension of this colonial control into the present.

During World War II, Fort Sill was utilized as an internment camp for Japanese Americans. In 1942, president Franklin D. Roosevelt issued Executive Order 9066, which led to the incarceration of around 120,000 Japanese Americans in internment camps during the war. Fort Sill was one such internment camp, housing several hundred Japanese Americans within its borders (Okihiro, 2013). The camp often operated as a space of repression and sometimes death for its inhabitants. In one account, Fort Sill guards shot and killed Kanesaburo Oshima, who had been forcefully separated from his family and out of frustration attempted to climb the fence to escape (Okihiro, 2013). After Oshima's death at Fort Sill, a funeral for him was held. The funeral was surrounded by guards pointing machine guns at the mourners for fear that they might rebel (Okihiro, 2013). In this way, Fort Sill not only acted to contain perceived threats to the outside but also worked to control and surveil practices of mourning on the inside.

Since then, Fort Sill has continued to operate as a major U.S. military base. After World War II, the base continued to support U.S. interventions in the following decades, including the Vietnam War (Janda, n.d.). It became a permanent operation base of the U.S. Army Field Artillery in 1930 and established the Fort Sill Museum (formerly known as the Field Artillery Museum) in 1934 (Janda, n.d.), and these aspects of the base continue in operation until this day. Nancy Marie Mithlo, a Chiricahua Apache, visited the Fort Sill Museum and recounted the way in which the museum continues to glorify the post's history, thus actively erasing the colonial violence present at the base. As Mithlo explains, "as a society, we still have not acknowledged the complete destruction of unique native cultures that absorbed the impact of Western expansion. The Fort Sill story embraces this denial as a part of its history" (1995, p. 54). In this way, Fort Sill continues to operate as a space of colonial and racial domination, both as an active base supporting U.S. military intervention and as a museum that narrates and glorifies a colonial history of violence.

In June 2019, the Trump administration announced that it planned to use Fort Sill to house migrant children. Though it had been used to house primarily Central American migrant children under Obama as well, it was Trump's declaration that ignited a political firestorm (Kates, 2019). Under Trump, Fort Sill was supposed to house around 1,400–1,600 children. Because it would be located on federal land, it would not be subject to statewide child welfare inspections, raising concern over the safety of the camps for the children who would be there (Kates, 2019). Here, we can see the complicated politics of space at play; immigrants are framed as threats to the spatial and ideological borders of the U.S. nation-state, and as a result, land is appropriated to contain those who have crossed those borders. In response, however, Japanese American, Native American, Latina/o/x Americans, and other communities drew precisely on the painful history of violence at Fort Sill in order to challenge the administration's actions. Indeed, many communities were outraged precisely because of Fort Sill's historical use for racial violence, seeing the base's planned designation as a migrant detention camp as the latest instantiation in a larger legacy of violence. By naming the way Fort Sill indexed the interconnected and intergenerational nature of their different histories and oppression, activists rhetorically drew on this violent legacy in order to facilitate coalition.

Vernacular Discourses of Coalition at Fort Sill

In response to the announcement that migrant children would be incarcerated at Fort Sill, multiple different groups mobilized against these actions. In Oklahoma, community organizations including United We Dream, BLM Oklahoma City, Oklahoma Call for Reproductive Justice, Indigenous Environmental Network, Tsuru for Solidarity, Bend the Arc, American Indian Movement, and Dream Action Oklahoma, among others, held a protest in Oklahoma on July 20, 2019 (Bouhid et al., 2019, July18). A number of similar protests held by community organizations were planned throughout the summer as well, including protests in Oklahoma as well as solidarity actions in states throughout the nation including Washington, Texas, and California (Bouhid et al., 2019, July 18; Nakagawa, 2019). Organized by immigrant youth, Latina/o/x Americans, Jewish Americans, Asian Americans, Black Americans, Native Americans, and a number of other groups, the protests surrounding the camp galvanized cross-racial solidarity in the face of injustice, a phenomenon likely not unrelated to the fact that many groups shared personal relationships to violence at Fort Sill. By the end of July, the Trump administration announced it was no longer going to use Fort Sill to house children, though they reserved the right to do so in the future. Though they cited a drop in migrant child referrals to the Department of Health and Human Services as their reasoning, it is possible that the protests and public outcry throughout June and July also influenced this decision (Frazin, 2019).

In the midst of the Fort Sill controversy, multiple vernacular discourses emerged as various communities sought to criticize the state's decision to use the base to incarcerate migrant children. In addition to helping to organize or attend protest actions, many groups released public statements on their websites or in news sources, including statements criticizing the violence at Fort Sill, retrospective accounts that recounted what happened at the protests, and joint statements authored by multiple organizations. These various sources showcase the multiple overlapping vernacular discourses that criticized Fort Sill. In examining these discourses, I identified three major interrelated themes; first, place-based discourses that drew on the historically charged nature of the Fort Sill site specifically to name interrelated systems of violence; second, discourses articulating a personal relationship that an individual or their community had to the site; and third, those that sought to highlight a "shared" or "common" oppression as the basis for coalition.

Fort Sill as a Site of Interconnected Violence

A recurrent theme in the discourses protesting Fort Sill was the way in which many groups named the place of Fort Sill as indexing larger forms of interconnected violence. For example, Cristina Jiménez from United We Dream, an immigrant-youth-led organization that challenges the oppression of undocumented individuals in the United States, stated:

> People are dying at the hands of the deportation force; Johana, Simratpal, Abel, Augustina, Roxsana, Huy Chi, Felipe, Jakelin, Claudia and many others. We have said it before and we will say it again—we must end the inhumane practice of incarceration and deportations. (as cited in Bouhid, 2019, June 21)

In naming those migrants who have died at the hands of ICE, Jiménez not only decries the violence at Fort Sill but connects it to a broader interconnected system of immigration-related violence within the United States. Though their stories, identities, and circumstances were not the same, each was subjected to forms of state-sanctioned racialized violence of the U.S. immigration system; for instance, Roxsana Hernandez Rodriguez was a transgender Honduran woman who died in ICE custody after coming to the United States seeking asylum, and Huy Chi Tran was a Vietnamese American man who died in ICE custody while awaiting deportation. By naming these individuals, Jiménez connects the violence at Fort Sill to violence being enacted by ICE against several immigrant communities at multiple detention sites across the United States, thereby illuminating how Fort Sill's designation as a detention center was not an isolated instance but part of a broader interconnected system of racial violence.

Groups named Fort Sill's connection to other contemporary ICE detention centers and its historical role in reproducing racial violence against Japanese American and Indigenous groups as well. In a press release by United We Dream, a number of activists from different organizations shared statements regarding the camp and their actions protesting it. Brenda Lozano from Dream Action Oklahoma, an immigrant justice community organization, stated:

> Let's remember why we are all here together, because for too long the government has incarcerated, abused and killed people of color. Generations of Japanese, Native American, and Black people have all been hurt by Ft Sill and we will not allow history to repeat itself with a concentration camp for immigrant children. We will not stop fighting until the camps are closed, all our people are released and the deportation force is out of Oklahoma! (as cited in Bouhid, 2019, July 20, para. 5)

Here, Lozano names the interconnected nature of the violence at Fort Sill, referencing its history of violence against different racialized groups. These connections thus encompassed forms of violence that spanned not only multiple racialized groups but also multiple generations throughout U.S. history. Lozano's declaration that "we will not allow history to repeat itself" was echoed by other organizers. In the same press release, Mary Topaum of the American Indian Movement-Indian Territory stated, "We will continue to stand in solidarity and fight for the injustice and racism that is done to our Indigenous communities. We say no more to history continuing to repeat itself" (as cited in Bouhid, 2019, July 20, para. 11). Here, Topaum connects the racial violence at Fort Sill to a legacy of colonial domination against Indigenous communities, stating the imperative to resist the repetition of history. Densho, an organization dedicated to documenting the experiences of Japanese American internees, also produced a statement of solidarity on their website. In it, they relate the violence at Fort Sill to other camps including detention centers in Dilley, Texas, and Lordsburg, New Mexico, the latter of which was also a former internment site for Japanese Americans. As Wallace and Varner write:

Sites like Fort Sill, Lordsburg, and Dilley need to be permanently closed. . . .
And we must also acknowledge that every single one of these sites exists on
stolen land, and the majority of Central American migrants currently detained
are Indigenous people. The battle we're fighting today started in 1492, not 1942.
(2019, para. 11)

Here, Densho draws connections between Fort Sill, other contemporary
immigrant detention centers, and Japanese American internment camps. Then,
in pointing out that many of the migrants currently detained are themselves
Indigenous Central Americans and declaring this battle began "in 1492, not
1942," Densho situates Fort Sill as an extension of a larger, interconnected matrix
of colonial and racial power.

By capitalizing on the repeated way Fort Sill has been used as a base for
demonizing marginalized communities throughout history, activists drew
on Fort Sill's intergenerational history of violence to build collective struggle
across different groups. These discourses are significant insofar as they demonstrate vernacular discourses of coalition that drew on the site of Fort Sill as a
convergence point for multiple overlapping histories of oppression in order to
decry the Trump administration's actions. In this regard, we can see elements
of what Ono and Sloop (1995) call "pastiche"; that is, the vernacular discourses
surrounding Fort Sill did not exist in isolation from dominant discourses, but
rather drew on the dominant history surrounding the particular site of Fort
Sill to demonstrate the interlocking nature of their oppression. Moreover, these
discourses not only draw attention to a form of pastiche between dominant and
vernacular discourses, but also between multiple vernacular discourses from
Latina/o/x American, Japanese American, and Native American communities.
Finally, these vernacular discourses of coalition were formed through a uniquely
place-based rhetoric; that is, the place of Fort Sill was not a passive backdrop
to the actions being taken, but an active medium insofar as the activists drew
on the history of the site to stage collective struggle.

Naming Personal Relationships to the Site

Many of the groups protesting Fort Sill related their or their community's
personal experiences of trauma at the base to the present day. In doing so,

they not only produced a stringent critique of state violence, but further highlighted the use of place as a basis for forming coalition. In a joint statement released by the Japanese American Citizens League (JACL), National Congress of American Indians, Asian & Pacific Islander American Health Forum, and UnidosUS, Jefferson Keel of the National Congress of American Indians explained, "Fort Sill is a visceral symbol of the federal government's policy to colonize Native people by forcibly removing them from their homelands. Many of us across Indian Country still wrestle with the trauma that policy left in its wake" (as cited in Japanese American Citizens League, 2019, para. 3). Here, Keel recalls Fort Sill's role in a history of colonization and the forced displacement of Indigenous communities, a trauma that continues to impact them today. Japanese Americans also recalled their experiences with anti-Asian violence at Fort Sill as an impetus to resist the Trump administration's actions. Satsuki Ina, formerly incarcerated at the internment camp in Tule Lake, stated:

> As Japanese American survivors and descendants of U.S. concentration camps, we know that imprisoning parents and children causes deep harm that is passed down from generation to generation. We will not stand by quietly as this administration seeks to inflict the pain on others that our community suffered in World War II. (Ina, 2019)

In this statement, Ina emphasizes her own experience as a survivor of Japanese American concentration camps to relate to the psychological damage imposed on children and parents who are incarcerated in camps. In these cases, an intimate knowledge of the intergenerational violence of incarceration at camps like Fort Sill motivated Indigenous and Japanese American communities to relate to, speak out against, and resist the violence at Fort Sill. Here, naming a personal connection to the specific place of Fort Sill represented an important part of the vernacular discourses at play; doing so enabled activists to produce an incisive critique of Fort Sill's repeated role in state-sanctioned violence while also facilitating coalition.

Similarly, the Indigenous Environmental Network who participated in the protests also spoke about the relationship between the violence inflicted on Indigenous communities at Fort Sill to the present day. As they explain:

For twenty years beginning in 1894, our Apache relatives were held as prisoners of war at Fort Sill. We, as Indigenous peoples, know the pain and generational trauma that comes from Fort Sill and camps just like it. It is our moral responsibility to take a stand with our Indigenous relatives trying to cross the so-called "border." Generations of Indigenous youth have suffered and have been forced to assimilate at Fort Sill's boarding school. We cannot stand by as this happens again. (Indigenous Environmental Network, 2019, para. 2)

In this statement, the Indigenous Environmental Network names their own relationship to the site to produce a moral argument against its present designation as a detention center. Long familiar with the way in which Indigenous communities are uprooted, by referencing the "so-called 'border'" the Indigenous Environmental Network names the way who is constructed as an undocumented migrant is the product of the colonial imposition of unnatural borders. In this regard, the Indigenous Environmental Network connected their own community's experience at Fort Sill specifically to draw connections between historical colonization practices and present-day detention centers. In this way, the Indigenous Environmental Network also describe their intimate knowledge of the violence of Fort Sill, using the overlapping histories of violence produced by Fort Sill as a source for building cross-racial and cross-generational coalitions.

A related dynamic can be gleaned in the participation of a number of Buddhist priests who cooperated with United We Dream and other immigrant-youth-led organizations to plan a collaborative action. As Duncan Ryuken Williams (2019), one of said Buddhist priests present at the protests, recounted on his personal website, the activists had collectively planned for the Buddhists to march behind the Latina/o/x DREAMers leading the marching and chanting until they reached the fence line of Fort Sill, at which point the Buddhists would set up an altar. The alter contained a photo of Kanesaburo Oshima—the Japanese American internee shot and killed by the Fort Sill guards—as well as a *maile lei* from Oshima's family in Hawai'i, and a Buddha statue that had been carved in the Manzanar Japanese American internment camp. Buddhist leaders then intoned the Heart sutra, and as Williams explains,

This Buddhist form of free speech was not only dedicated to those who had suffered at Fort Sill in the past, but also a prayer that history would not repeat itself with the reports of an imminent transfer of 1,400 Central American migrant children here. (Williams, 2019, p. 6)

In this regard, Buddhist practitioners brought their own religious practices and rituals of mourning to bear on the protests, espousing a vernacular discourse that connected the experiences of Japanese American internees to the present-day detention of migrant children through their own relationship to the place. The altar of Oshima that they set up speaks to the personal connection these Buddhist priests and other Japanese Americans had to the site; here, mourning and naming the racial trauma at Fort Sill that affected Japanese American communities served as an important basis for relating their experiences of oppression to the present day and for producing coalition.

Articulating a Common or Shared History of Oppression

A final theme that I wish to touch on in this chapter is that many of the groups specifically framed the interconnected nature of their oppression through the language of "shared history." Tsuru for Solidarity, a Japanese American–led direct-action group involved in organizing some of the protests, stated on their website that their mission is to demonstrate solidarity in protesting detainment across the United States and to "coordinate intergenerational, cross-community healing circles addressing the trauma of our shared histories" (Tsuru for Solidarity, n.d.). At the same time, as part of a joint statement, David Inoue of the JACL stated that "it is unconscionable that we are now considering holding children at Fort Sill, a facility once used to imprison American resident Japanese immigrants . . . this same trauma is now being inflicted upon migrant children through our government's policy" (Japanese American Citizens League, 2019, para. 5). By describing the present actions at Fort Sill as the "same trauma" as that inflicted on Japanese Americans, Inoue uses analogy to create a relational, one-to-one correspondence between Japanese internment and border policing. Relatedly, Dream Action Oklahoma expressed their intentions to unite "against a common settler colonial violence to find in that united resistance, a possibility for a future, freed" (2019, para. 3). In these instances, solidarity is staged in the name of a shared, common experience, connected both through the convergence point of Fort Sill and the larger generalization by which anti-immigrant border practices are rendered analogical to other forms of violence.

This aspect of the vernacular discourses at play, the appeals to a common or shared oppression, presents complicated implications for the politics of coalition. On the one hand, activists at Fort Sill strategically deployed the language of shared oppression to produce counterhegemonic vernacular discourses of coalition that challenged the way Fort Sill affected multiple communities. Nevertheless, on the other hand, further research revealed that not all of the groups committed to demonstrating solidarity at Fort Sill were willing to show that same solidarity in other instances. For example, after Chinese American New York Police Department officer Peter Liang shot and killed Akai Gurley—a Black American going to visit his significant other in an apartment complex—controversy erupted in response to Liang being convicted when other white officers who had killed Black Americans had not been. In the wake of this controversy, the JACL—one of the aforementioned groups that spoke out against Fort Sill in a joint statement—also released a statement in the wake of Liang's conviction. In it, however, they write:

> It is fair to call into question the training of these officers or the state of the public housing complex, as symptoms of deeper systemic issues that enabled this tragedy. It is also fair to question the underlying racial implications of this case, as there is no question that Liang, an Asian American, was treated differently from other police officers who have not been held accountable for actions against unarmed men and women of color. (Ouchida & Moy, 2016, para. 3)

In this statement, the JACL implicitly compares the racial discrimination faced by Gurley to the fact that Liang was convicted when other white officers were not. However, to render these two dynamics comparable or equivalent mystifies Liang's role in anti-Black violence. Indeed, as Liu and Shange (2018) explain, in the case of NYPD officer Peter Liang shooting and killing Akai Gurley, the idea of a "shared history" of oppression led many Asian Americans to claim Liang, too, was a victim of the "same" or similar violence that Gurley was, thus occluding interracial violence committed by Asian Americans like Liang against Black Americans like Gurley. In the JACL's statement, they produce a similar narrative of equivalency by comparing the racism faced by Gurley to the conviction faced by Liang, suggesting it is "fair" to question both sides of the story without making any meaningful distinction between anti-Black police murders and Liang's conviction as a Chinese American. Moreover, it is notable that in the entirety of the press release, the JACL fails to acknowledge or use the language of anti-Black racism at all (Ouchida & Moy, 2016). The closest they get is in the aforementioned quotation when describing the "deeper systemic issues" in the training of police officers and public housing, neither of which acknowledges that Asian Americans specifically, including Liang, are part of systematic anti-Black violence in the United States. Consequently, we might apprehend some of the limits to the language of shared oppression, insofar as it can occlude dynamics of violence between marginalized Asian American and Black American communities.

In a related dynamic, just one year prior to the protests at Fort Sill, the Jewish American advocacy group Bend the Arc, who also participated in the solidarity actions taken surrounding Fort Sill, drew criticism from the Jews of Color and Sephardi/Mizrahi Caucus for its silence on the Israeli government's genocidal actions against Palestinians (Cohen, 2018). Bend the Arc demonstrated a willingness to show solidarity at Fort Sill, in part due to the experiences of Jewish individuals in concentration camps, yet remained silent in the face of Israeli settler colonial domination of Palestinians. In this regard, the unwillingness of Bend the Arc to show solidarity in the case of Palestinian genocide, and the unwillingness of the JACL to recognize Liang's unique role as a Chinese American in perpetuating anti-Black violence against Gurley both point to some of the potential limits of this framing.

Put differently, if this shared experience at the site of Fort Sill did not exist, would the same wide coalition of groups still respond in this way? Would they be willing to recognize instances in which their own communities were involved in the oppression of another, and demonstrate solidarity with oppressed people nonetheless? Of course, it is impossible to answer this question for every individual group that resisted Fort Sill, and I do not seek to categorically condemn every group who demonstrated solidarity and resistance to Fort Sill's designation as a detention center. Rather, I simply seek to point out that the fact that both the JACL and Bend the Arc can express solidarity in the case of Fort Sill but perpetuate or obscure anti-Black and colonial violence in other instances exemplifies some of the limits of using "shared" history or oppression as the basis for coalition. Thus, while Fort Sill represented a moment of cross-racial solidarity that productively garnered critical mass for opposing Fort Sill, it is important at the same time to acknowledge the potential limitations of the language of shared oppression and analogy more broadly as the basis for anti-racist coalition building.

Conclusion

Amid dominant racial discourses that work to criminalize them, marginalized communities use vernacular discourses to rewrite, critique, and think beyond these restrictive logics. This volume's vision demonstrates that migrants make a world for themselves by producing a sense of collective identity, redefining their history, and rewriting racist representations through creativity. In this chapter, I have chosen to focus on the multiple vernacular discourses responding to Fort Sill, including those from Latina/o/x American, Native American, and Japanese American activist communities. I discussed three themes that emerged in these vernacular discourses: those that used the *place* of Fort Sill to name the interconnected nature of the various groups' histories, those that described a personal relationship to the Fort Sill site, and those that named a "shared" or "common" oppression as the basis for coalition. Together, they represented vernacular discourses of coalition that drew on the historically charged nature of the Fort Sill site to name interlocking histories of oppression and formulate collective resistance. Consequently, the dynamics surrounding Fort Sill point to broader implications for considering the interrelated nature of coalitional politics, vernacular discourse, and space and place. First, they exemplify Ono and Sloops's (1995) concept of "pastiche" as it relates to space and place; that is, activists drew on the dominant history of the Fort Sill site to name various histories of oppression as interrelated. In this sense, place was a fundamental element in the production of pastiche within vernacular discourses of coalition, insofar as place shapes the dominant culture that vernacular discourses draw on, play off of, and resist.

Additionally, the vernacular discourses of coalition at Fort Sill demonstrate not only the interplay between dominant and vernacular discourses, but also the simultaneous interaction between multiple vernacular discourses. Considering this interplay represents an important avenue through which one apprehends the politics of coalition; that is, in examining this interaction, scholars might consider the different ways in which communities link seemingly divergent struggles to an interconnected matrix of power. In the case of Fort Sill, vernacular discourses connected Fort Sill to a broader, present-day assault on immigrant lives in the United States as well as the intergenerational connections between multiple groups whose communities had been incarcerated there. Activists drew connections across both temporal and racial lines, demonstrating how place served as a rhetorical meeting point for different marginalized communities to name the interconnected nature of oppression and drawing connections to their own experiences of racial trauma at the base. Ultimately, Fort Sill pushes scholars to consider not only the interplay between dominant and vernacular forms of discourse in the politics of coalition, but also the way multiple vernacular discourses can use space and place to interact with one another and stage collective resistance.

Finally, the controversy surrounding Fort Sill presents important implications for considering how the basis of "shared oppression" and analogy operates in anti-racist coalitional politics. Indeed, this language helped draw support from a broad number of groups in opposing Fort Sill. Nevertheless, forging solidarity on the basis of common oppression risks, in some instances, limiting those expressions of solidarity to moments of interest convergence. Such a dynamic can be gleaned, for instance, in Bend the Arc's willingness to oppose Fort Sill but not Israeli violence against Palestinians. At the same time, the language of a common oppression can also serve to obscure structural violence between oppressed groups, as was the case in which Asian Americans compared Liang's conviction and Gurley's death as both outcome of the same racist system, obscuring the role Asian Americans play in anti-Black violence.

To highlight these instances is not to categorically denounce or homogenize all the groups involved at Fort Sill—indeed, it is important to recognize that coalition and activist work is always messy and heterogeneous—but rather to approach the dynamics at Fort Sill with a critical perspective on the vernacular discourse and coalitional politics at play. It was important, in the case of Fort Sill, that activist groups connected their experiences through their relationship to a particular place. Doing so enabled a vocabulary that named interweaving and enduring historical processes of anti-Asian violence, settler colonial violence, and anti-immigrant violence. In light of these dynamics, then, I believe it is worth asking what forms of coalition might become possible that both illuminate intertwined histories of oppression while recognizing their differences.

Might it be possible to produce, for instance, a vocabulary that recognizes the interconnected relationship that Japanese American, Indigenous, and immigrant communities have to Fort Sill, without reducing that relationship to one of a common oppression? Indeed, as scholars such as Soto Vega and Chávez (2018) have discussed, it is important to recognize dynamics of settler colonialism and anti-Blackness *within* communities of color. Following these insights, it is worth asking what critical and nuanced discourses of coalition might be produced by, for instance, recognizing how the *place* of Fort Sill represents a site of convergence for different interrelated forms of oppression without presuming they are therefore *synonymous*. Doing so may provide possibilities for coalitional politics that interrogate the interrelated yet irreducible relationship between settler colonialism, internment, border policing, and other forms of racial violence.

REFERENCES

Aiello, G. (2011). "From Wound to Enclave: The Visual-Material Performance of Urban Renewal in Bologna's Manifattura delle Arti." *Western Journal of Communication*, 75(4), 341–366.

Bouhid, B. (2019, June 21). "We Must Not Forget Our Country's Shameful History." *United We Dream.* https://unitedwedream.org/2019/06/we-must-not-forget-our-countrys-shameful-history/.

Bouhid, B. (2019, July 20). "Protests to Close the Camps Escalate at Action by Immigrant Youth, Japanese Americans, Indigenous, Jewish, Veterans and Racial Justice Groups Who Demand the Government Stop Repeating History." *United We Dream.* https://unitedwedream.org/2019/07/protests-to-close-the-camps-escalate-at-action-by-immigrant-youth-japanese-americans-indigenous-jewish-veterans-and-racial-justice-groups-who-demand-the-government-stop-repeating-history/.

Bouhid, B., Nazarett, J., & Barbara, J. (2019, July 18). "Demand to #CloseTheCamps Escalates with Actions throughout the Summer." *Portside.* https://portside.org/2019-07-18/demand-closethecamps-escalates-actions-throughout-summer-doing-nothing-not-option#1.

Chávez, K. (2009). "Remapping Latinidad: A Performance Cartography of Latina/o Identity in Rural Nebraska." *Text and Performance Quarterly, 2*(1), 165–182.

Chávez, K. (2010). "Spatializing Gender Performativity: Ecstasy and Possibilities for Livable Life in the Tragic Case of Victoria Arellano." *Women's Studies in Communication, 33*(1), 1–15.

Cohen, I. B. (2018). "How Can Bend the Arc Claim to 'Unite a Progressive Jewish Voice for Justice for All' but Ignore Israel?" *Mondoweiss: News & Opinion About Palestine, Israel & the United States*. https://mondoweiss.net/2018/07/progressive-jewish-justice/.

De Certeau, M. (2011). *The Practice of Everyday Life*. 3rd ed. Berkeley: University of California Press.

Dream Action Oklahoma. (2019, August 5). "On Fort Sill: Communal Resistance against Phantasms of Coloniality." *Medium*. https://medium.com/@DAOK/on-fort-still-communal-resistance-against-phantasms-of-coloniality-4581b1ed84d3.

Endres, D., & Senda-Cook, S. (2011). "Location Matters: The Rhetoric of Place in Protest." *Quarterly Journal of Speech, 97*(3), 257–282.

Fort Sill Indian Agency Cemetery. (2011). "Fort Sill: A History of Fort Sill." https://www.findagrave.com/cemetery/2401080/indian-agency-cemetery.

Frazin, R. (2019, July 27). "Trump Officials Say Children Won't Be Held at Oklahoma Migrant Shelter." *The Hill*. https://thehill.com/latino/455016-trump-officials-say-children-wont-be-housed-at-oklahoma-migrant-shelter/.

Guo, L., & Lee, L. (2013). "The Critique of YouTube-Based Vernacular Discourse: A Case Study of YouTube's Asian Community." *Critical Studies in Media Communication, 30*(5), 391–406.

Ina, Satsuki. (2019). "Statement by Satsuki Ina on the Federal Regulation Announced Today to Permit Indefinite Detention of Migrant Children." *Tsuru for Solidarity*. https://tsuruforsolidarity.org/statement-by-satsuki-ina-ph-d-mft-on-the-federal-regulation-announced-today-to-permit-indefinite-detention-of-migrant-children/.

Indigenous Environmental Network. (2019, July 21). "Indigenous Peoples Led Shutdown at Ft. Sill Immigration Detention Center." https://www.ienearth.org/indigenous-peoples-led-shutdown-at-ft-sill-immigration-detention-center/.

Janda, L. (n.d.). "Fort Sill." *The Encyclopedia of Oklahoma History and Culture*.

Japanese American Citizens League. (2019). "Joint Statement Condemning Decision to Hold Migrant Children at Fort Sill." *Japanese American Citizens League*. https://jacl.org/statements/joint-statement-condemning-decision-to-hold-migrant-children-at-fort-sill.

Kates, G. (2019, June 11). "U.S. Will Use Fort Sill Army Base in Oklahoma to Shelter Migrant Children." *ABC News*. https://www.cbsnews.com/news/migrant-children-to-be-kept-at-armys-fort-sill-in-oklahoma/.

Lechuga, M. (2020). "Mapping Migrant Vernacular Discourses: Mestiza Consciousness, Nomad Thought, and Latina/o/x Migrant Movement Politics in the United States." *Journal of International and Intercultural Communication, 13*(3), 257–273.

Light, E. (2018). "Aesthetic Ruptures: Viewing Graffiti as the Emplaced Vernacular." *Communication and Critical/Cultural Studies, 15*(2), 179–195.

Liu, R., & Shange, S. (2018). "Toward Thick Solidarity: Theorizing Empathy in Social Justice Movements." *Radical History Review,* (131), 189–198.

McKittrick, K. (2011). "On Plantations, Prisons, and a Black Sense of Place." *Social & Cultural Geography, 12*(8), 947–963.

Mithlo, N. M. (1995). "History Is Dangerous." *Museum Anthropology, 19*(2), 50–57.

Morrissey, M. E. (2013). "A DREAM Disrupted: Undocumented Migrant Youth Disidentifications with U.S. Citizenship." *Journal of International and Intercultural Communication, 6*(2), 145–162.

Nakagawa, M. (2019, June 26). "Tense Moments as JA Activists Protest at Fort Sill." *Rafu Shimpo: Los Angeles Japanese Daily News.* https://rafu.com/2019/06/tense-moments-as-ja-activists-protest-at-fort-sill/.

Okihiro, G.Y. (2013). Fort Sill. In *Encyclopedia of Japanese American Internment,* edited by G. Y. Okihiro. Westport, CT: Greenwood.

Ono, K. A., & Sloop, J. M. (1995). "The Critique of Vernacular Discourse." *Communication Monographs, 62*(1), 19–46.

Ouchida, P., & Moy, J. (2016). "JACL Statement on Liang Decision." *Japanese Americans Citizens League.* https://jacl.org/statements/jacl-statement-on-liang-decision.

Pham, V. (2017). "Reviving Identity Politics: Strategic Essentialism, Identity Politics, and the Potential for Cross-Racial Vernacular Discourse in the Digital Age." In *Theorizing Digital Rhetoric,* edited by A. Hess & A. Davisson (pp. 153–165). New York: Routledge.

Shome, R. (2003). "Space Matters: The Power and Practice of Space." *Communication Theory, 13*(1), 39–56.

Soto Vega, K., & Chávez, K. (2018). "Latinx Rhetoric and Intersectionality in Racial Rhetorical Criticism." *Communication and Critical/Cultural Studies, 15*(4), 319–325.

Tsuru for Solidarity. (n.d.). "What Is Tsuru for Solidarity?" *Tsuru for Solidarity.* https://tsuruforsolidarity.org/mission-history/.

Wallace, N., & Varner, N. (2019, June 12). "Fort Sill Is a Site of Ongoing Trauma." *Densho Blog.* https://densho.org/catalyst/fort-sill-is-a-site-of-ongoing-trauma/#:~:text=Fort%20Sill%20is%20not%20an,Americans%20were%20incarcerated%20during%20WWII.

Wanzer-Serrano, D. (2006). "Trashing the System: Social Movement, Intersectional Rhetoric, and Collective Agency in the Young Lords Organization's Garbage Offensive." *Quarterly Journal of Speech*, *92*(2), 174–201.

Williams, D. (2019). "Making Paper Cranes Fly: A Report from Fort Sill, Oklahoma." www.duncanryukenwilliams.com.

Yueh, H. (2020). "Theorizing Vernacular Discourse in Sinophone Transnational Space: On Namewee's YouTube Music Videos." *Critical Studies in Media Communication*, *37*(2), 174–187.

My Home/lands and Belonging beyond the Borderlines

An Oral History Performance of a Burmese Media Activist and Refugee in Diaspora

Eunbi Lee and Leda Cooks

In early December 2012, M, a Burmese migrant worker, political refugee, and media activist living in exile in South Korea, got the opportunity to teach media literacy in a Karen refugee camp on the border between Thailand and Myanmar. To M, the camp promised the opportunity to teach fellow refugees, Karen ethnic groups, the Christian minority in the Buddhist state, who had been forcibly relocated to the refugee camp on the Thailand-Myanmar borderlands due to the heinous state violence that began in 1949, when the Karen group started fighting for independence (Callahan, 2013). Furthermore, he could again cross the border to visit Myanmar and his family.

As he stated:

> I crossed the border from Myanmar to South Korea with my temporary work visa. However, after 18 years, I am neither a Burmese nor a Korean in the document, instead, I became a refugee. I could not go back to my country officially, so I had to bribe the border guards in the Thai-Burma borderland in order to visit my home. (M, personal communication, March 11, 2014)

Knowing that crossing the border was illegal for refugees, he had not done so since he moved to South Korea eighteen years earlier. Now, however, the closeness to his former home and the many years since he had left his family provided the incentive he needed to risk everything by crossing borders. Even as a migrant worker in Korea, M kept fighting for democracy in Myanmar, a country where the military regime had suppressed ethnic minorities and imprisoned thousands of pro-democracy protesters since the 8888 Uprising against the junta. As a result, thousands of protesters were killed, and Aung San Suu Kyi, a representative of the democratic party, was placed under house arrest (*BBC News Magazine*, 2011, December 2). For this reason, the military junta has prohibited M from returning to his country. Although he remains a refugee in Korea, M has dedicated himself to the promotion of media literacy and to the production of community media for migrants there. Also, he continues to teach media literacy to other Burmese refugees each year on the border between Thailand and Myanmar. Among these layers of his life that are impacted by national boundaries and diasporic cultures, how can we understand his narrative of traveling between homes?

Home can indicate a core physical and geographic space, a site of shelter and nurturance, as well as a symbolic location that can be explained through the experience of living in, leaving, and returning to that place. Such a construction presumes that home is everlasting, fixed, and safe, whereas leaving home is temporal, mobile, and dangerous. When we leave and come back home, we can elaborate on what home means to us and articulate its affective valances. Once we expand this thought to the idea of living in/leaving a nation-state, we can see the meanings of living, leaving, coming back to a nation-state, or living in different nation-states in the context of home (Ahmed, 1999; Puar, 1994). That is, homes and nations can be explained through human actions of place making. Given this basis for defining "home," however, we want to clarify that this chapter does not focus on those who have the privilege of being able to leave and come back home with the security of citizenship. Rather, we consider those who have had to give up their homes and cross into other countries to survive amid the collision of political upheaval and neoliberal capitalism-driven globalization—oppressed migrants, refugees, and asylum seekers.

Thus, the meanings of home and homeland for these migrants can be multiplied by telling their life stories, as they choose or are forced to leave, to fight again for their survival, and try to create a sense of belonging elsewhere.

As such, these stories are not so much based on state-related facts such as birth, nationality, race, ethnicity, and gender, but more on the construction of experiences through communicative practices (Naficy, 1993). By communicating those experiences in the present through storytelling, texts, and visual images, all under the influences of various aspects of history, cultures, society, and subjectivities (Taylor, 2007), memories of home, homeland, and belonging become materialized so as to connect the subject and their world. Remembering home, homeland, and belonging are mediated actions through which one adjusts to live, survive, defy, and imagine a better life.

With an understanding of home as a constructed and communicative act, this chapter describes M's life as a Burmese migrant worker, refugee, and media activist in South Korea. Specifically, we examine his lived experiences, going back and forth between different places he calls home. We explore the ways his visceral feelings and knowledge create meaning-making around and beyond discourses of global migration. We read these as performances of relations of power at the intersections of capitalism, ethnocentrism, nationalism, and classism—performances of oppression and dehumanization that provided incentive for M to create a mediated diaspora for migrants across different social locations. In doing so, we bring theoretical frames from post(de)colonial, feminist, Indigenous, and communication studies to explicate the polysemic meanings of home, homeland, and belonging.

Oral History as Performance

This chapter uses oral history performance as a method to combine the afore-mentioned theoretical frames with a focus on M's performance of self in relation to various people and institutions in his life. Oral history performance approaches the memories of others in a way that brings sensuous experiences, held in marked bodies, to their expression in the present time, to be shared with others in public. To be specific, this is not simply the retelling of past events but a conscious process of bringing stories of the past to the present with full affect, wherein tellers assemble, reassemble, enunciate, forget, and add new meanings to the memories at different moments. That is, oral history performance is a transformational process. It translates subjectively remembered events into embodied memory acts, moving memory into an action of re-membering (Pollock,

2000). Also, the action of remembering is not limited to verbal communication; it includes nonverbal communication such as gestures, crying, laughing, smiling, and gazing into the distance (Zarina, 2013). Hence, oral history performance relies upon sensuous actions that are embedded in bodies.

Moreover, oral history performance is avowed as personal experience and affirmed as a history in form and content by an audience—and that telling and audiencing occurs at the intersections of social group identities such as race, gender, sexuality, and nationality (High & Little, 2014). It is distinguished from oral history, which is framed within the conventional interview setting where interviewees simply answer questions from researchers. Traditional oral history research regards acts of remembering as testimonies that deliver what happened in the past. Viewing testimony as a receptacle for history overlooks the moments of meaning-making, when tellers and listeners exchange stories and feelings together that performance studies can capture. In this way, oral history performance deepens the magnitude of the performative moments (Pollock, 2000).

The first time M and I (Eunbi Lee) met was in an academic setting, where I was conducting research on oral history performance in 2009. As time passed, however, we often saw each other to share memories, stories, and mundane events in our respective everyday lives. Although I learned that I had to hold an objective view of him as a source for my research, we easily became friends. Sharing our stories about home and homeland, smiles, laughs, tears, and big hugs when we say goodbye are sensuous memories that we can look back upon now, after thirteen years of friendship. Hence, oral history performance (rather than traditional oral history) is a suitable method to thank and privilege the relationship between M (teller) and Eunbi.

Knowing the positionality and privilege with which scholars are able to maintain accountability, authority, and responsibility for representation and interpretation of others through academic language (Madison, 2012), in this chapter we share stories that span over a long period of M's life trajectory: from his upbringing in Myanmar, to his migration to South Korea, to his media activism. Throughout, we describe his feelings of pain and joy when he brings senses of home, homeland, and belonging to the present, and when we listen and react to the stories together. This chapter coalesces around three questions: 1) What meanings come together around "home/homeland" for M as a migrant worker and a refugee? 2) What purpose does M's development of a media network serve him and the migrant community? 3) How might the sense of belonging impact his life both as a migrant and a media activist? For Carey, communication is a process through which our realities are brought into being: "we first produce the world by symbolic work, and then take up residence in the world we produce" (1989, p. 30). M's world making is remarkable and worthy of studying, precisely because taking up residency and building community under labels like "alien," "migrant," "exiled," and "other" is symbolically and materially uneasy, contradictory, and defiant. Through sharing his oral history performance, we demonstrate how M expresses sensual memories of home, homeland, and belonging in the course of border crossing, as well as how building a media community for migrants and refugees creates meaning-making beyond the discourse of global migration.

Sensual Memories of Home, Homeland and Belonging in a Diasporic Life

M says, "My home is neither in Myanmar nor in Korea. It exists in my memories from childhood" (personal communication, October 25, 2017). For him, home does not exist in countries but exists in his memories. If so, how do we epistemologically understand "home" in the contexts of his life? In our/the authors' lives, home is inside the walls of houses where we were born, grew up, or currently live: For one of the authors, it means apartments in cosmopolitan cities, and for the other author it means houses in cities or in more rural locales. For us, home is a space where we can think of our families: for Eunbi, celebrating every family member's birthdays together every year until my brother and I moved outside Korea, and for Leda, leaving family at a young age but always returning in times of need. For us, home is a space where we can reminisce through sensual feelings—smells, visions, tastes, and touch, and a space where we feel (un)safe and (un)comfortable by imaginary national protections. As such, home doesn't indicate only the physical place that one inhabits; it brings together multiple meanings that convene with sensual memories in which a person made and are making their lives.

Building on these ideas, Ahmed (1999) explicates the layers of what home means to us in the course of living/leaving home. She argues that scholars in cultural studies tend to see home as a stable space, existing inside strong walls that bound us from the outside; in turn, living at home becomes a safe and comfortable action, whereas leaving home becomes an unsafe and dangerous action, inseparable from strangeness. In this sense, home is a familiar space, whereas outside home is foreign. It also means that one who is at home is a member of the family and a neighbor, whereas someone outside the home is a stranger. This logic of home applies not only to homes and villages but also to nations. Here, Ahmed applies the meaning of home to that of a nation:

> We could recognize strangers within, rather than just between nation[al] spaces. To argue otherwise, would be to imagine the nation as a purified space, and to deny differences within that space: it would be to assume that you would only encounter strangers at the border. (1999, p. 340)

In a sense, home implies a space that generates identities only for those who inhabit home in their native countries: dwellers, residents, and citizens—not for others who left their homes and nations, namely nomads, migrants, refugees, and asylum seekers. However, we want to go further to think of the act of leaving home and nation in terms of global migration. Anderson argues that "nationalism invents nations where they do not actually exist" (2006, p. 6), that the borderlines that mark national territories on the map lead to the imagination of state power and militarized border authorities. Although globalization across borderlines has celebrated a world where labor markets, global production, and cultures are able to travel based on Western-oriented economies and politics, the increase globally in militarization places control over people's physical mobility. This control results in displacement, dislocation, and immobility based on race, gender, class, and nationality (Mendez & Naples, 2015). That is, national borderlines are geographical as well as rhetorical and cultural lines that dominate legalization and restrict mobility of humans. We can extend this notion of national borderlines to critique popular ideas of diaspora that refer to spaces where people of the same ethnicity live abroad and assimilate to the host country or return to their countries of origin when faced with the inadequacy of national models (Connor, 1986; Falzon, 2003). Instead, we might understand diasporas as complex spaces that contain the feelings and experiences of those who are forced into displacement. Typically, constant global migrations shift meanings of home, based on Western capitalism and labor exploitation (Puar, 1994). Therefore, nations and diasporas are more than spaces where hegemonic systems mark the legitimacy of who is eligible to belong. These spaces are created through communicative actions; we "sentimentalize the space to belong to" (Ahmed, 1999, p. 341). This sense of belonging *to* somewhere is related to a matter of how one feels or fails to feel about home in between situations of living and leaving between nations and diasporas.

Embracing this sentimentalism of spaces, Ahmed further theorizes a sense of belonging to home and diasporas as "the lived-experience of locality through feelings" (1999, p. 341). That is, a sense of belonging is about the lived experience of being in a space that one remembers through smell, vision, sound, and touch, and which also connects to how we sense the world we live in. Here, we can think of the world not as constituted by nations but as "land" through the view of Indigenous studies. Indigenous studies hold the power to decolonize land, acknowledging land "not as something to be owned and divided by borders but as the basis of life of all beings" (Arvin, 2019, p. 349). Adopting this view means seeing lands as occupied territories that cannot be purchased; this perspective argues that land cannot be "owned" or in other words held by landowners and nations. This view calls into question spaces where oppression of migrants and the poor occurs, and where space is used in the destruction of nature for capitalistic gains. We wish to see lands as wellsprings where our lives have evolved through connections with nature, kinfolk, and cultures. In a sense, our homes/lands become "skin" (Ahmed, 1999, p. 341) that create a sense of belonging between our lives and lands and become communicative spaces for people who share similar and different senses of home/land beyond geographical spaces.

From this sensual configuration of home/land as the communal source of our being, various feminists in cultural and communication studies, such as Puar (2007) and Manning (2006), add theoretical vocabularies to grasp how we share a sense of belonging with others. Puar uses the word "contagion" (2006, p. 172) meaning that communication between bodies infects us with sensation, vibration, and irregularity through indeterminacy and contingency, and Manning promotes "touch" (2006, p. 57) as a political action that apprehends a connection between two different bodies, not as a meeting of two different subjects but as continually readjusting themselves to the movements of desire. For Puar, contagion accentuates a particular moment of (dis- and re-)connecting between two bodies as well as how people from different social locations are repositioned as they resonate with other's stories.

On the other hand, Manning's word, "touch," highlights the way in which people adjust and adapt themselves to create change. This is not a temporal moment of connection but is a long journey of confronting, understanding, and listening to each other. Puar and Manning use different words, but both articulate stances that are critical of the structures through which different bodies are traditionally thought to convene to achieve social change. Puar and Manning take a post-structural view to theorize how sensual and contingent connections between bodies have the potential to build a sense of collective belonging in a specific time and space. In this sense, we can use the words "contagion" and "touch" to grasp how migrants, refugees, and asylum seekers might share similar and different stories of home/lands and create a collective sense of belonging.

Contagion and touch can move us from indifference to belonging through collective performances of remembering home. Given that remembering is a verbal and nonverbal action of sharing lived experiences, feelings, and emotions that are inseparable from history, culture, and the society in which we live, language and nonverbal cues become mediums of materializing memories in social and cultural contexts (Zelizer, 2005). Furthermore, without recounting our past experiences with listeners, memories cannot obtain social meaning. That is, remembering is not a unilateral communication but is the process of tellers sharing their stories and listeners hearing them, reacting to them, and allowing them to resonate by adding personal experiences and feelings. This act of remembering, telling stories, breaks down the wall between tellers and listeners in public spaces, and leads participants to take stories in a special way, one that creates deeper meanings and a sense of intimacy (Langellier, 1999). Moreover, the meeting of storytelling with digital media technologies has changed the boundaries of space and time. As such, storytelling, in general, which used to occur in the present and in the presence of others, now takes place in a virtual space where people are geographically and temporally dispersed but are virtually connected together. Within the context of this chapter, it is important to note that sensual memories of home/lands and touch and contagion among oppressed migrants manifest and can proliferate in digital spaces.

For M, both touch and contagion occurred during protests on the street with other migrant workers and led him to create a sense of collective belonging through media activism.

In the winter of 2003, the Korean government declared massive crackdowns on illegal migrant workers. We protested for our human rights and freedom, but the Korean government did not stop arresting us, and mass media depicted us as illegal migrants occupying public spaces. Consequently, we decided to establish our own media station to deliver our real voices. (M, personal communication, October 25, 2017)

M's project, to elevate the connections he felt with others who were mis- and under-represented in the media, worked to communicate both the stories of migrants and the affective relationships produced in the act of storytelling in digital spaces. To elaborate, when raced/gendered/migrant bodies share their stories, emotions, and feelings about home/lands together in public, their voices permeate the listeners' lives, and listeners' reactions and feelings also permeate the lives of the storytellers. Moments of contagion lead to touch, building solidarity in migrants across the world. Much like commensality, these communal moments create a sensual commonality at the intersections of different bodies. Therefore, a sense of belonging does not come from necessarily sharing the same race, gender, nationality, or language, but from contagion and touch that are created when different bodies are constantly (dis- and re-)connected with each other in communities. Belonging thus becomes a communicative action that is generated when marginalized people across races, nationalities, ethnicities, genders, sexualities, and classes are connected to each other over stories.

Several communication scholars have advanced studies of identity and/ as liberation through belonging to a global community of displaced peoples in action. For instance, Langellier (2010) examined the storytelling of Caaliya (pseudonym), a young, Black, Somali, Muslim, and refugee woman in Lewis-ton, Maine, in which Caaliya embodied and performed her identities amid the tensions of cultural differences layered with diasporic experiences. Through following Caaliya's story that put her own vivid language in conversation with the authors' feminist and academic language, the project enlivened Caaliya's subjectivity and agency, rather than the determinism of her state-related identities. In doing so, the narrative performance and analysis show the possibilities for performing a migrant's identities that are not immersed in the global discourse of migration but resonate with the counteractions revealed in a local story.

Similarly, Calafell (2010) unfolds fragmented but connected narratives in her encounters with her great-grandmother. Throughout the chapter, from confronting Immigration and Customs Enforcement (ICE) agents with her Chicana friend in Arizona, to her love story interwoven with immigration, citizenship, and islamophobia after 9/11, she centers her desire to know her great-grandmother who crossed the border from Mexico to the United States. The borders crossed in each narrative happened in different spaces and times, but they emerge together in one moment of expressing love of friends, partners, and families who stand between national borderlines. Extending the affection and emotion found in performative writing and poetry, we imagine how home/land, memories, and belonging in space and time are materially embedded in our lives and bodies.

Moving from this theoretical journey through the complexities and tensions in ideas of home/land, diasporas, and belonging, this chapter turns again to amplify the experiences of M, in order to examine how home and homeland are shaped by the contingencies of belonging in his life story thus far. We humbly share his story of loss and how he created belonging. Furthermore, M's contribution of building community media for migrants and refugees across different ethnicities, nationalities, and genders expands the boundaries of affective belonging discussed earlier to include marginalized, illegal, or otherwise invisible bodies in creative world making.

Home/lands in, between, and beyond Borderlines

M remembers a time of innocence, when he enjoyed spending time with family and friends in the beautiful space he called home, Kyauktu, Burma. However, when he was eleven, in 1988, he witnessed his family and neighbors protesting for democracy in the streets. In turn, the military regime responded by killing people in his community. He viscerally recalls the smell of blood and the dead. He recalls seeing the injured bodies of neighbors everywhere throughout the town. After that experience, M yearned to live in democratic countries, where people possibly could be free from the fear of military violence. In 1994, he decided to move to Korea to experience living in a democratic system of government and hoped to earn money with a temporary work visa. When he arrived in Korea, however, he was immediately labeled a migrant worker.

Unidirectional migration for work is a by-product of economic globalization. In the struggle between globalization and nationalism, borders become hybrid sites where labor markets and global production cross national territories, and cultures travel. Therefore, humans, too, cross borders for political and economic survival and better lives. However, the global increase in the militarization of places controls people's physical mobility and is an intimidating the feature of borders (Naple & Mendez, 2015). Borders become a threshold, pushing people toward the global labor market and, at the same time, pushing them into sites of displacement, dislocation, and immobility. Through this portal, M's body crossed the border as a migrant worker in a developed country—a body marked by the myriad faces of racial and ethnic discrimination and hatred.

> I came to Korea to learn about a democratic system, but I never had the chance to observe it. I spent all my time at a factory. I was exposed to hazardous working conditions and mistreated by Korean bosses at the factory. Outside the factory, I felt the unsolicited gaze of people on the street and a few Koreans yelled at me "go back your country." At that time, I learned that Myanmar was not an exception, the suffering of the oppressed exist everywhere. (M, personal communication, March 11, 2014)

Although he had imagined a brighter future in Korea, he found little to hope for in this strange land where hypercapitalism, racism, and ethnocentrism seemed to pervade the atmosphere. In South Korea, under the influence of U.S. military power, neocolonial control, and globalization, Americanized capitalism and whiteness are seen as an ideal racial and economic system. To better compete, the Korean government started to bring cheap labor from developing countries to meet the standard of neoliberal globalization (Lee, 2015; Watson, 2010). In this context, M was just a Burmese migrant worker who had relatively darker skin than Koreans. His body was needed to fill the void of 3D (Dangerous, Dirty, and Difficult) labor, such as factory work and farmwork, since South Koreans, who were better off economically, were able to avoid such jobs. For M, the military regime that determined the public world of Myanmar gave form to his upbringing, while labor exploitation and discrimination against his darker skin and nationality shaped his adulthood in Korea. Estrangement and oppression marked his experiences in both countries. Neither of these countries provided him with safety, happiness, or a sense of home.

Life was hard. I was always working and it was difficult to adjust to Korean culture. However, I could not give up and go back to my country, where the Burmese government had killed my people. I had to keep living and surviving in Korea. When I was going through such difficult times, I always recalled my memories from childhood. (M, personal communication, April 24, 2020)

According to the national discourse of birthright and citizenship, M belonged to Myanmar, but he never felt he belonged in a country where the state physically oppressed its own people. Moreover, his host country, South Korea, tolerated his existence as a laborer, not as a human being. M had to endure difficult working conditions, prejudice, and hatred from the South Koreans. He has never felt comfort inside national borders. However, he recalls feelings of home through his sensual memories of his childhood. This memory-based home and homeland indicate physically the same space where he grew up in the national territory of Myanmar, but he re(de)constructs the space through the ways in which he remembers particular moments. Specifically, M recalls his childhood home as influential:

At my home, I ran to catch insects, freely roamed around hills and along the streams. At the same place, I learned political visions from my family and neighbors and witnessed how they fought for our future against the military dictatorship. This home did not offer me safety, but it was there that I shaped my senses and visions. (M, personal communication, April 24, 2020)

Here, we see that home exists in M's memory as a place where he moved freely and where he developed his own senses and thoughts, but home was also a place where his family and neighbors demonstrated courage in their power to fight against oppression. His home does not remain in scattered or frozen images of the national territory. Rather, it is actually re-created in the current moments of remembering through his senses, in his actions and visions (Ahmed, 1999).

M's meaning and valence for home/land are constantly shifting in how he reflects on his life, and how that life anchors and confirms his stories of the world and his subjectivity from the past and the present. As with the discussion of home/land, reflections on home/land become a transformative communication practice that mirrors the complex and dynamic experiences of dis/emplacement in everyday life. To be specific, when M speaks of nationalism and economic globalization, he remembers home based on "land" (Arvin, 2019), not as a secure place within national territories. As a place *for* his subjectivity, home loses its present presence as national space and becomes only a place that he experienced, both in nature and in political turmoil, a budding sense of who he is, what he thinks, and who he hopes to be in the world. As Ahmed (1999) observed home becomes the "skin" between his life and the world; home and homeland are ontological roots of M's life that cannot be located in the artificial demarcation of borderlines. Although the vocabulary of nation, borders, and boundaries necessarily shape its objects, discourses of inclusion and exclusion also offer the opportunity for different forms of (be)longing.

M never stopped thinking about the oppression of others living under military violence and national ideologies. In his heart, he saw himself embedded in a home/land where he experienced nature and the world and learned about (in)justice from his kin and larger community. In doing so, he created a sense of belonging to the larger community and people in various home/lands. By following his sense of home/land from his childhood and his understanding of the roots of his oppression in racism, ethnocentrism, and capitalism in his adulthood, he moved from his own sense of displacement to form connections by taking action for people living in similar circumstances. For M, building a community around media literacy and production was the best way to bring together his concerns for social justice and sharing the stories and experiences of fellow migrants and refugees.

Mediating Home/land for Diaspora beyond Borderlines

M's decision to build a community through media and media literacy was, in large part, driven by his determination to tell stories that would not otherwise be heard, to recognize and be recognized as subjectivities in and through migration. The circuits of communication technology are twisted in a paradox that brings people together to communicate with each other beyond territories, strengthening or loosening the bonds of nationalism and diaspora, while also representing them as citizens and alienized migrants. That is, communication technologies, such as mass media, that are driven by state power and media corporations disseminate imaginary belonging to groups and communities through national ideologies. Those who are marginalized, alienated, and excluded often use online grassroots media networks to resist those narratives and produce their own content, amplify their voices, connect, and build community through their stories. Several communication scholars have advanced critical discussion about how online media networks facilitate social and political movements for migrants. For instance, Wanning (2014) has researched how rural migrants in China engage in media and cultural practices in order to create counter-stories against representation of migrants in mass media and deliver their own content that represents their dreams, hopes, and justice. Rae, Holman, and Nethery (2018) have examined how detainees in Australia's offshore immigration detention centers use social media to disperse their stories of border crossing and experiences of immigration detention and make a connection with people outside facilities to create a political movement for social justice. Grassroots media thus offer a platform for migrant and displaced peoples to fight against representation and prejudice and build a sense of belonging across the world.

The places where migrants resist or reverse the power of surveillance can carve spaces of mobility against the border authorities. This action to create or secure spaces for their lives/living does not stem from the logics of national territories, but from home/land where belonging is not a simple matter of inclusion or exclusion but one of autonomy and connection. They form these relationships through and beyond stories of violence and oppression—particularly through media. With communication technologies, home/lands do not remain in memory but expand to the public where migrants across different social locations can convene, stay, resist, and hope for better lives. In these media spaces, migrants reveal their collective voices, actions, and mobility beyond border regimes.

When M and his migrant friends picked up cameras and microphones on the street, those streets were temporarily and performatively displaced—transforming sites of surveillance into sites of resistance. After a year of strikes and documenting protests, in 2004 they were able to establish an online community media station, called Migrant World Television (MWTV). MWTV's media content can be accessed anywhere in the world through their website (Lee & Kang, 2013; Sun & Park, 2006). This community media station aims at conveying diverse voices and stories of migrants as well as training them to be media activists.

We produce our news and documentaries that deliver migrant workers' opinions. Also, I've taught media literacy classes to migrant workers for 10 years. The purpose of the media literacy classes is to work with migrants who are potential media activists so that we can sustain our community media. (M, personal communication, September 6, 2010)

At MWTV, M connects his story with others to form and communicate a collective diasporic consciousness; he has been documenting the lives of migrant workers and refugees on the streets, at factories and farms, and in borderlands. For example, he reported deaths and work accidents of migrant workers at factories, promoted internet campaigns for donation for the workers' medical expenses, and produced videos and photos of other Burmese refugees who protested for democracy in Myanmar. Also, he produced a video of a trip with fellow migrant workers to Jeju Island, one of the most famous tourist destinations in Korea. The video documented the multidimensionality of the migrants' lives outside their workplaces. Through his media productions, M tries to deconstruct lived experiences of migrant workers and refugees and then experimentally assemble the scenes, reflecting the subjectivity and resistance inherent in their stories in the media productions. In these texts, host countries and borderlands where alienized migrants were isolated can become a playful place of possibility where he and others reflect critically and aesthetically on the power of their collective voice.

Not only does M work with other displaced people to produce media for communities; he also shares media knowledge with others in order to expand the media production network for migrants. He combines media literacy classes with human rights education so that migrant workers in the class understand the connection between media power and human rights. As a result, most of the media productions that migrant workers craft in the class show the discrimination and struggles that they face in Korean society and reveal defiance against the stereotypes of migrant people on mass media, such as illegal workers, cheap bodies, and potential criminals.

As the reach of MWTV has grown, M has brought his media projects closer to "home," to refugee camps between Thailand and Myanmar. In the camps, he documents the lives of Burmese refugees who, like him, were persecuted by the military regime. After gathering their stories, M holds media literacy classes for the refugees where they discuss the dominant media representations of refugee life and critique them in relation to their own lives. Additionally, through donations from nonprofit organizations in South Korea, he has brought used digital cameras to the camps and taught refugees how to record and produce a short video of their lives.

Through this media activism, migrant workers and refugees can amplify their voices and tell their own stories about their identities and lived experiences—stories considered to be of little value in national and global discourses. Furthermore, through MWTV, migrant workers and refugees across Korea and Myanmar who live in different countries and social locations simultaneously create resistant moments that cannot be limited by border regimes. In promoting and mediating these connecting stories, MWTV becomes the circuit for building a sense of belonging across different bodies. When oppressed migrants and refugees reveal their feelings and actions and resonate with each other's voices together through alternative media, they create a sensual belonging that crosses over different cultures, nationalities, languages, and bodies. This diasporic media does not locate itself in national territories; rather, it inspires people to rethink borders that dehumanize them and to (re)place their bodies around and beyond the borderlines.

M's journey—living under the border authorities, documenting the lives of migrants and refugees, teaching media literacy to fellow migrants and refugees in different places, and eventually creating diasporic connections—has been composed of sensual moments of (be)longing across time and in different spaces with different people. How, then, has he come to feel this sense of belonging in his life?

(Be)longing beyond the Borderlines

Unlike national belonging which is already constituted and filters people through ideologies, the sense of belonging that M and his community create is never already constituted but is built through people's bodily actions and feelings. The immanence of belonging among migrant workers and refugees occurs in making media content that convey feelings, emotions, and narratives from their lived experiences. This connection is not retained in or determined by privileged cultures and politics. Rather, it is released in the moments when painful bodies share affects, emotions, and feelings and feel affiliation with each other across different social locations. In these moments, M and MWTV contribute to the creation of that diasporic circuit where different bodies across social locations are able to affect each other through a moment of "touch" (Manning, 2006) and "contagion" (Puar, 2007) in which they transmit feelings, voices, and actions, connecting with each other in resistance to dominant narratives. Every moment of connecting, readjusting, and reconnecting among different bodies with hopes for the better world becomes a spark of belonging.

As he tells his story, M, too, resurrects these moments of finding home/land and locates spaces of inclusion within the people he learned from there.

> Missing home evoked feelings of loneliness, and returning home made me feel scattered. However, home and homeland are the places where I was nurtured by my people. I built my vision and dreams from watching my family and neighbors' lives at home: resistance and endurance. I follow my heart, and that is rooted in my home and my homeplace. (M, personal communication, April 24, 2020)

Remembering home/land does not provoke nostalgia in M; rather, the memories evoke a spirit of resistance and defiance that has grown in him through learning from family and neighbors who had chosen independence over the military regime. It provided him with the catalyst for building his subjectivity beyond the discursive power of national borderlines. In other words, resistance against the dominant system as well as the worth and dignity of all humans are at the core of his actions and emanate from his experiences of home. The culture of belonging that he had organically learned in the spaces he calls home shapes his visions and dreams today, as he embraces a sense of belonging with other people working toward social justice and equity beyond borderlines. M manifests sensual memories of home/land through his own voice and actions. He has built a communal and digital space in order to create a sense of belonging with migrants beyond borders.

Conclusion

This chapter explored the oral history performance of M, a Burmese migrant worker, refugee, and media activist residing in South Korea. We write his story of remembering home as an expression of sensual be/longing; we write and follow his story as he tells it in relation to others, to Eunbi, to his family and friends, to fellow migrants across borders and nations. These are stories told that give rise to action and processes of contagion and touch that build connections among migrants and refugees in the digital media space of MWTV.

Home is shaped by and through discourses of inclusion and exclusion in national spaces that can leave people feeling disenfranchised, oppressed, and hopeless. However, when home is considered through affect, created by and through the lived experiences of being in a space of *feeling*, it becomes a sensual medium that connects the past and the present—and maybe the future. In M's memories, home/land is situated in the story of his childhood when he learned love and resistance and where he built his way of being in the world. Although he cannot officially return to his home and has felt like a stranger after risking so much to go back there, these spaces are where he learned to believe in the power of people to take action and change their lives for the better. Home exists as a sense-memory, and it vividly nourishes his current life. It enables him to be an activist for the equitable world of which he dreams; that is, this spirit of home/land that he experienced is the root of both his singularity and his community.

Based on his visions of home/land, M built a media network for migrants and refugees to raise their collective voice through stories that are embedded in their own affects and emotions. In the work of MWTV, he embraces a sense of belonging that is not territorial but moves fluidly through the spaces where people share their own experiences and feelings of the world across national borders. A sense of belonging that resonates with affects, emotions, and feelings from painful bodies is enabled through performance—through an alternative media circuit that moves beyond dominant narratives.

Through sharing M's oral history performance, this chapter contributes to communication studies of migration by highlighting the sensual, temporal, and relational aspects of both home/lands and (be)longing for migrants and refugees and for M, in particular. M's experiences of building community through MWTV also demonstrate the ways media literacy and production might expand the boundaries of affective belonging to include marginalized, illegal, or otherwise invisible bodies in creative world making. As M said, "MWTV is the place where we can connect with each other and share a vision of the world together" (M, personal communication, April 24, 2020).

NOTE

Acknowledgment: This project does not meet the definition of human subject research under federal regulations, according to the Human Research Protection Office at University of Massachusetts Amherst. To protect the safety of the narrator's life under his current circumstances, the narrator and Eunbi agreed that we would use a pseudonym (M) in the informed consent process.

REFERENCES

Ahmed, S. (1999). "Home and Away: Narratives of Migration and Estrangement." *International Journal of Cultural Studies, 2*(3), 329–347.

Anderson, B. (2006). *Imagined Community*. New York: Verso.

Arvin, M. (2019). "Indigenous Feminist Notes on Embodying Alliance against Settler Colonialism." *Meridians: Feminism, Race, Transnationalism, 18*(2), 335–357.

BBC News Magazine. (2011, December 2). "Who, What, Why: Should It Be Burma or Myanmar?" https://www.bbc.com/news/magazine-16000467.

Bünte, M., & Dosch J. (2015). "Myanmar: Political Reforms and the Recalibration of External Relations." *Journal of Current Southeast Asian Affair, 34*(2), 3–19.

Calafell, B. M. (2012). "Love, Loss, and Immigration: Performative Reverberations between a Great-Grandmother and Great-Granddaughter." In *Border Rhetorics: Citizenship and Identity on the US-Mexico Frontier*, edited by R. D. Dechaine (pp. 151–162). Tuscaloosa: University of Alabama Press.

Callahan, M. P. (2013). *Making Enemies: War and State Building in Burma*. Ithaca: Cornell University.

Carey, J. (1989). *Communication as Culture*. New York: Routledge.

Connor, W. (1986). "The Impact of Homelands upon Diasporas." In *Modern Diasporas in International Politics*, edited by G. Sheffer (pp. 16–45). New York: St. Martin's Press.

Falzon, M. (2003). "Bombay, Our Cultural Heart: Rethinking the Relation between Homeland and Diaspora." *Ethnic and Racial Studies, 26*(4), 662–683.

High, S., & Little, E. (2014). "Introduction." In *Remembering Mass Violence: Oral History, New Media and Performance*, edited by S. High, E. Little & T. R. Duong (pp. 3–32). Toronto: University of Toronto Press.

Langellier, K. M. (1999). "Personal Narrative, Performance, Performativity: Two or Three Things I Know for Sure." *Text and Performance Quarterly, 19*(2), 125–144.

Langellier, K. M. (2010). "Performing Somali Identity in the Diaspora 'Wherever I Go I Know Who I Am.'" *Cultural Studies, 24*(1), 66–94.

Lee, K. J. (2015). "The Black Amerasian Experience in Korea: Representation of Black Amerasians in Korean and Korean American Narratives." *Korea Journal, 55*(1), 7–30.

Lee, E., & Kang, J. S. (2013). "Chaiwa sosuseongeul wihan ijunodongja midieogyoyuge daehan jiljeong yeongu pengkn ijunodongja midieogyoyung gyosuja min hakseupjawaui jiljeong simcheunginteobyureul jungsimeuro." *Hangugeollonhakbo, 57*(6), 441–468.

Madison, D. S. (2012). *Critical Ethnography: Methods, Ethics, and Performance*. Thousand Oaks: Sage Publications.

Manning, E. (2006). *Politics of Touch*. Minneapolis: University of Minnesota Press.

Naficy, H. (1993). *The Making of Exile Cultures: Iranian Television in Los Angeles*. Minneapolis: University of Minnesota Press.

Mendez, J, & Naples, N. (2015). "Introduction." In *Border Politics: Social Movements, Collective Identities, and Globalization*, edited by N. Naples & J. Mendez (pp. 1–31). New York: New York University Press.

Pollock, D. (2000). "Introduction." In *Remembering: Oral History Performance*, edited by D. Pollock (pp. 1–15). New York: Palgrave Macmillan.

Puar, J. (1994). "Writing My Way 'Home.'" *Socialist Review, 24*(4), 75–108.

Puar, J. (2007). *Terrorist Assemblages: Homonationalism in Queer Times*. Durham: Duke University Press.

Rae, M., Holman, R., Nethery, A. (2018). "Self-Represented Witnessing: The Use of Social Media by Asylum Seekers in Australia's Offshore Immigration Detention Centres." *Media, Culture & Society, 40*(4), 479–495.

Rapport, N., & Andrew, D. (1998). "Introduction." In *Migrants of Identity: Perceptions of Home in a World of Movement*, edited by N. Rapport & A. Dawson (pp. 3–20). Providence: Berg.

Sun, B. S., & Park, C. W. (2006). "Junodongjaui midieo munhwahwaldonggwa jeongcheseong jeongchi ijunodongjaui bangsong[pengkt]saryereul jungsimeuro." *Hanguksahoehakoe gitaganhaengmul* (pp. 223–243).

Taylor, Diana (2007). *The Archive and the Repertoire*. Durham: Duke University Press.

Wanning, S. (2014). *Subaltern China: Rural Migrants, Media, and Cultural Practices*. Lanham: Rowman & Littlefield.

Zarina P. (2013). "Forgetting to Remember the Performance of Memory, History, and Gender in John O. Killens' the Cotillion or One Good Bull Is Half the Herd." *Journal of African American Studies, 17,* 328–329.

Zelizer, B. (1995). "Reading the Past against the Grain: The Shape of Memory Studies." *Critical Studies in Mass Communication, 12*(2), 214–239.

Resisting Constructions of "Refugee" Identity through Narrative Performances during a Colorado Refugee Speakers Bureau Event

Natasha Shrikant

Studies in communication and related disciplines illustrate how authoritative discourses—such as legal documents, political debates, nonprofit discourses, and news media—construct the refugee identity category as homogenous despite refugees' diverse ethnicities, experiences, geopolitical origins, and host countries of residence (e.g., Ehmer, 2017; Every & Augoustinos, 2007; Ghazal Aswad, 2019; Lynn & Lea, 2003; McAllum, 2019; McKinnon, 2016; Powell, 2015; Sambaraju & McVittie, 2017). Authoritative discourses erase the diversity of refugee origins and experiences and instead construct refugees as homogenous outsiders to their various host countries through morally evaluating refugees as hostile invaders, as victims in need of saving, or through questioning the legitimacy of their belonging in a host country. Other studies show how diverse refugees construct their own identities in ways that align with these moral evaluations. For example, in narratives told during asylum-seeking processes in Belgium and the United Kingdom, refugees foreground their identities as victims in ways that align with legal definitions of who counts as a victim deserving of entry into a host country (Blommaert, 2001; Kirkwood,

2016). Interview studies illustrate how diverse refugees construct their identities through addressing and refuting negative evaluations of authoritative discourses (Leudar et al., 2008; Wroe, 2018).

These studies highlight how moral stances taken by authoritative discourses reproduce a broader moral order (Jayyusi, 1984/2014) that constrains the way that people, including refugees, construct the refugee identity category. The current study analyzes how personal narratives of three refugee women—one from Bosnia and two from Iraq—living in Colorado resist the constraints of dominant moral orders that negatively evaluate the refugee category. This chapter addresses the following questions: How do narratives from these three refugee women construct identities of themselves and various others? How are moral stances embedded in this identity construction? How do the personal narratives analyzed in this study reproduce, negotiate, or challenge dominant moral orders that position refugees as homogenous outsiders?

The data analyzed is from an annual public storytelling event hosted by the Colorado Refugee Speakers Bureau (CRSB). The CRSB is a nonprofit organization that "was founded in 2016 as a way to help share the rich stories and experiences of Colorado's refugee, SIV [special immigrant visa], and immigrant community."[1] All performers, through performing as a part of a CRSB event, are adopting the identity of refugee, yet their stories diversify meanings associated with the refugee identity category through foregrounding individual daily experiences. Unlike previous studies, this study explores a context where participants tell their own stories without prompts, guidance, or imposition from government institutions or the researcher about the topic or the means of their discussions. Furthermore, different from critical ethnographies that document struggles of the migration journey for particular ethnically and spatially tied refugee communities (Besteman, 2016; Tang, 2015), this study focuses on identity negotiation of ethnically diverse refugees who are tied to one another through their institutional involvement in the CRSB and their current residency in Colorado. Although the CRSB is supportive of refugees, Coloradans generally vary in their stances toward refugees, and the U.S. president at the time this data was gathered—President Trump—repeatedly negatively evaluated immigrants and refugees and placed a temporary ban on U.S. acceptance of refugees. Thus, everyday narratives and participation in the CRSB become an important avenue through which participants build community in contexts where people are simultaneously supportive of and hostile toward refugee communities.

In the following section, I explain this chapter's discourse analytic approach to analyzing identity negotiation and moral stances as emergent through everyday interaction. I then review personal storytelling as a discursive practice that provides agency for participants to creatively reconstruct their own and others' identities and experiences through language and embodiment (Ochs, 2004). I then discuss how participants' use of membership categories during their narratives provides insight into ways that participants construct moral stances toward their own or others' identities and behaviors (Jayyusi, 1984/2014). Analyses of three stories highlight ways that membership categories during these women's narratives construct diverse identities and moral stances. I conclude by discussing the link between these women's narratives and moral orders surrounding refugee identity, thus highlighting the political functions of these personal narratives (Lazaar, 2008).

Discourse Analytic Approaches to Identity and Morality

Refugee identity, like identities more generally, is negotiated through everyday interaction in contexts of inequality (Asante et al., 2016; Bucholtz & Hall, 2005; Hall, 1990; Shrikant, 2018). The ways that authoritative discourses construct refugee identity align with ways that dominant populations position colonized populations (Hall, 1990). In the United States, legacies of colonialism are visible through processes of racialization. The United States was built on foundations of slavery, where white Europeans exploited the labor and land of Black and Indigenous peoples. Throughout history, new migrants have been racialized as white or as various non-white groups, with privileges reserved for those who count as white (Brodkin, 1998; Ignatiev, 1995; Omi & Winant, 2014; Roediger, 2005). Refugees and asylees are involuntary migrant groups forced to flee from their countries of origin only to be racialized and excluded in their new host countries (Powell, 2015). Authoritative discourses contribute to constructing an imagined immigrant who is "always spoken for, yet rarely heard from" (Ghazal Aswad, 2019, p. 364). Everyday discourse can provide marginalized groups with agency to negotiate identities on their own terms, thus resisting dominant portrayals of their groups (Shrikant, 2014, 2018).

This chapter takes an ethnomethodological approach to studying morality, orienting to moral stances as emergent via everyday discourse and moral orders as constituted and reconstituted through everyday discourse (Jayyusi, 1984, 2014; Stokoe, 2003). Through closely analyzing participants' narratives, this chapter reveals the participants' stances about "whether human conduct and character is right, good, and reasonable" (Robles, 2015, p. 1032). Grounding the study of morality in everyday interaction allows for the exploration of the diversity of moral stances constructed by participants and highlights the agency of everyday interaction to disrupt taken-for-granted moral orders perpetuated by authoritative discourses.

Personal Narratives and Identity

This chapter positions "refugees as experts of their own experience" (Wroe, 2018, p. 340) through analyzing ways that participants reconstruct identities and experiences through storytelling. During narratives, storytellers—both verbally and through embodiment—construct relationships between events and identities in the past and those in the present context (Cooren et al., 2013; Koven, 1998; Merino et al., 2017; Wortham, 2001). Storytellers draw connections between the past and present through shifting from narrating past events to overtly commenting on those events to their current listeners or audience members (Koven, 2002). Narrators also use quotation, where they quote people in their stories—including themselves—and in doing so take stances toward theirs and others' past selves (Bakhtin, 1981; Koven, 2002). Last, storytellers draw connections between past events and the current context of storytelling through embodying changes in their identity as they tell a story (Wortham, 2001).

Membership Categorization Analysis, Morality, and Refugee Identity

Membership categorization analysis (MCA) traces how participants construct social worlds through the ways they name, characterize, and position identity categories (Fitzgerald & Housley, 2015; Hester & Eglin, 1997; Sacks, 1972; Stokoe, 2012). Jayyusi (1984/2014) discusses how tracing categorization work in everyday discourse provides insight into ways that people construct moral stances. Similarly, multiple studies analyzing how non-refugees negotiate the refugee identity category have illustrated specific ways that participants construct moral stances as intertwined with refugee identity.

Participants construct moral stances through the choice of the category itself. Studies analyzing refugee identity illustrate how news media and politicians switch between categories such as "boat people" versus "refugees" or "bogus refugee" versus "genuine refugee" (Lynn & Lea, 2003; Rowe & O'Brien, 2014). The choice of the category implies whether the refugees referenced are good people who deserve help and protection or are manipulating their way into a new country. In addition, studies highlight how morality is embedded in the ways refugee groups are characterized through category-tied predicates that describe the category, and category-bound activities that construct refugees as naturally engaging in certain kinds of activities (Every & Augoustinos, 2007; Goodman et al., 2017; Goodman & Speer, 2007; Leudar et al., 2008; Nightingale et al., 2017; Wroe, 2018). Every and Augoustinos's (2007) analysis of Australian parliamentary debates, for example, illustrates ways that politicians use category-tied predicates like "actually have money in their pockets" (p. 419) or category-bound activities such as "seeking to abuse the system" (p. 420) to question the moral character of asylum seekers, ultimately positioning asylees as not deserving entry into Australia.

Last, people display moral stances through the ways they construct relationships between refugee and other identity categories. Participants construct standardized relational pairs, or "pairs of categories that carry duties and moral obligations in relation to the other, such as 'parent-child'" (Stokoe, 2012, p. 281). Thus, simply naming categories can imply moral obligations between them (i.e., good parents should take care of their children). Another pair is an activity-occasioned pair, where people do not name categories but make categories—and the relationship between them—relevant through "involvement in a joint transaction" (Leudar et al., 2008, p. 194). For example, Leudar et al. (2008) show how the category "failed asylum seeker" appears alongside the categories "children of failed asylum seekers" and "parents" in a news article. An example of a standardized relational pair is parent-child: the news article frames "failed asylum seekers" as bad parents because they failed to provide their children with a safe home. An example of an activity-occasioned pair is between "government" and "asylum-seeking parents": the newspaper article states, "parents whose asylum claims have been rejected"

(Leudar et al., 2008; p. 193). In this case, the category "government" is not named but is made relevant through the category-bound activity "have been rejected"—the government is the authority who rejects but is not named as an agent in the process.

These examples illustrate how MCA is a productive analytic approach for studying the relationship between morality and refugee identity negotiation, yet the majority of these studies analyze how non-refugee authorities construct refugee categorization and, through doing so, maintain the excluded, racialized position of refugees in their host countries. This chapter analyzes how refugees mobilize categories, category-bound activities, and category-tied predicates when constructing their own identities. Through analyzing categories, activities, and predicates as embedded in personal narratives, I examine how participants draw connections between past and present identities in ways that resist dominant characterizations by outsiders. Thus, tracing categorization work during personal narratives provides insight into ways that personal narratives are political (Lazar, 2008).

Discourse Analytic Methods

Discourse analysis encompasses a variety of methods focused on how people accomplish social action through specific discursive strategies (Tracy, 2015). This chapter analyzes how refugees accomplish the social action of identity negotiation through closely examining their choice of categories, category-bound activities, and category-tied predicates as they occur during personal narratives.

The three audio- and video-recorded excerpts analyzed here occurred as part of a larger event held by the CRSB in October 2019. The three-hour CRSB annual showcase event was open to the public and live streamed on a social media platform. I attended the event in person, and with the permission of the participants, I recorded audio and video. The event was attended by refugees, advocates, and members of the general public. There were nine speakers at the event and an emcee (a refugee herself) who hosted the event. The emcee introduced the event with her own story and introduced each speaker with their name, their country of origin, and other biographical details. The audience (including the performers) was highly supportive of the performers. During the event the emcee discussed storytelling as doing two things: 1) educating the public about refugee experiences in hopes of humanizing refugees, and 2) providing recently resettled refugees with a sense of community across their diverse cultural, linguistic, and religious backgrounds.

Part of discourse analytic research is the descriptive and interpretive process of translating a complex lived experience into written form in a way that meets practical aims for analysis. Including detailed transcriptions of narratives helps foreground refugees' voices and interpretations of their own experiences as an important part of the analysis and findings. Of course, any transcription is a partial representation of an event that is a product of the choices made by the transcriber. In this chapter, I use verbatim-enhanced transcription conventions (Craig & Tracy, 2021). I transcribed all words, partial words, vocal sounds (e.g., uhs and ums), and pauses; I used symbols to indicate nonverbal qualities such as emphasizing words or using rising and falling tones; Last, I added significant gestures in double parentheses. (See the appendix for transcription symbols.) Transcribing words, paralinguistic features, and gestures meets analytic aims to analyze how the refugee women both construct and enact their own and others' identities during storytelling. Although this was a public event, for purposes of confidentiality, I used pseudonyms for participants' names.

Findings

I present transcriptions of three stories, each of which highlights different facets of refugee experience and illustrates ways that refugees take moral stances when constructing their own and others' identities.

Example 1: Shedding "Shame" through "Sharing Stories"

Analysis of the following video-recorded excerpt illustrates how the CRSB emcee, Amina, constructs her transformation from an ashamed refugee to a courageous refugee through the ways she narrates and enacts her past and present identities. In doing so, Amina reconstructs negative moral evaluations that refugees associate with shame they feel about their own experiences into a source of strength. Amina introduces herself as a refugee from Bosnia and then tells a story about her experiences with the CRSB.

EXAMPLE 1

1	Amina	I was actually one of the initial members of the Refugee
2		Speaker's Bureau, I was a part of cohort one. Um, and I
3		can't <u>tell</u> you and say enough of, what sort of
4	–	transformation it's had in my life. Um, when <u>I</u> initially,
5		was, introduced to I – to the idea of sharing my story or
6		being a part of something like this, I, I was more than
7		apprehensive. I was like, there will be – you will never
8		see me talk about (.) <u>my</u> trauma and my hardship, and you
9		will <u>nev</u>er see me cry in – in public. And that's what I
10		envisioned that this process would be like. And so I got
11		pulled into a meeting. And I remember I had a friend who
12		was organizing all of this um: and she, she sat me down,
13		she sincerely asked me is, you know, I don't want to
14		force you to do this. But is this something that you want
15		to do? And I remember just feeling like, I can't possibly
16		(.) go up in front of all these people and tell them what
17		I've been through. An:d when I finally just pushed
18		myself, and I, I did our first showcase, and I shared my
19		story and after that I – I began sitting on panels, I
20		<u>real</u>ized that (.) the <u>piece</u> of me, that the reason that
21		I'm having so much trouble was because I was ashamed of
22		who I was. I was a<u>sham</u>ed of this story. And that's
23		something that (.) you – you may hear often in the
24		community? You hear a lot about resistance and res-like
25		resilience and bravery and courage. But I think something
26		that we don't talk enough about on on top of other things
27		that we don't talk about in the refugee community, but we
28		↑don't talk enough about (.) feeling a<u>sham</u>ed, feeling
29		ashamed of these (.) abnormal situations that we are
30		placed in. Sort of feeling like we will never belong in a
31		(.) ((air quotes)) normal society ((close air quotes)).
32		And so I <u>nev</u>er wanted to if – if this makes sense anyone in
33		the room I honestly just never wanted to share my story

34	Amina	because I didn't want anyone to think I was weird. Or
35		broken. And here I am. Uh, it's been two years? Two or so
36		years? And I:: I'm standing in front of you telling you
37		I'm a former refugee=
38	Audience	=woo! [WOO! ((applause)) woohoo!]
39	Amina	[And that's a huge. hhh] That is a hu::ge (.)
40		accomplishment for me. I have gained so much (.) courage,
41		and it – it just, I have really been able to shed some of
42		that shame, and I'm still working on it but I've been
43		able to shed some of that shame.

Amina names the categories "initial members" and "cohort one" (1–2), thus identifying herself according to her institutional role as an experienced member of the refugee community, and of the CRSB in particular. Amina states that her membership in the CRSB "transformed" her, thus separating her past self from her current, transformed self (4). Throughout her narrative, Amina centers her transformation around the category-bound activity expected for CRSB members: "sharing my story" (5). Amina positions her past self as "apprehensive" about sharing her story. When quoting her past self, she uses category-bound activities: "never see me talk about my trauma," "never see me cry in public" (8–9), and "can't possibly go up in front of all these people" (15–16), thus creating a scared, vulnerable past identity. Amina narrates her transformation through several category-bound activities: she "pushed herself," "shared her story," and now "sits on panels" (17–19). In addition to narrating her transformation, Amina is also publicly and confidently sharing her story as an experienced member of the CRSB and the emcee of this event. Amina's current enactment of a confident identity overlaps with her narration of her transformation.

Amina then introduces a category-tied predicate as an explanation for her reluctance to share her story: being "ashamed" (21).[2] Amina ties this predicate not only to herself but also to "the [refugee] community" (23–27). Amina lists other category-tied predicates like resistance, resilience, bravery, and courage, which are more morally valued rather than shame, an emotion people often seek to hide (24–25). Amina opposes the category "refugee community" and instead uses the category "normal society"; refugees feel shame about their "abnormal experiences," which excludes them from integrating into "normal" (non-refugee) society. Amina again names the category-bound activity "sharing her story," and names category-tied predicates that non-refugees might attribute to refugees if they share their stories: "weird" or "broken" (34–35). Amina closes by addressing her audience directly, using the category-bound activity "standing in front of you telling you I'm a former refugee" and stating that she has gained "courage" and "shed some of that shame" throughout her transformation process (35–43). As Amina narrates, she speaks confidently and directly to her audience, thus embodying her transformation from scared and ashamed to courageous.

Through the ways she constructs and evaluates her past and current selves, Amina reconstructs taken-for-granted moral orders both within and outside of the refugee community. Amina's narrative suggests that there are preferences for the kinds of stories that need to be told, and the kinds of stories or experiences that should be hidden. However, shame is not something that should be considered immoral; rather, it is something that should be talked about, and in doing so, refugees (like herself) can build a stronger, more courageous self.

Example 2: Constructing Moral Obligations between "Americans" and "Refugees"

Analysis of the following example illustrates how Farah, one of the CRSB speakers, reconstructs moral obligations between "Americans" and "refugees" through narrating her past negative experience with a man from the United States, and then drawing connections between this experience and broader logics that U.S. Americans, more generally, use when evaluating refugees. Through doing so, Farah is morally evaluating U.S. Americans, refugees, and the relationships they have with one another. Farah is introduced as an "autism mom," an artist, and a radio host. Farah emigrated to the United States on a Special Immigrant Visa that she received because she and her family worked for the U.S. military and therefore were in danger in Iraq.

Farah names the category "this old guy" (1) and constructs the "old guy" as aggressive through using the category-bound activity "verbally attacked me" (2–3), quoting this man as repeatedly telling her to leave the country (3–6), replying to Farah with sarcasm when she asks if he is talking to her (8–10), and using aggressive hand gestures when enacting this man's identity during

EXAMPLE 2

1	Farah	<u>Two</u> weeks back hhh, I ran — I ran into this old guy in
2		one of the stores in Denver, who hhh verbally attacked
3		me by saying, we don't want you here people. And I
4		thought he was talking to somebody else, but apparently
5		he was talking to me ((touches her chest)), and he
6		repeated it by saying we <u>don't</u> want you <u>here</u> people
7		((emphasizes each word with arms)). <u>Sir</u>, are you
8		talking to me? Duh:: you're the only one in the aisle
9		here. I'm not supposed to talk about the chickpea can
10		on the shelf, yes I'm talking to you. I was like,
11		<u>ho</u>ly guacamole.
12	Audience	((soft [laughter]))
13	Farah	[Am I ready for this? It was a bad day already.
14		(1.0) I went to him and I go like, I am so sorry sir
15		that you're feeling this way. And I truly appreciate
16		your concern, ↑but I'm a little afraid that its ↓not
17		your call for me to be or not be here. ((steps back and
18		throws arm up in the air))
19	Audience	Woo! Yeah! ((applause))
20	Farah	And I shoved my way out of that aisle heading to
21		another aisle to get an extra bottle of [wine needed
22		for that heck of a night.
23	Audience	[((laughter))
24	Farah	Yeah I know it was funny. It was funny until it was not
25		when I found myself bursting into tears in my car. I
26		didn't cry because I was sad. I cried because I was
27		angry. That's what wine made for, right you guys?
28		((points at audience))
29	Audience	((laughter))
30	Farah	But it's it's it's it's I'm not a drinker. I'm a
31		thinker. So that's why I spend the whole thinking
32		about <u>where</u> this guy is <u>com</u>ing from. Luckily I am a
33		photographer, I can put different — put on different

34	Farah	lenses and see from different perspectives so I <u>know</u>
35		and I <u>get</u> it when people, they don't know they fear.
36		People fear what they don't know. And when they fear,
37		they judge and when they judge, they attempt to
38		control, and when they cannot control they attack. And
39		I get it. I get it. He was scared like most of
40		Americans, I was angry. His fear is as valid as my
41		anger. He was scared. I was angry. We both are human,
42		and it's totally fine. And I told him, it is not your
43		call, to decide whether I should be here or shouldn't
44		be. But also I'm telling you guys, it is not his call
45		also to delve into it and to dig deeper and explore who
46		I am. Why people like me had to leave their countries;
47		what my background looks like? Or what I have to
48		sacrifice in order to come here yet is my
49		responsibility to stand tall for me and for people like
50		me to tell the whole world, American people, why I'm
51		here, what they want or what they need to know about
52		me. For that, I'm dedicating, and I wrote my last part
53		for him, so I pretend that he's present in the room,
54		and we're gonna have this dialogue together, so bear
55		with me.
56	Audience	((laughter))

quotation (7). Farah positions herself as a victim of the "verbal attack" and as confused, yet respectful (quoting herself using "sir") toward this man at a grocery store (3–11). Through quotation, Farah makes relevant the categories of "migrant/refugee" and "U,S. American," and constructs migrants (like herself) as often victimized by aggressive U.S. Americans. Farah closes her story by voicing her past self as strong: she uses the category-bound activity of "went up to him" and then quotes herself as acknowledging this man's feelings yet dismissing his words with direct criticism. Farah's enactment of her own identity as she tells the story supports her construction of herself as strong: she uses a high-pitched tone, often associated with being indirect or unsure, when saying "but I'm a little afraid that it's" and contrasts it with a deep, authoritative tone when saying "not your call for me to be or not be here" (16–17). Farah also follows her criticism by throwing her arm up in the air (similar to a mic-drop gesture). Through her response to this man, Farah takes the moral stance that it is not she who is unwanted but this "old guy" who is overbearing, rude, and hurtful.

Although this story seems relatively straightforward, Farah follows it with extensive commentary. This was not simply a one-off experience where Farah cleverly put down an "old guy" never to think of the experience again. Rather, she cried afterward and thought at length about this man's perspective. Farah connects her personal experience with one man to moral orders that "people" (35, 36) have generally used to justify who deserves to be here, who gets judged, or who deserves to be controlled or attacked (35–38). Farah clarifies that the "people" who pass judgment on migrants and refugees are "Americans" (40), and she separates herself from the category "Americans" through using the category "people like me" (46). By "people like me," Farah means refugees. As seen through the category-bound activities, she adds: "leave their countries" and "have to sacrifice" (46, 48). Then, Farah, through using a category-bound activity, constructs a relationship between "Americans" and "people like me": "People like me" have to "stand tall . . . and tell the whole world, American people, why I'm here" (49–50). Farah constructs Americans as not needing to "delve into" (45) understanding refugees, but constructs refugees as having the "responsibility" (49) to educate Americans. Farah continues through reenacting her conversation with the "old guy," this time voicing common negative beliefs that Americans have about refugees and her own responses to these beliefs.

Example 3: Criticizing Hypocritical Moral Stances of "Classmates" and the "U.S. Army"

Analysis of the final example illustrates how Saira, a college student and refugee from Iraq, connects her personal experiences to those of her classmates. She often refers to political relationships between the U.S. military and foreign, innocent civilians. By criticizing her classmates' and the U.S. military's moral stances toward war. Saira narrates a classroom experience discussing "morality," where most of her classmates agree that killing innocent civilians is a justifiable

EXAMPLE 3

1	Saira	I'm a senior in college now and just about done with
2		everything. I'm in my war and morality class, philosophy
3		class. An:d, of course, foreign morality, the issue of
4		terrorism comes up. The question? Should we bomb schools
5		and community centers in those places that are terrorist
6		invested? Because, you know, we don't have very specific
7		army targets, fo:r those terrorist groups that would make
8		our win, complete. Of course, no, for me, but I was
9		fla(h)bbergasted. And all of my classmates seem to agree
10		with the logic. You see, we have to win this war, this war
11		that no one really knows what it's about, really. We have
12		to win it and in order to win it, we might have to bomb
13		some schools and mosques and like, who ca::res, really, if
14		a few innocent people, die. (2.0) I was sitting there, in
15		beautiful CU Boulder, surrounded by kindhearted
16		liberals. The same people who put up signs at coffee
17		shops. That say you're welcome here. And they were okay
18		with that. Slowly I raise my hand and I put forth the
19		radical thesis that, hey, maybe if we destroy the
20		community infrastructure, those people will be driven.
21		To the exact same groups that we claim to protect them
22		from. And my classmates look at me as ((if)) I've just come from
23		a different planet. I feel like I just come from a
24		different planet. [six lines omitted where she comments on
25		other stories she told previously] When my classmates a —
26		talk about uhm, talk about terrorism like that, or when
27		they think that I feel alien to them because of the way
28		that I talked about it myself, it's because you know, they
29		value diversity until you say something that they don't
30		agree with. And the:n they're like, no, we don't want
31		that. We just want the number that you buy.

cost of winning a war against terrorists. Saira opposes her classmates, both within the story and in her comments to her audience.

Saira constructs her identity as a student through naming the category "senior in college" and discussing her class—one that focuses on "morality" (1–2). Saira quotes a question asked in class, "bomb schools and community centers in those places that are terrorist invested" (4–5). Through naming the activity ("bomb"), Saira voices the relationship that her class constructed between U.S. Americans (who bomb) and foreigners (whom U.S. Americans bomb). Saira continues quoting the class discussion and, in doing so, invokes the category of the U.S. army when using the predicate "don't have very specific army targets"—and then names the category "terrorist groups" as the enemy of the U.S. army against which the army must "win" (7–8). Saira voices her past self as adamantly against bombing in this situation, but as extremely confused ("flabbergasted," 9) by her classmates' response. Saira positions the categories "classmates" and the "army" as aligned with one another through voicing their shared moral stances; winning the war against "terrorists" is more important than preserving "innocent lives" (10–14). Here Saira is criticizing the U.S. military as well as her classmates' stance as immoral. Saira continues expressing her confusion toward her classmates' stance through juxtaposing their immorality with the supposed liberal qualities of people in Boulder. Saira uses the category "liberals" and adds category-tied predicates of "kind-hearted" and category-bound activities of "putting up signs" that welcome refugees (15–17). Saira criticizes her classmates who live in Boulder as hypocritical because they claim to be welcoming while not actually valuing human life.

Saira returns to narrating her classroom experience, and when narrating her response she uses category-bound activities of "destroy" and "people will be driven" to negatively evaluate the United States, and the U.S. military, as destroying lives of innocent people and causing people to join terrorist groups (18–20). Saira also uses the category-bound activity "claim to protect," which highlights contradictions between what the United States claims to be doing (fighting wars to protect from terrorism) and what the U.S. military actually supports doing (destroying lives of innocent civilians for purposes of winning wars) (21). Saira then narrates the shift in the relationship between herself and her classmates; she is not a fellow classmate but rather an "alien" from another planet (23–24, 27). Later, Saira attributes her classroom experiences to her classmates' narrow definition of "diversity." Saira constructs her classmates' moral stance as only "valuing diversity" as long as "diverse" people align with the moral values of her classmates (29–30). Thus, Saira again criticizes the moral commitments of her classmates who claim to support diverse communities, yet only do so if these communities align with her classmates' own beliefs.

Discussion

This study illustrates how a close analysis of these three stories provides insight into ways that the personal is political (Lazaar, 2008); each story diversifies meanings and moral stances associated with the refugee identity category. The stories also illustrate ways that these women draw connections between everyday experiences and sociopolitical inequalities. Through participation in the CRSB and through invoking the category "refugee," each woman does orient to being a refugee as a relevant identity. However, their narratives expand the kinds of qualities associated with the category. Many of these narratives foreground emotionally tied qualities that pervade these women's experiences: feeling ashamed, being brave, feeling upset, trying to be understanding, being angry, or being confused. These identities are both verbally stated and nonverbally enacted and embodied through storytelling (Wortham, 2001). Furthermore, since stories connect past and present identities and experiences (Koven, 2002), these participants were able narrate how their identities fluidly changed over time and in different contexts (i.e., from ashamed to brave, from direct to upset, from surprised to angry).

Similarly, these women narrated a diversity of moral stances and dilemmas through the ways they used, characterized, and organized categories (Jayyusi, 1984/2014). For example, Amina narrates dilemmas about how "sharing her story" could position her as being "brave" but also as "weird" or "broken." Farah attempts to reconcile being direct and shutting down U.S. Americans with trying to understand U.S. American perspectives and help them. Saira navigates feeling hurt and ostracized in class versus criticizing and holding her classmates (and the U.S. military) accountable for their stances. Interesting to note is that Farah and Saira take opposing stances about moral obligations between refugees and U.S. Americans; Farah argues that refugees should understand and explain their experiences to U.S. Americans, whereas Saira argues that refugees should hold

U.S. Americans accountable for their hypocritical stances. The diversity of ways that each refugee woman constructs her own identities and moral dilemmas functions to disrupt authoritative discourses (Bakhtin, 1981) that position refugees as homogenous outsiders through evaluating them as invaders, victims, or as having questionable legitimacy in their host countries (e.g., Ehmer, 2017; Every & Augoustinos, 2007; Ghazal Aswad, 2019; Lynn & Lea, 2003; McAllum, 2019; Sambaraju & McVittie, 2017).

The stories these women told also serve political functions because they comment on and criticize dominant ideas about refugee identity. This analysis illustrates how each woman drew connections between personal experiences and broader political struggles and inequality through category work during their narratives. Each of the women positioned her personal stories as political through shifting between personal identity categories used to reference specific people in a narrative (e.g., Farah and "the old guy") and political categories referencing larger groups of people and inequalities among them (e.g., "refugees" and "Americans"). Thus, these women narrate personal stories about public speaking, going grocery shopping, or attending class as inseparable from political experiences of navigating shame and dealing with xenophobia and racism.

In addition, performing these stories publicly, foregrounding diversity of experience, and being supportive of critical stances are values that each refugee woman displayed and upheld through her narrative and, more generally, through participation in this CRSB event. Similar to DiDomenico's (2015) findings about how storytelling practices at an LGBTQ organization helped build community among storytellers, the storytelling practices at the CRSB provide space for these women to build a sense of community across diverse, otherwise unconnected identities in contexts where they often face shame and hostility.

Conclusion

This chapter analyzed how three refugee women constructed identities of themselves and various others, how moral stance-taking was embedded in this identity construction, and how participants' everyday discourses challenge dominant moral orders that position refugees as homogenous outsiders. This study's discourse analytic approach highlighted the agency of participants to, through choices they make about categorization and narration, navigate and reconstruct the outsider-imposed refugee identity category on their own terms. Through drawing from discourses of refugees and closely analyzing categorization during personal narratives, this study showed that macro categories like refugee are complex, emergent, and negotiated in moment-to-moment interaction by people who are positioned as part of this category. Thus, using a discourse analytic approach highlights concrete ways that intersections between the personal and political are constituted via everyday interaction.

Analyzing how everyday interaction constitutes intersections between the personal and political among refugees, and migrant communities more broadly, is especially important in the current political climate with a heightened, pervasive demonization of migrant groups in the United States and internationally. Sacks long ago noted relationships between everyday categorization work and social change:

> The important problems of social change . . . would involve laying out such things as the sets of categories, how they're used, what's known about any member, and beginning to play with shifts in the rules for application of a category and with shifts in the properties of any category. (1979, p. 14)

Most work on categorization and refugee identity has focused on "laying out" ways that authoritative voices name and use categories. Very few studies focus on the ways that everyday groups resist authoritative characterizations through their own storytelling and categorization practices (for an exception, see Shrikant, 2014, 2018).

Findings of this study illustrate how, through their narratives, these women are creating social change through "playing with" categories, relationships, and moral stances associated with them. Future work should expand on these findings through highlighting how voices of often marginalized or excluded communities disrupt authoritative discourses through playing with assumed forms of categorization. As researchers, we should work toward creating more empathy and understanding of these communities on their own terms, and categorization analysis of refugee narratives is one fruitful way to do so.

Appendix. Transcription Conventions

(modified from Jefferson, 2004)

:	Stretched sound, more colons demonstrate longer stretches
__	Indicates emphasis
↑	Indicates raised intonation
[ ]	Overlapping talk: "[" (open bracket) indicates beginning of overlap; "]" (closed bracket) indicates end
—	An abrupt stop in speaking
=	Contiguous utterance
(( ))	Contains analysts' comments, label nonverbal activities
?	Rising inflection
.	Fall in tone
,	Continuing intonation
( )	Unclear or inaudible speech
(hhh)	Hearable exhalation

NOTES

1. https://coloradorefugeespeakersbureau.wordpress.com/.
2. For a review of the notion of "shame," particularly as it applies to understanding migrant women's experiences, see Tonsing and Barn (2017).

REFERENCES

Asante, G., Sekimoto, S., & Brown, C. (2016). "Becoming 'Black': Exploring the Racialized Experiences of African Immigrants in the United States." *Howard Journal of Communications, 27*(4), 367–384.

Bakhtin, M. M. (1981). *The Dialogic Imagination: Four Essays.* Austin: University of Texas Press.

Besteman, C. (2016). *Making Refuge: Somali Bantu Refugees and Lewiston, Maine.* Durham: Duke University Press.

Blommaert, J. (2001). "Investigating Narrative Inequality: African Asylum Seekers' Stories in Belgium." *Discourse & Society, 12*(4), 413–449.

Brodkin, K. (1998). *How Jews Became White Folks and What That Says about Race in America*. New Brunswick: Rutgers University Press.

Bucholtz, M. & Hall, K. (2005). "Identity and Interaction: A Sociocultural Linguistic Approach." *Discourse Studies, 7*(4–5), 585–614.

Cooren, F., Matte, F., Benoit-Barné, C., & Brummans, B. H. J. M. (2013). "Communication as Ventriloquism: A Grounded-in-Action Approach to the Study of Organizational Tensions." *Communication Monographs, 80*(3), 255–277.

Craig, R., & Tracy, K. (2021). *Grounded Practical Theory: Investigating Communication Problems*. San Diego: Cognella.

DiDomenico, S. M. (2015). "'Putting a Face on a Community': Genre, Identity, and Institutional Regulation in the Telling (and Retelling) of Oral Coming-Out Narratives." *Language in Society, 44*(5), 607–628.

Ehmer, E. A. (2017). "Learning to Stand on Their Own: Contradictory Media Representations of Burmese Refugees by Nonprofit Organizations." *Critical Studies in Media Communication, 34*(1), 29–43.

Every, D., & Augoustinos, M. (2007). "Constructions of Racism in the Australian Parliamentary Debates on Asylum Seekers." *Discourse & Society, 18*(4), 411–436.

Fitzgerald, R., & Housley, W. (2015). *Advances in Membership Categorisation Analysis*. Los Angeles: SAGE.

Ghazal Aswad, N. (2019). "Biased Neutrality: The Symbolic Construction of the Syrian Refugee in the *New York Times.*" *Critical Studies in Media Communication, 36*(4), 357–375.

Goodman, S., Sirriyeh, A., & McMahon, S. (2017). "The Evolving (Re)categorisations of Refugees throughout the 'Refugee/Migrant Crisis.'" *Journal of Community & Applied Social Psychology, 27*(2), 105–114.

Goodman, S., & Speer, S. A. (2007). "Category Use in the Construction of Asylum Seekers." *Critical Discourse Studies, 4*(2), 165–185.

Hall, S. (1990). "Cultural Identity and Diaspora." In *Identity: Community, Culture, Difference*, edited by J. Rutherford (pp. 222–237). London: Lawrence & Wishart.

Hester, S., & Eglin, P. (1997). *Culture in Action: Studies in Membership Categorization Analysis*. Lanham: University Press of America.

Ignatiev, N. (1995). *How the Irish Became White*. New York: Routledge.

Jayyusi, L. (1984/2014). *Categorization and the Moral Order (Routledge Revivals)*. New York: Routledge.

Jefferson, G. (2004). "Glossary of Transcript Symbols with an Introduction." In *Conversation Analysis: Studies from the First Generation*, edited by G. Lerner (pp.

13–31). Amsterdam: Benjamins.

Kirkwood, S. (2016). *Language of Asylum*. London: Palgrave Macmillan UK.

Koven, M. (1998). "Two Languages in the Self/The Self in Two Languages: French-Portuguese Bilinguals' Verbal Enactments and Experiences of Self in Narrative Discourse." *Ethos, 26*(4), 410–455.

Koven, M. (2002). "An Analysis of Speaker Role Inhabitance in Narratives of Personal Experience." *Journal of Pragmatics, 34*(2), 167–217.

Lazar, M. M. (2008). "Language, communication and the public sphere: A perspective from feminist critical discourse analysis." In *Handbook of Communication in the Public Sphere*, edited by R. Wodak & V. Koller, 89–110. New York: Mouton de Gruyter.

Leudar, I., Hayes, J., Nekvapil, J., & Turner Baker, J. (2008). "Hostility Themes in Media, Community and Refugee Narratives." *Discourse & Society, 19*(2), 187–221.

Lynn, N., & Lea, S. (2003). "'A Phantom Menace and the New Apartheid': The Social Construction of Asylum-Seekers in the United Kingdom." *Discourse & Society, 14*(4), 425–452.

McAllum, K. (2019). "Refugee Resettlement Volunteers as (Inter)cultural Mediators?" *Journal of International and Intercultural Communication, 13*(4), 1–18.

McKinnon, S. L. (2016). *Gendered Asylum: Race and Violence in U.S. Law and Politics*. Champaign: University of Illinois Press.

Merino, M.-E., Becerra, S., & De Fina, A. (2017). "Narrative Discourse in the Construction of Mapuche Ethnic Identity in Context of Displacement." *Discourse & Society, 28*(1), 60–80.

Nightingale, A., Quayle, M., & Muldoon, O. (2017). "'It's Just Heart Breaking': Doing Inclusive Political Solidarity or Ambivalent Paternalism through Sympathetic Discourse within the 'Refugee Crisis' Debate." *Journal of Community & Applied Social Psychology, 27*(2), 137–146.

Ochs, E. (2004). "Narrative Lessons." In *A Companion to Linguistic Anthropology*, edited by A. Duranti (pp. 269–289). Hoboken: Blackwell.

Omi, M., & Winant, H. (2014). *Racial Formation in the United States*. New York: Routledge.

Powell, K. M. (2015). *Identity and Power in Narratives of Displacement*. New York: Routledge.

Robles, J. (2015). Morality in Discourse. In *The International Encyclopedia of Language and Social Interaction*, edited by K. Tracy, T. Sandel, & C. Ilie (1st ed., Vol. 2, pp. 1032–1037). Hoboken: Wiley Blackwell.

Roediger, D. R. (2005). *Working toward Whiteness: How America's Immigrants Became White; The Strange Journey from Ellis Island to the Suburbs*. New York: Basic Books.

Rowe, E., & O'Brien, E. (2014). "'Genuine' Refugees or Illegitimate 'Boat People': Political

Constructions of Asylum Seekers and Refugees in the Malaysia Deal Debate." *Australian Journal of Social Issues, 49*(2), 171–193.

Sacks. (1972). "On the Analyzability of Stories by Children." *Directions in Sociolinguistics,* 325–345.

Sacks, H. (1979). "Hotrodder: A Revolutionary Category." In *Everyday Language: Studies in Ethnomethodology,* edited by G. Psathas (pp. 7–14). North Stratford: Irvington Publishers.

Sambaraju, R., & McVittie, C. (2017). "The European Union and the Refugee Crisis: Inclusion, Challenges, and Responses." *Journal of Community and Applied Social Psychology, 27,* 99–104.

Shrikant, N. (2014). "It's like, 'I've Never Met a Lesbian Before!': Personal Narratives and the Construction of Diverse Female Identities in a Lesbian Counterpublic." *Pragmatics, 24*(4), 799–818.

Shrikant, N. (2018). "'There's No Such Thing as Asian': A Membership Categorization Analysis of Cross-cultural Adaptation in an Asian American Business Community." *Journal of International and Intercultural Communication, 11*(4), 286–303.

Stokoe, E. (2012). "Moving Forward with Membership Categorization Analysis: Methods for Systematic Analysis." *Discourse Studies, 14*(3), 277–303.

Stokoe, E. H. (2003). "Mothers, Single Women and Sluts: Gender, Morality and Membership Categorization in Neighbour Disputes." *Feminism & Psychology, 13*(3), 317–344.

Tang, E. (2015). *Unsettled: Cambodian Refugees in the New York City Hyperghetto.* Philadelphia: Temple University Press.

Tonsing, J., & Barn, R. (2017). "Intimate Partner Violence in South Asian Communities: Exploring the Notion of 'Shame' to Promote Understandings of Migrant Women's Experiences." *International Social Work, 60*(3), 628–639.

Tracy, K. (2015). "Editor's Introduction." In *The International Encyclopedia of Language and Social Interaction* (pp. 1–22). Hoboken: John Wiley & Sons.

Wortham, S. E. F. (2001). *Narratives in Action: A Strategy for Research and Analysis.* New York: Teachers College Press.

Wroe, L. E. (2018). "'It Really Is about Telling People Who Asylum Seekers Really Are, Because We Are Human Like Anybody Else': Negotiating Victimhood in Refugee Advocacy Work. *Discourse & Society, 29*(3), 324–343.

Online Latina/o/x Vernacular Discourse

CHIRLA's Crafting of Home and Resistance through Activism

Victoria A. Cisneros and Sergio Fernando Juárez

Day One: Narciso, 22, is residing in the United States with Deferred Action for Childhood Arrivals (DACA) protections. He has two sisters who are U.S. citizens. Like them, he knows no other home but here. #homeishere #riseforDACA—the words sit below an image of this young man posted to Instagram by the Coalition for Humane Immigrant Rights Los Angeles (CHIRLA). This post and others by CHIRLA not only call attention to the ongoing political struggle by migrant communities in the United States but also resist the anti-immigration rhetoric that became increasingly prevalent under then president Donald Trump's administration. President Trump utilized an anti-immigrant platform to win the 2016 election and continued that rhetoric throughout his administration. During his presidency, he also adopted several anti-immigrant policies such as ending the DACA program. Ultimately, former president Trump's rhetoric and presidential policies contributed to his political downfall by activating pro-immigrant communities and organizations like CHIRLA. However, resistance by CHIRLA through grassroots organizing and public narratives are not new.

For the past four decades, CHIRLA has continued to employ forms of discursive resistance, and now some of these practices have begun to seep into the online sphere. Today, CHIRLA utilizes its Instagram account—an immensely popular social-networking application famous for featuring photos and videos that users engage with through captions, likes, and comments—to combat systemic oppression against migrants through several community-based objectives. CHIRLA uses Instagram to amplify its goals of providing access to low-cost legal services, outreach and education, and policy advocacy on local, state, and national levels.

In this chapter, we analyze CHIRLA's Instagram posts, particularly the captions that accompany the visual images, and explore how their online rhetoric works to resist the negative perceptions espoused by anti-immigrant rhetoric while simultaneously shaping migrants' own identities and definitions of citizenship and belonging. We argue that Instagram, specifically the applications' captioning function, is an online vernacular space where Latina/o/x communities can deploy resistive rhetoric that both provides an online home space and creates opportunities to affirm migrant identities, considering that the discourse surrounding migrants inevitably dictates their material realities. Groups like CHIRLA, who have struggled for migrant rights, utilize this space to connect to and be a voice for migrant communities. Their resistive work, showcased through their Instagram captions, is uniquely Latina/o/x and representative of a decades-long struggle for migrant rights. Centering CHIRLA's rhetoric within this analytical frame combats the tendency to obscure migrant voices and instead amplifies them.

CHIRLA's Efforts on DACA, ICE, and Migrant Detention Facilities

The Los Angeles–based organization has been on the front lines of resistance since the mid 1980s following the United States' efforts to expand immigration legislation and control over immigrant populations with the Immigration Reform and Control Act (IRCA) of 1986. IRCA provided a path to citizenship for undocumented individuals living in the United States before 1982 but also implemented employer sanctions, making it illegal for employers to hire undocumented workers (U.S. Citizenship and Immigration Services, n.d.). In an interview on CHIRLA TV, CHIRLA's executive director Angelica Salas notes that the organization was established to support immigrants who could benefit from IRCA's amnesty program, as well as those who faced labor discrimination because of the law's employer sanctions (Chirlavideos, 2018).

Although CHIRLA is active in providing legal services, educating communities, and fighting for legislation on a range of issues, it is important to narrow our focus to three topics that CHIRLA's Instagram account most frequently addresses: DACA, Immigration and Customs Enforcement (ICE) raids, and immigration detention facilities. In June 2012, President Trump's predecessor, President Obama, established DACA through an executive branch memorandum, granting individuals who immigrated to the United States as children and fulfilled several subsequent criteria, deferred action and the legal right to work (Department of Homeland Security, 2019). Comprehensive migration legislation was not likely to occur in 2012 and thus DACA was established by a presidential executive order to protect millions of young American residents who lacked documented status. In September 2017, after the Trump administration took office and the constitutionality of the program had been heavily debated, acting secretary of Homeland Security Elaine Duke, under pressure from the U.S. attorney general Jeff Sessions, revoked the Obama-era memo and offered up a plan to slowly dissolve DACA (DHS, 2019). Since then, federal courts in California and New York have ruled in favor of the program and issued national injunctions that allow DACA to continue as it did before September 2017, but do not require the acceptance of new applicants (U.S. Citizenship and Immigration Services, 2019). Furthermore, unlike the program's original provisions, after August 2019, U.S. Citizenship and Immigration Services will only allow recipients up to one year to renew their DACA status, complying with the department's most recent renewal policy following the September 2017 decision (U.S. Citizenship and Immigration Services, 2019).

Leading up to November 12, 2019, the date the Supreme Court heard oral arguments surrounding the federal government's decision to rescind the program, CHIRLA collaborated with other migration activist organizations to create the Home Is Here campaign and march from the Statue of Liberty in New York to the steps of the Supreme Court in Washington D.C. (Home Is Here, 2019). Although their campaign and eighteen-day march spread awareness about the issue, the future of DACA at the time seemed uncertain. Less than a year later, in June 2020, CHIRLA received a victory from the U.S. Supreme Court that overruled President Trump's directive to end DACA, forcing the president's administration to continue to receive DACA applications. CHIRLA remains hopeful and continues to support DACA recipients through their three main objectives, including providing services to renew DACA status, encouraging recipients to share their own experiences with the program, and advocating for the program's continuation (CHIRLA, 2018, July 12).

Alongside the fight for DACA, CHIRLA has opposed ICE and the role the department plays in enforcing immigration policies. ICE was created in 2003 and placed under the newly established Department of Homeland Security during a government reorganization process that came in direct response to the attacks on September 11, 2001 (U.S. Immigration and Customs Enforcement, 2019). CHIRLA firmly believes that ICE, along with the Department of Homeland Security, must significantly restrain its authority and exercise greater transparency (CHIRLA, 2018, June 27). CHIRLA also regularly holds demonstrations against ICE at locations and businesses frequently targeted for raids. The organization is both committed to driving ICE out of their communities as well as educating immigrants on their rights. This includes providing guidance on how to interact with ICE agents and distributing prewritten "Rights Cards" meant to signify to agents that the owner is invoking their constitutional right to remain silent (CHIRLA, 2018, February 20).

While ICE is responsible for many immigration-related arrests, it also plays a role in the operation of detention facilities. For groups like CHIRLA, immigration detention facilities have always been sites of concern; however, as the Trump administration continued to issue new policies, such sites have become political and rhetorical battlegrounds. On April 6, 2018, Attorney General Sessions announced a "zero-tolerance policy" that applies to all persons who attempt to or succeed in illegally entering the United States (Department of Justice, 2018). In later announcements regarding the policy, Sessions stated, "If you are smuggling a child then we will prosecute you, and that child will be separated from you as required by law. . . . If you don't like that, then don't smuggle children over our border" (Jordan & Nixon, 2018, para. 7). Such authority to separate families stands on the grounds of the 1997 Flores Settlement, which originally required unaccompanied minors to first be released to either their parents or a relative; however, if such accommodations were not feasible, children were placed in licensed facilities (Preston, 2015). A 2015 expansion to the settlement by California Federal Judge Gee extended the release requirements to accompanied minors and their parents. The 2016 appeal reversed the settlement's applicability to parents but upheld its applicability to all minors (Preston, 2015; Flores v.

Lynch, 2016). Therefore, undocumented children are either released or placed in facilities while their undocumented, detained parents face their own charges.

The treatment of migrants in both adult and child facilities has been under investigation by the House of Representatives Committee on Oversight and Reform since mid-2019 (Committee on Oversight and Reform, 2019). The committee continues to receive reports of wrongful treatment resulting in the distress and sometimes death of detainees under government custody. Reports of negligence and failure to meet medical needs add to the committee's concerns over the treatment of such persons and their continued investigation into the use of for-profit contractors. While these investigations are ongoing, CHIRLA continues to fight against the inhumanity of such facilities and encourages the public to join them. Through their activity on Instagram, CHIRLA urges its audience to see the Trump administration's zero-tolerance immigration policy as a "zero humanity policy" (CHIRLA, 2018, June 27). Some of their posts addressing detention facilities depict small children whose faces are wrought with fear. Others show images of activism and advocacy as CHIRLA organizes large-scale protests, specifically the organization's trip to Southern California's High Desert Detention Center in Adelanto, where members have protested both the family separation policy and the treatment of detainees (CHIRLA, 2019, August 6).

Even as CHIRLA celebrates both small and large victories, their work is never fully done. The organization continues to fight against the seemingly unending cascade of state-sanctioned violence and uses Instagram to both contextualize and amplify the voice of migrants.

Online Vernacular Discourses

A primary goal of our chapter is to privilege the perspectives of migrant communities. We center the rhetoric of CHIRLA, an organization led by migrants that is engaged in the political struggle for immigrant rights. We also aim to honor Alcoff's (1991) challenge of not speaking for others as we centralize the perspectives of migrants to illuminate obscured knowledge. Ono and Sloop's (1995) vernacular discourses privilege historically marginalized perspectives, center on the local by critiquing text that is self-produced by local communities, interrogate complex power relations, and consider the role of critics themselves in the process of a critique. As such, the messaging of CHIRLA can be understood as what Ono and Sloop (1995) describe as a vernacular discourse, which they argue is everyday talk, text, music, and more, but can be understood as discourse that resonates and originates from historically underrepresented communities. Scholars have turned to vernacular discourse to study the experiences of Latina/o/x migrant communities (Anguiano & Chavez, 2011; Cisneros, 2014; Lechuga, 2019).

Howard (2008) describes spaces like Instagram as part of an online vernacular web where discursive performances are illuminated through dialectical tensions, and where the "subaltern" contrasts particular perspectives against dominant institutions. We uncover the tensions by analyzing a hundred thirty-one of CHIRLA's Instagram posts, specifically the captions that represent resistive themes, between 2018 and 2019. CHIRLA's language, emojis, and hashtags supporting migration offer their followers and other users their own unique and purposeful interpretation of a given image and serve as a tool for contextualizing their own content within the limit of 2,200 characters and 30 hashtags (Jackson, 2020). We argue that the content of the captions is revealing of an online vernacular, a framing of meaning of the images, because, like the images, captions are a direct indicator of intended meaning.

Although we recognize that Instagram is often characterized by its visual dominance and acknowledge that other scholars have primarily studied Instagram through a visual lens (Manovich, 2017), we focus our analysis on both the textual and visual aspects of CHIRLA's Instagram account. Simultaneously, we also consider how the imagery not only enhances the overall meaning of the posts but helps us understand the vernacular meaning. Our focus centers on both the visual and the linguistic aspects of CHIRLA's posts as we contend that the textual components are the essence of their vernacular. Without accompanying text, CHIRLA's posts, and all images posted to Instagram, would be left without context. We argue that CHIRLA's Instagram captions are a site of online vernacular discourse. Instagram posts are revealing of online vernacular meaning, and hashtags themselves are a form of vernacular language that function to link posts and people because they are also a searchable language (Sebastian, 2019). It is important to also note the capability to be searched across the Instagram platform so that users can connect with one another and possibly create online home spaces.

Online Latina/o/x Vernacular Discourse

Through Latina/o/x Vernacular Discourse (LVD), we uncover an online vernacular of Latina/o/x migrant communities that reflects a more nuanced relationship with the same institutions that attempt to exert their power over them. While in many respects we agree that the vernacular discourse of marginalized communities contrasts with dominant assertions, we also believe that through the lens of LVD, much more nuanced understandings of how power operates in these social relations can be illuminated. Tensions of resistance and compliance are notable in the utilization of a medium like Instagram. These tensions are notably evident within CHIRLA's captions, either through bilingualism, emojis, or hashtags. Oftentimes, these textual elements highlight the negotiations of border identities, community-building efforts despite state-sanctioned violence, and the redefinition of historically oppressive terms and symbols. To that end, we aim to focus on and explore the capabilities of self-representation found within Instagram's textual functions and better understand the ways in which CHIRLA uses this feature as a nuanced, vernacular space. For example, we argue that the use of Instagram is not inherently resistant to dominant ideologies; in at least two studies, researchers found that self-representations were often reproducing toxic or dominant norms (Caldeira & De Ridder, 2017; Hatfield, 2018). The utilization of Instagram itself to communicate is what Ono and Sloop would call "pastiche" (1995, p. 23); it is a recombination and reconstitution of dominant and marginalized ideologies. Instagram as a social media platform is an online space with an ever-changing practice where users voice a constant concern for local conditions and social problems.

LVD has been central in studying the rhetoric of migrant social movements because it allows scholars to focus on specific Latina/o/x contexts. We turn to LVD for its ability to focus on the local and to critically examine everyday sites where Latina/o/xs "struggle over, produce, engage, enact and/or perform culture, identities and community formation" (Holling & Calafell, 2011, p. 36). LVD allows scholars to make sense of the tensions facing migrants. In the case of CHIRLA, we aim to capture how this migrant activist organization conceptualizes belonging and resistance, and how it builds coalitions (Anguiano & Chavez, 2011; Chavez, 2013; Cisneros, 2014). We center the rhetoric of CHIRLA to better understand how an activist organization struggling for migrant rights constructs messages to relate with the migrant community and resist dominant anti-immigrant narratives.

Considering LVD as an extension of vernacular discourse provides a theoretical framework through which the perspectives of historically obscured/ marginalized voices that fall outside of the scope of dominant theories, can be examined. LVD scholarship is concerned with "everyday sites" where culture, identity, and community are enacted, but also sites where there is a collective empowerment and struggle (Holling & Calafell, 2011, p. 21). In an LVD critique of the documentary film *The Garden* (2008), Enck-Wanzer (2011) interrogates how south-central farmers of Illinois negotiate their Latina/o/x identity throughout the film. LVD is a theoretical lens that both foregrounds the necessity to understand discourse from a local perspective and privileges discourses of Latina/o/x communities (Enck-Wanzer, 2011).

It is in these everyday sites where identities are negotiated, and where Latina/o/x folks positively construct their communities and resist dominant rhetorics. Lechuga states that as a theoretical lens, LVD "affirms primarily the Latina/o/x community identity in addition to negotiating dominant and resistive logics attached to discourses in and about Latina/o/x communities" (2019, p. 262). Through an LVD framework, critics can elucidate complex power relations by shedding light on relationships between communities through explaining textual fragments of culture. Lechuga (2019) studies the narratives of the "No Papers, No Fear" pro-migrant campaign through an LVD frame and illuminates several binary tensions evident in the campaign.

LVD sheds light on the nearly imperceptible forces of power experienced by migrants, and privileging the perspectives of migrants that are otherwise obscured by anti-immigrant discourses that seek to marginalize and remove migrants and their perspectives from this country. LVD illuminates power relations between communities by exploring textual fragments of culture" (González et al., 2014, p. 57). To examine this text, we draw on LVD, whose intent is to reveal "liberatory and constraining dimensions" inherent in Latina/o/x discourses (Holling & Calafell, 2011). Using this lens, we recognize that the rhetorical strategies used by CHIRLA are embedded in a history of oppression toward immigrants and enmeshed in strategies of resistance and survival. This is what Ono and Sloop describe as "cultural syncretism" (1995, p. 21), which is theorized as a process of cultural expression that simultaneously affirms cultural understandings and protests dominant narratives or ideologies. CHIRLA's resistance often works within oppressive structures, recognizing the tensions inherent in immigrant identities. Overall, we hope to contribute to communication research centered on social media representations of Latina/o/x migrants because as of now research in this specific area is scant.

CHIRLA's Crafting of Home and Resistance through Instagram

CHIRLA's resistance often works within oppressive structures, recognizing the tensions inherent in immigrant identities. Such entanglements and tensions notably arise within CHIRLA's captions, either through emojis, hashtags, and bilingualism. Oftentimes, these textual elements highlight the negotiations of border identities, community-building efforts in spite of state-sanctioned violence, and the redefinition of historically oppressive terms and symbols.

Home through Bilingualism

CHIRLA, whose posts mostly target Latina/o/x communities, occasionally utilizes its captions to promote information in Spanish. A CHIRLA (2019, June 22) post regarding ICE sightings is paired with a Spanish caption that reads, "Vista a la migra? DOCUMÉNTALO!! No tengas miedo de documentar las acciones de ICE. Tu cámara o teléfono te pueden salvar la vida o la de otros. #Conoce-TusDerechos." Despite the use of a Spanish caption, the words are preceded by their English translation and the addition of the hashtag #CHIRLAhelps. In another post, this one dedicated to a father and daughter, Oscar Alberto and Angie Valeria Martinez Ramirez, showcases a Spanish caption followed by its English translation. "Esto duele hasta el alma [crying emoji] Continuaremos la lucha por ustedes con el anhelo de un día reencontrarnos [purple heart emoji]" (CHIRLA, 2019, June 29b). Many of CHIRLA's captions are written in Spanish and explicitly paired with their English translation, despite Instagram's capability to translate captions and comments for users with different language settings (Instagram, 2020a). This practice, then, speaks to CHIRLA's deliberate intentions to incorporate both languages when contextualizing their images. The implications of these intentions are threefold.

First, the use of both English and Spanish is an example of Ono and Sloop's "cultural syncretism" (1995, p. 21), in which CHIRLA attempts to express Latina/o/x culture while at the same time is constrained by the dominant ideology that all foreign languages must be translated into English. This pressure to preserve English as the dominant language folds into the subsequent implications. Second, to coalesce with other communities, CHIRLA must ensure that others have both direct access to their posts and the capability to understand them. Thus, through the social networking nature of Instagram, CHIRLA is able to reach audiences beyond their target demographic but is then committed to providing messages that penetrate a range of audiences. This recognition and experience with translation is part of Yosso's (2005) concept of "linguistic capital," or the knowledge and skills learned because of bilingualism and biculturalism. Just as communities of color often engage in translation and audience analysis when navigating dominant landscapes, CHIRLA employs this same tactic by including bilingual captions to both translate their message and speak to diverse audiences. CHIRLA's bilingual captions, then, evoke their linguistic capital and are one form of resistance evident in their vernacular discourse. Last, and perhaps most importantly, CHIRLA's use of bilingual captions acknowledges the border identities of the Latina/o/x community (Anzaldúa, 1987). The incorporation of both languages highlights CHIRLA's understanding that some Latino/a/x folks may not be well versed in either or both languages and that the immigrant experience, even the Latino/a/x immigrant experience, is not limited to a single language. This deliberate use of bilingualism showcases CHIRLA's own use of border rhetoric, while at the same time acknowledging and validating the border identities of its audience. In a similar vein, CHIRLA also reaffirms identities using collective language.

Emojis as an Online Latina/o/x Vernacular

CHIRLA's captions showcase forms of vernacular discourse that rework pieces of dominant ideologies to generate resistive discourses. These forms materialize through CHIRLA's use of emojis. Emojis, different from their predecessor emoticons, which only utilized keyboard symbols, are text-based pictures that require software to appear (Tang & Hew, 2019). We found that CHIRLA crafts a home space by utilizing specific emojis often, including a police siren, a square emoji that is tan to signify skin color, a raised fist, and flags of countries like Mexico, Guatemala, and Honduras.

Although emojis may belong to more recent technology, the raised fist symbol and its meaning is nothing new. Stemming from the image of John Carlos and Tommie Smith raising their fists in protest at the 1968 Mexico City Olympics, the meaning of the raised fist has become synonymous with resistance and yet has taken on various meanings given its changing contexts (Osmond, 2010). As it is used by CHIRLA, the raised fist emoji appears in almost every caption that is paired with an image of protest. The fist emoji appears across several campaigns, including #homeishere, #familiesbelongtogether, and #knowyourrights.

In a post from June 2018 promoting a demonstration against President Trump's zero-tolerance immigration policy, the posted graphic depicts three fists of varying skin tones paired with information on the date, time, and location of the protest. The caption ends with, "Let's hold those who allowed this to happen accountable [raised fist emoji, brown skin tone emoji] Sign Up—LINK IN OUR BIO" (CHIRLA, 2018, June 27) Similarly, a post from May 2018 promoting International Workers' Day, a day on which immigrant communities especially draw attention to workers' rights, depicts a raised fist emoji and asks followers to join the organization for a march in downtown Los Angeles. This caption states, "It's a beautiful day to take the downtown streets of Los Angeles with your comunidad [raised fist emoji, brown skin tone emoji] 12 PM" (CHIRLA, 2018, May 1). CHIRLA uses emojis to create an extended sense of family, community, and solidarity across a range of identities. By calling on their followers to participate in the upcoming protests, the raised fist emoji manifests as a symbol that has been popularized by not only a culture of technology but also a culture of protest. Its symbolic re-placement in the context of CHIRLA and Latina/o/x/ discourses serves as a means of challenging oppressive immigration rhetoric, with a symbol often used to unite a range of audiences around a given issue and ultimately combat systemic oppression.

The police car siren emoji appears just as often as the raised fist; however, the former is used to attract attention to significant and timely posts. The police car's siren emoji is used in posts that announce updates on immigration policy, breaking news on issues like DACA, and information on protests or marches.

An April 2018 post reads, "BREAKING #DACA ALERT [police car siren emoji]:

Federal judge orders government to continue DACA and accept new applicants, in toughest blow yet to Trump's efforts to end program" (CHIRLA, 2018, April 24). The emoji is used again when referencing guidelines for interacting with ICE agents. "[police car siren emoji] SEE ICE? DOCUMENT IT!" (CHIRLA, 2018, May 1). Using the siren emoji to get the attention of their followers is rhetorically significant considering that Latina/o/x individuals, especially those who are undocumented, have a heightened awareness of and likeliness to encounter the police and government-sanctioned violence than those who are citizens. Using the siren emoji, CHIRLA is taking a historically oppressive symbol, often associated with law enforcement, and redefining its meaning. The siren no longer conveys an alertness grounded in fear of the government, police, ICE, or deportation; rather, it conveys an alertness grounded in resistance, activism, and change. Thus, its use serves to affirm the community in which the discourse arises while also dismantling the oppressive ideologies from which it stems.

The use of emojis not only enhances CHIRLA's resistive vernacular discourse, but it also blurs the lines between textual and visual forms of rhetoric. As some scholars suggest, emojis are often described as incorporating nonverbal communication into a text (Derks et al., 2008). However, emojis, like other forms of resistive vernacular employed by CHIRLA, embody border identities—not completely textual and not completely visual. The use of emojis, then, is both a testament to the immigrant experience and an opportunity to reclaim, repurpose, and recontextualize an image's meaning through its incorporation in the caption. Emojis can either outright replace their linguistic parallels in each text, or, as in the case of CHIRLA, can be used to enhance the meaning of the surrounding message. This versatility and ambiguity are the epitome of the immigrant identity whose purpose and value are also not confined to a singular meaning or function.

Crafting of Home through Hashtags

The #homeishere hashtag, which was part of the broader Rise for DACA campaign, was used as a part of a coalitional campaign among many migrant activist groups organizing to march together, creating a coalitional effort by multiple organizations that included narratives and images from activists highlighting multiple identities. The utilization of the #homeishere in support of DACA brought many migrant activists together, with the coalitional push for inclusion by CHIRLA and other grassroots organizations to protest the ending of DACA by president Donald J. Trump (FWD.US, 2019, October 2). Resistance to anti-immigrant rhetoric is evident throughout the #homeishere campaign. The hashtag includes the stories and perspectives of undocumented activists with a range of intersecting identities. A November 2019 post reads, "Migration is beautiful [butterfly emoji] we speak, look, and love differently but at the end we are all immigrants" (CHIRLA, 2019, November 1), ending with the hashtag #homeishere.

CHIRLA used #homeishere as they marched to Washington, D.C., before the Supreme Court heard oral arguments on DACA. Because of DACA, recipients have lived their lives in the United States, making their home here. They are resisting national rulings that may threaten their safety and identity. Threatening the DACA program is a threat to migrants' safety, feeling of belonging, as well as questioning their right to exist within the country. However, DACA recipients and their allies resist when evoking the natural occurrence of migration; they are framing their migration as a natural event, affirming their existence in the country. They are functioning as a form of cultural syncretism in which CHIRLA reaffirms the experiences of migrant communities and creates an online space for their resistive discourse. The phrase "home is here" reconstitutes the assertion that the United States is only meant to be occupied by people who are recognized with documentation while also affirming their right as citizens of the world to merely exist.

As the Trump administration enforced the separation of migrant families as part of its zero-tolerance immigration policy, CHIRLA works to resist such violence through multiple online campaigns like #homeishere, #keepfamilies-together, #polimigra, and #knowyourrights. The executive decision to separate families has been a major point of contention for organizations like CHIRLA who support migrant communities. These hashtags are another example of pastiche, because as CHIRLA uses Instagram captions and hashtags to humanize migrants by appealing to U.S. family ideals, the organization is also redefining what it means to be a democratic participant.

Still, while the hashtag campaigns #keepfamiliestogether, #polimigra, and #knowyourrights are liberatory and resist dominant narratives, it may be argued that the hashtags and their messages push for inclusion in a dominant system. To understand the power relations specific to the Latina/o/x migrant communities in their pursuit of inclusion, #homeishere requires a more nuanced understanding that can be better understood through Muñoz's (1999) "disidentifications." The concept of disidentification was theorized from queer experiences of survival, which Muñoz describes as "cultural, material, and psychic survival" and managing and negotiating historical trauma and systemic violence experienced by the queer of color community (1999, p. 161). Disidentification highlights a tension that lies outside the scope of Gramsci's hegemony,

There is a tension that occurs for Latina/o/x communities: while these individuals want acceptance from the very structures that oppress them, while it may seem contradictory, recognition by the state provides them with benefits and a sense of inclusion that also affirms the humanity of Latina/o/x migrants that is essential for survival. Lechuga (2019) describes this as tension between national and migrant identities, illuminating a largely misunderstood relation of power that this specific community experiences and recognizing that safety can be achieved from being legitimated by a nation state. State-sanctioned violence against Latina/o/x communities associated with the southern border is purposeful, the rhetorical construction of bodies as an "Other" that justifies state-sanctioned violence like the detention and deportation of migrant bodies (Cisneros, 2008; Gunn, 2004). This fight for recognition is a struggle for survival. Recognition by a nation-state should not be categorized as migrants' acceptance or resignation to being oppressed.

For migrants, the possibility of validation has material implications to the point of life and death. For some migrants, the return to their home country can mean imminent death; for others, it allows them access to health care, while for others it offers the opportunity to have a valid driver's license or access to education. It can mean the difference between something as simple as calling for help during a time of emergency, or not doing so because calling the police may lead to detainment and deportation. Rooted in queer and color performance scholarship, the concept of disidentification helps us understand how power operates through performance and offers a nuanced perspective of the claim that the United States is home regardless of citizenship status that is embedded within #homeishere. Struggle should not be essentialized as hegemony, as understood through Gramsci's classical notion of domination through consent that does not account for power and much less does not capture the complex relationship to power that is understood through this specific Latina/o/x vernacular (Lash, 2007).

Furthermore, it is through disidentification that we can better uncover struggle for inclusion as a form of cultural wealth. Many migrants recognize the development of a faux caste system based on recognition by the government. The struggle to be recognized by the U.S. government is not only a fight for inclusion but also a fight for safety. Queer migrant communities are aware of the U.S. migration system as well as the several layers of national status that are often overlooked but well understood by the Latina/o/x community. Although these differences in statuses are not a caste system, they play a similar role. Governmental programs like DACA validate individuals by recognizing certain life circumstances as valid, but in turn those life circumstances that are not state sanctioned are not only ignored but are further criminalized. Birthright citizenship, for example, is a national status that offers the most rights to an individual. Being a resident alien offers many rights, but does not include the right to vote, and residency may be revoked.

Constructing a home in the United States is complex, and undocumented migrants struggle with deciding whether to seek recognition by the government. On the one hand, DACA offers an opportunity for protections from deportation while allowing the recipient of DACA to be employed and, in some states, receive benefits such as obtaining a driver's license and state funding for education. Still, qualification for DACA is very restrictive with specific criteria and lacks a path to citizenship. Like DACA, Temporary Protected Status (TPS) protects recipients from deportation and provides opportunity for employment but also lacks a path to citizenship. Visas that allow migrants to be in the United States, such as H-2A and H-2B visas, are non-immigrant visas that allow employers to bring foreign nationals to the United States to fill low-skill, temporary, or seasonal agricultural and nonagricultural jobs for which U.S. workers are not available. Additionally, sexuality adds a layer of complexity to migration status that can preclude a migration application from being accepted or rejected. Understanding the varying degrees of status is an important concept subtlety recognized by many migrants, and awareness of these statuses is growing. The fact that a migrant can become "DACAmented" is an example of the complexity of migration in the United States. Regardless of status, the United States is home to many migrants because recognition by government authorities not only offers legal migratory validation but also affords migrants with varying degrees of safety. Yet many choose disidentification, choosing to create a home in the country and not seek DACAmentation.

Crafting Resistance though Hashtags

While use of the technology is considered pastiche, the phrasing of a hashtag like #polimigra is a form of cultural syncretism, because it resists dominant notions of governance by positioning migrants who have been victimized by state violence as justified democratic participants. In turn, nation-states, their migration laws, and government agents, like ICE and DHS, are positioned as immoral. The positioning of anti-immigrant laws and practices in the United States is evident in a post by CHIRLA (2019, October 2) that illustrates a man behind bars and reads "Compassion not cages." Here, the caption is: "This Thursday, CHIRLA will join the LA Raids Rapid Response Network and hundreds of community members at the Adelanto Detention Center to protest the inhumane and outright prison-like conditions at this facility" (CHIRLA, 2019, August 6). Through this post we can tease out how CHIRLA's syncretic discourse calls into question the possible notion that the U.S. government champions everyone in its democratic call for freedom and liberties. By highlighting the violence of imprisoning migrants while actively resisting through peaceful demonstrations, the post illustrates that migrants are championing democracy and are the victims of anti-democratic state violence. In another post, the positioning of the state as immoral is evident, in the image of "Homeland Security Kills." This framework works to resist dominant narratives of migrants as pollutants by humanizing the people harmed by anti-immigrant rhetoric and policy, and in turn it frames policies that tear families apart as immoral.

The combination of #polimigra, #keepfamiliestogether, and #knowyourrights humanizes immigrants through narratives and coalition building, as well as framing them as democratic participants. Although they may be undocumented and lacking protections, and they may be the targets of state-sanctioned violence, they can achieve liberty through democratic participation. Migrants are dying while trying to cross the border, and when they do cross, they are finding additional violence in the form of state-authorized detention of bodies. The ripping apart of families who have sought sanctuary, while it may be interpreted as legal, is still immoral state-sanctioned violence.

Just as emojis are a new addition to online rhetoric, hashtags and their slogans are relatively new tools that can not only be used to develop recognition and collectivity online but can also aid in the purposeful construction of an online homeland. Hashtags can create a sense of belonging through their ability to connect and tag posts. This hyperlinked connection ultimately creates an online home space where similar posts, such as those depicting CHIRLA's participation in the #homeishere march, live online. The use of a hashtag itself is pastiche, because #homeishere in this post not only connects it to other posts with the same hashtag but also encourages users of varying identities to use the hashtag as well. It is a recombination and reconstitution of a popular technology used to create a new Latina/o/x space (Ono & Sloop, 1995). The intention to craft an online home space is pastiche as a recombination and reconstitution of technology. The use of hashtags is a construction of new discursive spaces, a place where Latina/o/x and Chicana/o/x feminists can call home in a new, online context (Flores, 1996). Using hashtags, CHIRLA first "carv[es] out a space" of their own within Instagram's broader platform and then creates a homeland through tagged connections (Flores, 1996, p. 146). By constructing homelands through hashtags, CHIRLA rejects the border identities of its community in order "to move from the margins closer to their own center" (Flores, 1996, p. 146). Like the term "Latinx" itself, a hashtag can bring disparate migrant communities together in an online platform, unifying based on a shared experience of the United States. While one hashtag can create an online homeland, CHIRLA also acknowledges ties to other online homelands using several varying hashtags that represent the range of issues facing migrant communities.

Conclusion

In this chapter, we discussed how CHIRLA's Instagram captions serve as a form of LVDs that works to challenge dominant ideologies within its available means. We explained the functions of LVD as a theoretical framework to understand unique migrant perspectives, including the border identities inherent in their language use and emojis, in addition to the online homelands created through their use of hashtags.

Furthermore, we interrogated the process, through which Latina/o/x communities produce and disseminate culturally unique and self-affirming discourses. At the same time, we uncover the ways CHIRLA has created these self-affirming discourses while working within dominant structures. This is important not only because we add to the literature on media and migrants in a way that centers migrant voices, but also because we illuminate the tensions within migrant identities, such as the struggle to adhere to and break away from the English language; create resistance through building community; redefine cultural symbols, citizenship, and homeland; and reveal complex power relations. Still, the usage of the family-centered rhetoric for migrants is not without its own issues. While not minimizing the struggle to keep families together, Chavez points out the issues with appealing to family ideals by migrant organizations, stating that this framing "erases the reality that many families are not hospitable to queers or that family situations generally can be inhospitable for all of their members because of various kinds of abuse" (2013, p. 61). This critique is not one that minimizes the abhorrent violence Latina/o/x families have faced when arriving at the southern border. It is important to recognize that this appeal to dominant sensibilities needs to be explored further. This LVD critique points to the syncretism of dominant ideologies that are harmful and may come at the cost of obscuring issues faced by queer and feminist allies.

Our findings have significant implications for future research. Analyzing migrant rhetoric from a localized perspective allows scholars to pivot away from research practices that devalue migrant communities and toward practices that celebrate and uplift migrant voices. Research that only considers the dominant perspective has historically marginalized migrant communities and produced limited understandings of language, citizenship, and governance (power relations). Our research, however, recognizes the agency of migrant communities and the ways in which that agency is employed. Specifically, we reveal how Latina/o/x migrant communities produce vernacular discourses via Instagram to self-affirm their identities, create online home spaces, and resist anti-immigration rhetoric. Just as CHIRLA uses Instagram to frame the struggle of migrants like Narciso, capturing the tension of affirming their status while inspiring active resistance toward dominant structures, we challenge future scholars to engage migrant voices in ways that reflect the tensions of these realities rather than concealing migrants' lived experiences.

REFERENCES

Alcoff, L. (1991). "The Problem of Speaking for Others." *Cultural Critique* (20), 5–32.

Anguiano, C. A., & Chavez, K. R. (2011). "DREAMers' Discourse: Young Latino/a Immigrants and the Naturalization of the American Dream." In *Latina/o Discourses in Vernacular Spaces: Somos de Una Voz?*, edited by M. Holling & B. Calafell (pp. 81–100). Lanham: Lexington Books.

Anzaldúa, G. (1987). *Borderlands/La Frontera: The New Mestiza.* 1st ed. San Francisco: Aunt Lute.

Caldeira, S. P., & De Ridder, S. (2017). "Representing Diverse Femininities on Instagram: A Case Study of the Body-Positive @effyourbeautystandards Instagram Account." *Catalan Journal of Communication & Cultural Studies*, 9(2), 321–337.

Chirlavideos. (2018, October 12). "CHIRLA TV—Episode 1" (YouTube video). https://youtu.be/Liuckrxfnz8.

Cisneros, J. D. (2008). "Contaminated Communities: The Metaphor of 'Immigrant as Pollutant' in Media Representations of Immigration." *Rhetoric and Public Affairs*, 11(4), 569–601.

Chavez, K. (2013). *Queer Migration Politics: Activist Rhetoric and Coalitional Possibilities.* Champaign: University of Illinois Press.

Cisneros, J. D. (2014). *The Border Crossed Us: Rhetorics of Borders, Citizenship, and Latina/o Identity.* Tuscaloosa: University of Alabama Press.

Coalition for Humane Immigrant Rights Los Angeles (CHIRLA). (2018). "Abolish ICE: Just the Tip of the ICEBerg." https://chirla.org/sites/default/files/Abolish-ICE-Just-the-Tip-of-the-ICEberg.pdf.

Coalition for Humane Immigrant Rights Los Angeles (CHIRLA) [@chirla_org]. (2018, February 20). ICE was in Los Angeles last week serving i9 audits to over 100 businesses. (Photograph). Instagram. https://www.instagram.com/p/BfbxZuyAKyP/.

Coalition for Humane Immigrant Rights Los Angeles (CHIRLA) [@chirla_org]. (2018, February 22). SEE ICE? DOCUMENT IT! (Graphic). Instagram. https://www.instagram.com/p/BfguJPLAv-b/.

Coalition for Humane Immigrant Rights Los Angeles (CHIRLA) [@chirla_org]. (2018, April 24). BREAKING #DACA ALERT. (Graphic). Instagram.

Coalition for Humane Immigrant Rights Los Angeles (CHIRLA) [@chirla_org]. (2018, May 1). It's a beautiful day to take the downtown streets of Los Angeles with your comunidad [raised fist emoji] 12 PM. (Graphic). Instagram. https://www.instagram.com/p/BiPk32TB9PJ/.

Coalition for Humane Immigrant Rights Los Angeles (CHIRLA) [@chirla_org]. (2019, June 22). If you see #ICE, DOCUMENT IT! (Graphic). Instagram. https://www.instagram.com/p/BzBUM1gAzqY/.

Coalition for Humane Immigrant Rights Los Angeles (CHIRLA) [@chirla_org]. (2018, June 27). A federal judge ordered the reunification of the families torn apart by Trumps zero-tolerance policy. (Graphic). Instagram. https://www.instagram.com/p/BkiYp27h2f_/.

Coalition for Humane Immigrant Rights Los Angeles (CHIRLA) [@chirla_org]. (2018, July 12). The U.S. has failed to meet court mandates. (Graphic). Instagram. https://www.instagram.com/p/BlJgDheBoQz/.

Coalition for Humane Immigrant Rights Los Angeles (CHIRLA) [@chirla_org]. (2019, June 29). Esto duele hasta el alma Continuaremos la lucha por ustedes con el anhelo de un día reencontrarnos. (Graphic). Instagram. https://www.instagram.com/p/BzTgWIIgRjr/.

Coalition for Humane Immigrant Rights Los Angeles (CHIRLA) [@chirla_org]. (2019, July 1). DHS Kills. (Photographs). Instagram. https://www.instagram.com/p/BzZpw0vA27q/.

Coalition for Humane Immigrant Rights Los Angeles (CHIRLA) [@chirla_org]. (2019, August 6). This Thursday, CHIRLA will join the LA Raids Rapid Response Network and hundreds of community members at the Adelanto Detention Center. (Graphic). Instagram. https://www.instagram.com/p/B01Q6awAo2C/.

Coalition for Humane Immigrant Rights Los Angeles (CHIRLA) [@chirla_org]. (2019, October 2). Rise for DACA. (Photographs). Instagram. https://www.instagram.com/p/B4x6F6IAXhm/.

Coalition for Humane Immigrant Rights Los Angeles (CHIRLA) [@chirla_org]. (2019, October 19). Ana Chavez is a young woman from Hesperia who has #DACA. (Video). Instagram. https://www.instagram.com/p/B359QxnAjXh/.

Coalition for Humane Immigrant Rights Los Angeles (CHIRLA) [@chirla_org]. (2019, October 28). Scenes from day 3 of the #HomeIsHere march Today. (Photographs). Instagram. https://www.instagram.com/p/B4LZZHPgzuB/.

Coalition for Humane Immigrant Rights Los Angeles (CHIRLA) [@chirla_org]. (2019, November 1). Migration is beautiful [butterfly emoji] we speak, look, and love differently but at the end we are all immigrants. (Photographs). Instagram. https:// www.instagram.com/p/B4VfTnTAAnm/.

Coalition for Humane Immigrant Rights Los Angeles (CHIRLA) [@chirla_org]. (2019, November 9). Hey #SupremeCourt California is coming in full force to Washington DC. (Photograph). Instagram. https://www.instagram.com/p/B4qD1RiALCS/.

Committee on Oversight and Reform. (2019, December 23). "Committee Investigates Deaths of Immigrant Children and Adults" (Press Release). https://oversight.house. gov/news/press-releases/committee-investigates-deaths-of-immigrant-children-and-adults.

Derks, D., Fischer, A. H., & Bos, A. E. R. (2008). "The Role of Emotion in Computer-Mediated Communication: A Review." *Computers in Human Behavior*, *24*(3), 766–785. https://doi.org/10.1016/j.chb.2007.04.004.

Department of Homeland Security. (2019, September 23). "Deferred Action for Childhood Arrivals (DACA)." https://www.dhs.gov/deferred-action-childhood-arrivals.

Department of Justice. (2018, April 6). "Attorney General Announces Zero-Tolerance Policy for Criminal Illegal Entry" (Press Release). https://www.justice.gov/opa/pr/ attorney-general-announces-zero-tolerance-policy-criminal-illegal-entry.

Enck-Wanzer, D. (2011). "Race, Coloniality, and Geo-Body Politics: The Garden as Latin@." *Environmental Communication*, *5*(3), 363–371.

Exec. Order No. 13768, 3 C.F.R. (2017). https://www.govinfo.gov/content/pkg/DCPD-201700071/pdf/DCPD-201700071.pdf.

Flores, L. A. (1996). "Creating Discursive Space through a Rhetoric of Difference: Chicana Feminists Craft a Homeland." *Quarterly Journal of Speech*, *82*(2), 142–156. https://doi. org/10.1080/00335639609384147.

Flores v. Lynch (2016). 9th Cir.

FWD.US. (2019, October 2). "ICYMI: DACA Recipients, Broad Coalition of Immigrants' Rights Organizations Launch 'Home is Here' Campaign." https://www.fwd.us/news/ icymi-daca-recipients-broad-coalition-of-immigrants-rights-organizations-launch-home-is-here-campaign/.

González, A., Chávez, J., & Englebrecht, C. (2014). "Latinidad and Vernacular Discourse: Arts Activism in Toledo's Old South End." *Journal of Poverty*, *18*(1), 50–64.

Gunn, J. (2004). "The Rhetoric of Exorcism: George W. Bush and the Return of Political Demonology." *Western Journal of Communication*, *68*(1), 1–23.

Hatfield, J. E. (2018). "Toxic Identification: #Twinks4Trump and the Homonationalist Rearticulation of Queer Vernacular Rhetoric." *Communication, Culture and Critique*, *11*(1), 147–161. https://doi.org/10.1093/ccc/tcx006.

Holling, M. A., & Calafell, B. M. (2011). "Tracing the Emergence of Latin@ Vernaculars in the Studies of Latin@ Communication." In *Latina/o Discourses in Vernacular Spaces: Somos de Una Voz?*, edited by M. Holling & B. Calafell (pp. 17–30). Lanham: Lexington Books.

Home Is Here. (2019). "What We're Doing." https://www.homeisheremarch.org/.

Howard, R. G. (2008). "The Vernacular Web of Participatory Media." *Critical Studies in Media Communication, 25*(5), 490–513.

Instagram. (2020a). "See Translations for Comments, Captions and Profiles on Instagram." https://help.instagram.com/512686498916530?helpref=search&sr=1&query=translation.

Instagram. (2020b). "Verified Badges." https://help.instagram.com/854227311295302.

Jackson, D. (2020, August 3). "Know Your Limit: The Ideal Length of Every Social Media Post." https://sproutsocial.com/insights/social-media-character-counter/.

Jordan, M. & Nixon, R. (2018, May 7). "Trump Administration Threatens Jail and Separating Children from Parents for Those Who Illegally Cross Southwest Border." *New York Times.* https://www.nytimes.com/2018/05/07/us/politics/homeland-security-prosecute-undocumented-immigrants.html.

Lash, S. (2007). "Power after Hegemony: Cultural Studies in Mutation?" *Theory, Culture & Society, 24*(3), 55–78. https://doi.org/10.1177/0263276407075956.

Lechuga, M. (2019). "Mapping Migrant Vernacular Discourses: Mestiza Consciousness, Nomad Thought, and Latina/o/x Migrant Movement Politics in the United States." *Journal of International and Intercultural Communication,* 1–17.

Manovich, L. (2017). *Instagram and Contemporary Image.* Self-published.

Muñoz, J. E. (1999). *Disidentifications: Queers of Color and the Performance of Politics.* Minneapolis: University of Minnesota Press.

Ono, K. A., & Sloop, J. M. (1995). "The Critique of Vernacular Discourse." *Communication Monographs, 62*(1), 19–46.

Osmond, G. (2010). "Photographs, Materiality and Sport History: Peter Norman and the 1968 Mexico City Black Power Salute." *Journal of Sport History, 37*(1), 20.

Preston, J. (2015, July 25). "Judge Orders Release of Immigrant Children Detained by U.S." *New York Times.*

Sebastian, M. (2019). "Instagram and Gendered Surveillance: Ways of Seeing the Hashtag." *Surveillance and Society, 17*(1/2), 40–45.

Tang, Y., & Hew, K. F. (2019). "Emoticon, Emoji, and Sticker Use in Computer-Mediated Communication: A Review of Theories and Research Findings." *International Journal of Communication, 13,* 2457–2483.

U.S. Citizenship and Immigration Services. (2019, July 7). "Deferred Action for Childhood Arrivals: Response to January 2018 Preliminary Injunction."

U.S. Citizenship and Immigration Services. (n.d.). "Glossary." https://www.uscis.gov/tools/glossary?topic_id=i#alpha-listing.

U.S. Immigration and Customs Enforcement. (n.d.). "Fiscal Year 2018 ICE Enforcement and Removal Operations Report." pp. 1–22. https://www.ice.gov/doclib/about/offices/ero/pdf/eroFY2018Report.pdf.

U.S. Immigration and Customs Enforcement. (2019, March 4). "History." https://www.ice.gov/history.

Yosso, T. J. (2005). "Whose Culture Has Capital? A Critical Race Theory Discussion of Community Cultural Wealth." *Race Ethnicity and Education*, 8(1), 69–91.

Social Identity in the Queer Diaspora

The Use of Digital Media and the Middle Eastern Gay Refugee

Nathian Shae Rodriguez

esbian, gay, bisexual, transgender, and intersex (LGBTI) individuals around the world, as well as those perceived to be LGBTI, face persecution daily. Laws inflicting harsh repercussions, such as imprisonment, violence, and death, still exist in over seventy countries (76crimes.com, 2022); thus, many LGBTIs flee their native countries for safety and refuge in relatively more accepting countries. Since 2011, the United States has hosted refugees fleeing persecution because of their sexual orientation. In 2011, U.S. president Barack Obama released his administration's International Initiative to Advance the Human Rights of Lesbian, Gay, Bisexual and Transgender Persons, in which he instructed federal agencies to "promote and protect the human rights of LGBT persons" (White House, 2011, para. 2). In countries that do not recognize persecution based on sexual orientation or gender identity, the United Nations High Commissioner for Refugees has the authority to extend refugee status to individuals from these countries (ORAM, 2012).

This chapter examines how gay refugees and asylees use mediated communication, specifically digital media, to shape and maintain their social identities.

Identity, in this chapter's context, is seen as a process and is used interchangeably with the term "identification" (Jenkins, 1994, 2014). Employing the theoretical lens of social identity theory, six self-identifying gay refugees/asylees who have been granted asylum in the United States were interviewed. Each interviewee is a cisgender male who fled his home country in the Middle East and sought refuge and asylum in the queer diaspora of San Francisco. Interviewees were at various stages of the asylum process when interviewed, but all have identified with the category of refugee at one point in time. "Refugee" and "asylee" are closely related terms, but they are differentiated in the U.S. legal system. A refugee status is designated to anyone who "received legal recognition outside of the country and was officially accepted under the U.S. Refugee Admissions Program" (ORAM, 2012, p. 2), whereas an asylee is anyone who "first entered the U.S., with or without legal status, and later applied for and received refugee protection" (p. 3). The most significant difference is that an asylee is already in the United States, whereas a refugee may still be in another country pending resettlement. In this chapter, the interviewees will be referred to as "gay refugees/asylees."

I argue in this chapter that post-asylum, gay refugees/asylees must negotiate both negative and positive categorizations from their past and present in the construction of a social identity in the queer diaspora. Digital media assist in this negotiation by serving as tools of information seeking, relationship building, and acculturation. Social media allows users to represent social identity online regarding how their audience categorizes being gay. The refugees/asylees often censor information they post online, or they disconnect altogether. Digital media use does not occur in a vacuum, and issues related to the physical space of San Francisco's queer diaspora influenced how and why particular mediated platforms were utilized. The implications in this chapter highlight the iterative processes of identity negotiation in the queer diaspora that are dependent on the symbiotic relationship between the physical and the digital. In other words, the physical and digital are interconnected and not mutually exclusive.

Queer Diaspora

Refugees flee native areas for various reasons, including violence, war, and persecution, among others. Refugees commonly settle in new countries forming diasporas with those that share a cultural commonality (Hall, 1990). In its original conceptualization, the term "diaspora" was used to define any population living away from its original land and in a settlement, possibly in one or more nation-states (Alonso & Oiarzabal, 2010). The term has since been applied as a blueprint to define various marginalized and persecuted identity groups, including LGBTQI individuals (Alonso & Oiarzabal, 2010; Dhoest, 2019; Fortier, 2002; Karim, 2004; Manalansan, 2006).

Diasporas, however, are not simply passive identifiers for those on the move; rather, they are incessantly "constructed, debated, and reimagined" (Mandaville, 2003, p. 135). The identities of those living within a diasporic space are shaped by the context of history and the present, including social, cultural, temporal, and spatial factors (Karim, 2004). Stuart Hall refers to diasporas as a third new world presence that "is not so much power, as ground, place, territory" (1990, p. 234). A diaspora is often created out of existential angst (Fortier, 2002) and implicit issues of power and persecution, located in a liminal space between leaving and arriving (Eng, 1997). LGBTI refugees/asylees are not different. They do not arrive in their country of asylum and instantly assimilate; rather, they resume conflicts with heteronormative regimes of power (Manalansan, 2003). Often, LGBTI migrants and refugees are forced to spend time in intermediary countries, like Turkey in the case of refugees from the Middle East, on their way to western queer diasporas in North America and western Europe (Rodriguez, 2019).

Anne-Marie Fortier warns against reducing a definition of diaspora to those who have experienced forced dispersal, arguing it risks "engulfing diasporic populations into culturally unified groupings by virtue of their presumed 'common origin' and shared commitment to the homeland" (2002, p. 188). This theorization of queering the diaspora, as Puar (1998) labels it, is one of two main approaches employed by academics. A queering the diaspora approach disrupts normative, and most often heterosexist, assumptions of ethnic diasporas. The second approach, diasporizing the queer, places emphasis on the "transnational and multicultural network of connections of queer cultures and 'communities'" (Puar, 1998, p. 183). This study is positioned against Puar's diasporizing the queer, to examine how diaspora can serve as a space to consider queer issues and culture, particularly in relation to digital media.

A queer diaspora, for the purposes of this chapter, recognizes traumatic displacement as a distinctive (but not sole) feature, emphasizes inherent relations of power and inequality, and establishes connections between diaspora, queerness, and exile. This exile experienced by LGBTQIs in the queer diaspora "locates them outside the confines of 'home': the heterosexual family, the nation, the homeland" (Fortier, 2002, p. 188). Exile is negotiated in the queer diaspora through a sense of shared belonging fostered by mass media, technology, and other points of connection in pop culture (Schimel, 1997), further explicated later. The gay refugees/asylees interviewed in this chapter struggle to shape and maintain spaces (both physical and digital) of not only belonging but also safety, pleasure, identity, and culture.

A queer diaspora is ripe with difference as intersectional identities collide to produce interlocking experiences of oppression and, for some, opportunity. Race, ethnicity, and religion are some of these intersecting identities. The interviewees were all born and raised in Middle Eastern countries, mostly all indicated they were socialized in Islamic spaces, and then migrated to the San Francisco area as young adults. Although not one of the interviewees practiced Islam nor identified as Muslim, it is important to note that the two identities (Muslim and LGBTI) are often viewed as diametrically opposed to one another; "Muslim identities and values are seen as irredeemably patriarchal, unassimilable to western democracy and culture and, above all, a rejection of modernity" (Rahman, 2010, p. 945).

This is important for two reasons. One, the families of the gay refugees/ asylees remain in their respective Middle Eastern homelands and may harbor anti-LGBTI sentiment. Being gay is seen as a Westernized identity imposed on non-Western cultures (Puar, 2013), propagated by international LGBTI organizations protecting gay rights globally (Massad, 2002). This not only affects identify negotiation but can also affect the use of digital media for transnational communication, particularly if the gay refugees/asylees are not out to their loved ones (Rodriguez, 2017, 2019). Second, the gay refugees/ asylees may be categorized and treated as Muslim in the queer diaspora of San Francisco (Rodriguez, 2017). Thus, like individuals who do identify as gay Muslims, they exist in an intersectional social space between social and political structures, experiencing oppression (Rahman, 2010). In the queer diaspora, the gay refugees/asylees must grapple with multiple categorizations and subjugated oppressions of homophobia and Islamophobia as they shape and maintain their social identity.

Social Identity

When refugees of any kind arrive in their host country, they suffer from fragmented identities caused by forced migration (ORAM, 2012). Identity is specific to temporal, spatial, and cultural contexts attached to social roles and positions, networks, and histories (Ward, Bochner, & Furnham, 2001). Instead of promoting a vision of LGBTI refugees' quest for asylum as a heroic journey from repression to liberation, this chapter stresses the phenomenological experiences of these individuals as restructured inequalities, opportunities, and occurrences (Manalansan, 2003). LGBTI refugees/asylees must navigate a new culture while trying to make sense of their identities. These identities are always in flux and are intersectional, bringing together facets of gender, race, ethnicity, sexual orientation, religion, and culture (Dhoest, 2019; Hall, 1990; Hall & Jagose, 2012). Intersecting identities create overlapping systems of discrimination and oppression (see Crenshaw, 1991); LGBTI refugees/asylees of color may thus continually experience intersectional oppression in their host countries (Manalansan, 2006; Rodriguez, 2017), adding more complexity to their identity negotiation.

Identity, in its most fundamental form, is defined according to Jenkins as "the human capacity—rooted in language—to know 'who's who' (and hence 'what's what')" (2014, p. 5). Mead (1934) and Blumer (1969) highlight individuals' abilities to interpret symbolic actions and assign meaning through reflexive social interactions. Identity, then, is a symbolic representation of the self. Jenkins (2014) furthers this convention and argues that all human identities are social identities, because identifying ourselves and others is a matter of meaning, which always involves interaction. Identity is better understood as a process, rather than an object, which Jenkins terms "identification": "the specification of what things are and what they are not, entailing at the same time some specification of their properties" (2000, p. 7). Because an individual's identities are always in flux, identification is a process that is never settled. Identity is a constant comparison and contrast of relationships between and among individuals and collectivities (Jenkins, 2014).

The idea of including both similarity and difference, instead of only difference, is counter to the thinking of scholars such as Butler (1990) and Hall (1990), who assert difference against political heterogeneity and systemic hegemony.

While there is value in diversity and difference, more explanatory potential is present in comparing both the similarities and differences between individuals and groups to "identify what may be universal and variable about human cultures, as well as to discover reasons why the variation exists" (Ilesanmi, 2009, p. 82). Specific to this chapter, the gay refugees/asylees do not position themselves as "we" because we are not "them," which is highlighted in Tajfel and Turner's (1979) conceptualization of social identity theory. In this population, particularly, there is not a battle between in-group and out-group from the perspective of the gay refugee/asylee. Rather, because their identities are intersectional, there is an ongoing negotiation of self between many collectivities that, in specific moments, they identify with or deem as incongruent (Abdi & Van Gilder, 2016; Jaspal & Cinnirella, 2012).

Consider similarities and differences parallel with Jenkins's (1994) internal and external moments of the dialectic of identification. Social identity results from a continuous process of how one identifies herself/himself/themselves (internal process of identification) and how others identify her/him/them (external process of categorization). For the gay refugees/asylees, this means that each is subject to an internal identification process of himself juxtaposed with an external categorization process by others. Social identification is contextual and always in flux. Where the gay refugees/asylees are spatially and temporally in the migration journey will influence the process. In other words, social identification is dependent upon context and contingent upon both similarity and difference (Jenkins, 2000). Identities, then, are constructed and reconstructed by "embodied, socialized, individuals" interacting within various institutionalized contexts (2000, p. 14). Digital media is one way in which refugees/asylees negotiate the iterative processes of identity.

Digital Media and Identity in the Queer Diaspora

Transnational communication, which is propagated by both digital and traditional media such as television, radio, and print, allows linkages between global users (Karim, 2004). This global linkage aids in the ability for those in diasporas to remain in contact with people and issues in their home country (Papaioannou & Olivos, 2013). As individuals leave their homelands, either voluntarily or by force, they take the myths, languages, values, and traditions of their ancestry with them (Karim, 2004). These nostalgic relics carry bittersweet reminiscences of a physical place they love, but one that may not love them for being LGBTI. The post-asylum identity must incorporate not only these vestiges of the past but also the unfamiliar challenges of life in a new space and culture.

LGBTQI identities often follow a path similar to ethnic minority identities and tend to operate with both a cultural separatist stance and "an assimilationist one by the provision of material which directly posits symbolic components coded as cultural and community material" (Cover, 2002, p. 112). Media serves as assimilationist material; it can assist marginalized populations to accommodate a region and attempt to establish social and economic equality (Riggins, 1992). As mentioned earlier, most LGBTI refugees have no relational ties when arriving in the United States and may remain segregated from those who share the same country or region of origin (ORAM, 2012). Media, then, may function to both preserve what ties they have to their past, as well as fashion novel connections and spaces for their present and future.

Previous research in diasporic media use has evidenced this trend of groups simultaneously preserving the past while building new futures; however, this research focused primarily on culture and not on sexuality. Patterns of media use as a communicative tool between the diaspora and the homeland are found broadly across extant research, with digital media being labeled as a digital diaspora by some (Georgiou, 2006; Siapera, 2014). In Middle Eastern diasporas particularly, media play an integral role in identity formation. For Turkish migrants in Berlin, digital media facilitated affective feelings of affinity and hope during difficult times in the diaspora, making them accessible and shareable to the public (Savaş, 2019). Digital media has also been found to afford new stylings of diaspora culture, aiding in Iranian American identity formation in second-generation Iranian Americans in a Los Angeles diaspora (Alinejad, 2017). For Syrian diasporas in Canada, digital media helped advance transnational justice back in the homeland. For Syrian refugees displaced in diasporas in Jordan, Lebanon, and Turkey, digital media served as a tool for resettlement information, news on the Syrian war, and recuperating lost ties with loved ones back home (Miconi, 2020).

At the time of this writing, there exists very little research examining LGBTI media use in the context of a queer diaspora. Dhoest (2019), for example, has argued that a review of digital media use in diaspora highlights a general focus of maintaining transnational ties with loved ones in the homeland. Dhoest writes, "Not only is the focus on the family heteronormative in implicitly assuming that all families and their members are heterosexual; moreover, the one-sided focus on connections also obscures the possibility of forced or voluntary practices of disconnection" (2019, p. 390). In Dhoest's research on LGBTI migrants from twenty-six countries living in Belgium, he found mass media, film, and the internet to be important sources of LGBTI representations. Internet and social media, like Facebook, were central in the LGBTIs everyday lives and used to build connections in the diaspora. All LGBTIs disconnected in some degree from friends and family in the homeland, citing condemnation of their sexuality as the main reason. Dhoest noted that LGBTI refugee participants tended to remain closeted on social media, whereas LGBTIs who were not refugees posted a combination of LGBTQI and religious posts. Those who were second-generation migrants were more open on social media. His research evidenced that an intersectional approach to diasporic LGBTIs complicates heteronormative assumptions about the diaspora.

Though there may be some constraints to participating in online media, individuals are not bound by a particular space or culture when using digital media. They are, however, bound by physical space and culture as they navigate their post-asylum life in their host country in the queer diaspora. This tension created by online and offline spaces is factored into the identity negotiation process. Thus, this chapter examines the role of digital media in gay refugees/asylees' social identity in the queer diaspora of San Francisco.

Methodology

The target population of the chapter's study was any LGBTI refugee/asylee who was physically located in the San Francisco area who had fled their homeland due to persecution based on their sexuality. I visited San Francisco in person and contacted local LGBTI-specific nongovernmental organizations (NGOs) for interview participants. Two organizations forwarded my email to possible participants and only two individuals replied. One of them, Reza, became my informant and introduced me to two other participants, who in turn introduced me to others. Snowball sampling was used to compose a purposive sample. All the interviewees were cisgender males who self-identified as gay or queer, fled

TABLE. LGBTI Refugees/Asylees Interviewed

NAME	NATIVE COUNTRY	ASYLUM STATUS
Ibrahim	Iraq	Applied
Mahdi	Iran	Granted
Reza	Iran	Granted
Marwan	Syria	Granted
Nassim	Lebanon	Granted
Atif	Saudi Arabia	Applied

Note: (N=6). Each individual consented to being recorded. Pseudonyms were assigned to maintain anonymity.

Middle Eastern countries, and were assigned pseudonyms. Snowball sampling allowed me to contact and make inferences about a population that is difficult to enumerate and is socially stigmatized (Faugier & Sergeant, 1997).

The resulting sample included six participants (see table). Due to the precarious position of gay refugees/asylees, this is a difficult population to access, thus limiting the number of participants. In qualitative research there is no adequate predetermined sample number, but rather is relative to the quality of information, research method, and ultimate intention of the study (Sandelowski, 1995). This chapter's sample size satisfied this approach by utilizing participants whose positionality and lived experiences reflected the intention of the study. Also, the method employed lengthy face-to-face unstructured interviews, which allowed for nuanced feedback and saturation—the researcher continues to interview until patterns of data begin repeating themselves (Morse, 2000). All interviews were conducted in NGO offices, coffee shops, hotel lobbies, and were administered in English. Participants were asked about their life experiences pre- and post-asylum, the use of media and communication for representation, and the identity negotiation processes.

The interviews were recorded on an audio recorder and raw audio was sent to TranscribeMe, an academic transcription company, for transcription. A textual analysis employing open, inductive coding that followed Owen's (1984) qualitative method guidelines for distinguishing themes (repetition, recurrence, and forcefulness) was performed. The goal was to create a schematic representation that is conceptually meaningful, unambiguous, and succinct, yet comprehensive (Decuir-Gunby et al., 2011). The analysis yielded themes of queer diasporas, San Francisco as a symbol, advocacy, digital media, social media use, social media and family, and mobile apps.

Queer Diasporas

The interviewees all indicated they fled their Middle Eastern countries due to persecution for being gay. In Iraq and Syria, LGBTIs can face jail time and/or lashings, while in other countries like Iran and Saudi Arabia, they can face the death penalty (76crimes.com, 2022). Gay refugees/asylees also face verbal and physical violence from citizens, including family (Rodriguez, 2019). These homophobic rhetorics and behaviors from non-LGBTI immigrants were sometimes encountered in San Francisco. Reza directly experienced it with other Iranians living in the United States:

> I wanted to live in a free country. What's the difference? Still, I have to pretend, I have to hide. Then those people [non-LGBTIs in the United States] actually expressed negative things about gay people even though they have more contact with gay people. (Reza, personal communication, 2020)

When Reza moved to California, he still stayed away from non-LGBTI Iranians: "No, I don't want to have contact with Iranians anymore, because I'm coming to San Francisco to experience the freedom. I avoid all the Iranian friends and relatives or whatever. Still I'm avoiding them" (personal communication, 2016).

Ibrahim specifically stated, "For me, I don't normally mix with Middle Eastern people. I don't look for any straights because straight Middle Eastern people are pretty homophobic" (personal communication, 2016). He knows other Middle Eastern gay refugees/asylees, but his past has tainted his view of his culture of origin. "But I know Nassim. I know the Middle Eastern group, but I don't normally mix with them. I mix with anybody else." Ibrahim also mentioned that his lawyer was introduced to him through interpersonal networks: "I made connections, I made friends. So I made a friend who's Persian. And his lawyer, because he's also a refugee, his lawyer is also an Iranian" (personal communication, 2016). These networks help the refugees/asylees get in contact with vital LGBTI-specific resources and services.

Although the gay refugees/asylees preferred to interact with other LGBTI individuals, there was still an evident attraction to interact with other LGBTIs who shared cultural commonalities with them. Reza explained:

> I would say I know many gay Americans, but very few of them I see as real friends—they are like a far friend. The people that I feel much more as a friend are Middle Eastern friends. So those group of people are my real friends. (personal communication, 2016)

Interactions within the queer diaspora influences how Reza identifies with others occupying it. Human collectivity is the product of interaction between embodied individuals (Jenkins, 2002). Reza consciously identified collective characteristics with Middle Eastern LGBTIs; therefore, he formed a group identity with them. Other interviewees expressed similar attitudes; they saw themselves represented in the physical engagements with gay refugees/asylees from the Middle East. There appears to be a hierarchy among intersectional identities and cultural preferences: Middle Eastern LGBTIs, all gays, non-LGBTI San Franciscans, then heterosexuals in the diaspora.

San Francisco as a Symbol

LIFE magazine christened San Francisco the "Gay Capital of America" in 1964, creating a nationalized cultural linkage of "gay" with a geographical location (Ormsbee, 2010, p. 307). The city is home to gay rights activist Harvey Milk, the first U.S. lesbian organization (1964), the first U.S. gay community center (1966), the first U.S. pride parade (1970), the first gay games (1982), the first World AIDS Day (1994), and the first same-sex couple to be legally married in the United States (2015). The rainbow flag, a universal symbol of hope for the LGBTI community, was first flown in San Francisco in 1978, and one of the first U.S. gay neighborhoods is the Castro district. For many LGBTIs, including refugees/ asylees, the city is viewed as a beacon of safety and hope, "openly gay and non-apologetic in its queerness" (Rodriguez, 2017, p. 3). Identity is a symbolic representation of self (Jenkins, 2014) and San Francisco was a well-researched choice and emblematic of who the gay refugees/asylees "could" be. Nassim commented, "I always heard about San Francisco. Even before I came to USA, I always heard like all my friends that visited USA—it was the capital of the gays—so I chose here" (personal communication, 2016). Nassim also joked that he knew about the Castro's famous gay club 440 before he even arrived. He knew he could be openly gay and happy there.

Ibrahim recalled, "It has the highest rates of acceptance to refugees—especially to gay refugees, and I don't have to wait as long as the rest of the states" (Ibrahim, personal communication, 2016). San Francisco provided the refugees a collective social identity of being gay, an outlet to express their sexuality, and a tangible space to represent themselves by performing and communicating their gay identity. Ibrahim elaborated:

> I want to live a normal life, being open, not afraid. This is the most important thing I have, not to be afraid of having a date and if I'm grabbing his hands in the middle of the road and not getting any homophobic shitheads telling me, "No, you can't do that." I wouldn't have to worry about that. (personal communication, 2016)

For Reza, he knew he wanted to move to the United States at an early age, thinking, "San Francisco is such a liberal city, gay-friendly." Reza searched for images online:

> Oh, how does it look in California, San Francisco? There's ocean! I wanted to see where the ocean starts, so then I used the Google Street. So that part I saw when I was in Iran from Google Maps . . . when I came I drove, suddenly I remembered, "Oh, my God. I've seen this before." (personal communication, 2016)

Digital media provided a sense of place and Western culture, particularly U.S. gay culture. Reza, who once feared for his life when walking the streets of Iran, found comfort and safety in the Castro: "I never would imagine my first march in gay pride New York and then next year march in San Francisco. . . . I marched with the Middle Eastern group" (personal communication, 2016). Now marching in the parade is a yearly tradition for Reza; he walks in solidarity with other

LGBTIs and gay refugees/asylees. Reza also recalled looking through his teenage diary and finding a drawing he had made of the Golden Gate Bridge. He said, "That was my dream—when I was a teenager—to come to San Francisco!"

San Francisco was symbolic of the expression of the interviewees' sexuality. It represented being openly gay and directly shaped how they saw themselves. They categorized gays in San Francisco as open, free, and happy. They then identified with that categorization, forming their social identities (Jenkins, 2002). There were more positive categorizations and behaviors in San Francisco than in the gay refugees/asylees' Middle Eastern homelands; therefore, they came to think in more positive terms about their identities and themselves.

Digital Media in the Queer Diaspora

Most of the refugees turned to television and pop culture for cultural representations to help them assimilate in their new home. Ibrahim said, "I did watch *Glee* . . . when I came here, I hooked up with Netflix and I was watching *Queer as Folk*" (personal communication, 2016). Ibrahim also watched *Little Britain* and felt like the program played a big role in informing him about Western popular culture and its identity. Nassim watched digitally based services on his computer, tablet, and mobile phone. His favorite show was *RuPaul's Drag Race* because it was so different from what he saw in the Middle East:

> I have Netflix, I watch everything. I watched all the gay movies that are not found in Lebanon, back home. They're like movies for a gay life. I only knew about one movie before, the *Brokeback Mountain*, that's it, because it was international. (personal communication, 2016)

Media in the queer diaspora provided representations of gay people and culture for Nassim and Ibrahim that were not available to them in Middle East. The men categorized the representations as positive and identified with them, employing them as a reference point on Western gay identity.

Mahdi did not have to catch up very much on Western gay culture when he moved to San Francisco:

American culture was not a complete unknown to me. I watched a lot of movies, a lot of series. I read a lot about what's happening here and media somehow keeps this line alive. So, I wasn't really far behind when I came here, but still there was lot of shock. I knew I had to change some of my concepts, because I used to live somewhere completely isolated where nothing was happening socially. My life experiences don't necessarily fit in with a society where people have been living freely and been expressing their feelings and they have formed a lifestyle around this concept. But I still think it's much here. (personal communication, 2016)

Mahdi used the media post-asylum to learn about American culture and to investigate how to adapt to his new environment, but it still did not fully prepare him for his post-asylum experiences. His physical social interactions in the queer diaspora helped further clarify what it meant to be gay in the United States. Meaning was reshaped through both digital and physical interactions (Mead, 1934), shaping his social identity as a Western gay man.

Digital media was heavily consumed by the interviewees and was utilized more than traditional media to help inform life in the queer diaspora. Mahdi used digital media daily to stay updated on American and gay culture: "I'm still learning about that, like last night I was just reading about the definition of a U.S. person" (personal communication, 2016). Mahdi also used digital chatrooms to practice his English skills with other gay men. He stressed that his online interactions with a friend from Ohio aided in shaping the meaning of gay culture in the United States and, ultimately, his gay identity.

For all the interviewees, digital media helped access representations of Western gay identity that served as information on how to perform their social identity. They all compared their past conceptualizations of gay culture with novel ones in the queer diaspora. This is reflective of Jenkin's (1994) proposition that identity is both nominal (a name) and virtual (an experience). The virtual is essentially what the nominal means and can change while the nominal identity remains the same. The reverse is also true. Both the nominal and the virtual unite in an "ongoing production and reproduction of identity and its boundaries" (Jenkins, 1994, p. 218). The gay refugees/asylees' virtual experiences changed their categorizations of what it meant to be gay, which they in turn identified with.

Mobile apps on smartphones also provided digital content with new categorizations of sexuality. Mobile phones are innately individualistic yet connect each individual socially to the broad world of the internet and social media (Ling et al., 2020). Ibrahim used gay dating mobile apps as a way of meeting other gay men in his area:

> I normally find other gay people everywhere. I can't find somebody who you would want to date on GROWLr, [it] is pretty difficult—it's just more a hookup. Of course, I still use GROWLrs, SCRUFF, not a lot of Grindr, but now Tinder is getting gay now. (personal communication, 2016)

GROWLr was also a popular app for Nassim, directly linking to his identity as a gay bear, an identity typified by hair and a girthy body build. He explained, "There's the GROWLr and there's bars for bears and leather and stuff like that" (personal communication, 2016). Nassim meets other bears on the app and then interacts with them in person at clubs and bars. His identity as a bear evidences his internalization of Western gay identity that was cultivated and performed both online in the apps and offline in the queer diaspora.

Reza also utilized apps and (after some research) came to identify with another Western gay label: "I'm an otter based on the description like body type." Reza uses mobile apps not only to meet local people but also to keep in touch daily with friends and family in Iran and other parts of the Middle East. At one point he used Viber and WhatsApp, but the apps change due to government intervention. Reza said:

> All of the Iranians used this app [WhatsApp] until they find out the government block it and then they find something else. And this one, it automatically encodes everything. So then really the government cannot do anything. But still can send your own sexual pictures or political opinions, so that's kind of safe to do that. I have all these apps. For a month, for a year. (personal communication, 2016)

Reza's commentary demonstrates that an LGBTI identity is viewed as pejorative in his homeland and even using an app to discuss LGBTI issues places his loved ones in precarious situations. It also highlights the use of apps as a space to foster relationships on an individual basis, rather than collectively like Facebook, where your content can be viewed by all friends. Apps were targeted specifically for their privacy. Thus, gay refugees/asylees are more able to perform their identity without fear of unintended recipients seeing personal communication.

For some interviewees, interactions on digital media facilitated confidence and public content creation. Reza started a YouTube channel to perform his social identity:

> Most of my life, first it was online. At some point I feel comfortable to make YouTube video talking about being Iranian gay. So, I put them online, but I hide my face because still I was scared people would find me and kill me or make problem for my family. (personal communication, 2016)

He internalized the positive categorizations that others posted about him under his videos, which aided in his identification of a gay social identity (Jenkins, 1994). Not only did the positive identification encourage Reza to make more videos; it also encouraged him to march in his first pride parade.

Reza's story is reflective of experiences among most of the gay refugees/asylees. Their lives were spent online, in closeted virtual spaces. They used digital media in their homelands to escape, learn, and interact with other LGBTIs in the West (Rodriguez, 2019). Once they arrived in the United States, they still used digital media (and social media to an extent as outlined later) to meet other gay men; however, they then turned to physical interactions in the queer diaspora to foster these relationships. Real-world tangible experiences replaced the digital confinements of their pasts. Nassim stated:

> We're friends on Facebook, so we support each other. Like it would be real life more than Facebook, we don't post about this on Facebook. In real life we meet every two to three days or every one week every weekend. So, we talk about everything that happening with us. So, we support each other in real life more than Facebook. (personal communication, 2016)

Previous research has typically pointed to the reverse of what the refugees indicated with interpersonal and mediated communication. More frequent digital media use was associated with the loss of members in a social circle, suggesting that online interactions displace strong social ties (Sparks, 2016).

Social relationships online are fostered at the expense of others offline. Here, the reverse is evidenced. Gay refugees/asylees utilize digital media to instigate and nurture those in the physical spaces of the queer diaspora. This is consistent with the research of Reich et al. (2012), who found that online time was spent making offline relationships stronger.

Facebook Use in the Queer Diaspora

Social media was noted as a space where representation and identity converged, particularly Facebook. Interviewees indicated that social media created a tension between past and present social identities, a space that was constantly being shaped and reshaped. Living in a queer diaspora did not always equate to projecting a gay identity on mediated platforms that were accessible to friends and family members back home in the Middle East. A majority of the gay refugees/asylees expressed various reactions from loved ones that made them either censor or change their actions on social media.

Mahdi stated that his Facebook profile was a constant negotiation between his advocacy with the NGO he worked for and his own personal connections with his family and friends. Mahdi alters his behavior on social media and tries to find a balance due to his apprehension of family and friends in Iran finding out about his sexuality. Each area of his life is separate, yet all are interrelated:

> There's still a lot of stigma connected to the issue back in Iran and I have a lot of connections, I have a lot of contacts, I have almost all my family back there in Iran, and no matter how hard you try, it's still got a backlash. If I post something really overt then I'm sure it's going to go back home so I usually go somewhere in between. (personal communication, 2016)

Mahdi's commentary demonstrates the conscious effort he puts into choosing which information to post on his Facebook. Even though he is living in the queer diaspora of San Francisco, he is still concerned about how loved ones in the homeland categorize him. Mahdi uses social media to control what information others are privy to. He represents himself on social media much differently than he does in person in the queer diaspora.

Reza was also hesitant to openly advocate for LGBTIs on Facebook: "That's my ultimate goal and passion, but there's a challenge because still I'm not out to the world. I'm just out to my mom, brother and sister in Iran." His advocacy was confined to physical events in San Francisco. He said, "Now I feel local. I mean I feel comfortable if I go and talk. But global, I'm afraid. I mean afraid just because of my family." This fear of family and friends finding out he was gay also triggered Reza to remove his YouTube videos mentioned in the previous section:

> So, then I thought it still is dangerous if they find out or I thought the Iranian government is very sensitive. They want to kill you or put you in jail because they will say you are advertising Western culture. Because of those reasons I thought maybe it's not smart, so I removed them. (personal communication, 2016)

Although Reza had expressed internalization of positive gay categorizations in the queer diaspora, he was still aware that pejorative categorizations still existed in his native country of Iran. Reza did not want to bring about danger to his family back home, so he altered the way he represented himself on social media by creating two Facebook accounts: "But one is my gay Facebook. The other one is my straight Facebook [account], which is my Iranian families, relatives back in Iran, here. And I have my gay one which has almost all the gay friends" (personal communication, 2016). He aggregates his content between the two, making sure not to post too much about his gay lifestyle on his Iranian-facing page.

I argue that Mahdi's non-gay performance on social media and Reza's use of two Facebook accounts is like what Goffman describes as "bounded regions" (1959, p. 82). Front regions are where a particular performance is being enacted, and back regions are where action occurs that is related to the performance but is inconsistent with the front (Goffman, 1959). For Mahdi, his Facebook page would be considered a front region and his in-person identity a back region. Both of Reza's accounts are front-region performances. On his "straight" Facebook page that he uses to communicate with his family, Reza performs a neutral sexual identity, and on his "gay" Facebook page, he performs a gay identity. In person, Reza stated his identity is more like the one exhibited on his gay Facebook page. For both participants, their front-region performance is bounded by cultural expectations of gender. They must act masculine and heteronormative. The interviewees stated they employed this impression management based on how they thought others categorized them. People see themselves how others see them and often present acceptable representations of themselves by concealing characteristics or details that may be in direct conflict with societal expectations and norms in each situation (Goffman, 1959).

Other interviewees did not attempt to sync their performative identities with their audiences. Ibrahim refused to participate in any type of negotiation when it came to the mediated performance of his gay identity, regardless of his family's online presence. He stated, "What they see is what they get!" Ibrahim did, however, use Facebook to monitor LGBTI injustices in the Middle East and to stay abreast of other issues in Lebanon. This compliments the research of Papaioannou and Olivos (2013), who found that Facebook was employed to connect with the diaspora outside of Libya and to foster feelings of nationalism through pictures and videos. In this sense, Ibrahim is fostering a sense of gay pride and activism, in addition to nationalism, between Lebanon and the queer diaspora in San Francisco.

In a similar fashion, Nassim also posted whatever he felt like posting or sharing. His ability to control his social media communication came from monitoring his Facebook friends, rather than his messages or posts:

> My brothers know about me, but my mother and father, I think they know but we've never ever talked about that—never. I post sometimes shirtless pictures, whatever. At the gay bars, I get tagged. Because my mother and family, they don't know English that much, so they don't know what they're reading or just seeing. I got some bad comments from friends in Lebanon, so I removed them from Facebook. That's it! I'm not in Lebanon anymore. (personal communication, 2016)

Nassim felt pressure from his native culture to represent himself in restricted ways. The representations of, and categorizations from, his social environment heavily influenced how he identified. On social media, if he encounters negative categorizations, he can simply disconnect. This strategy has also been employed with other LGBQIs in the queer diaspora who disconnected by "keeping their timeline 'neutral,' by not using Facebook for contact with family members, or by keeping family members apart from gay friends" (Dhoest, 2019, p. 397).

Conclusion

In summary, the external categorizations the gay refugees/asylees encountered post-asylum were contrary to those they encountered in their native Middle Eastern countries. Persecution of their sexual orientation served as a catalyst for seeking refuge outside of the Middle East. They turned to the queer diaspora of San Francisco, particularly for its representation of LGBTI liberation and happiness, to find categorizations that were less pejorative. The categorizations encountered in the queer diaspora post-asylum were congruent to existing group identifications; therefore, they reinforced each other (Jenkins, 2014). The participants internalized the more positive categorizations represented in digital media and interpersonal communication and identified with a gay social identity. In the queer diaspora, the interviewees still had to negotiate some negative categorizations from other non-LGBTI individuals from their home countries and cultures. Therefore, like previous research on queer Iranian women, the interviewees created cultural distance from non-LGBTIs (Abdi & Van Gilder, 2016) and were drawn to other gay men—particularly if those gay men were also refugees or gay Middle Easterners.

Distinctions between mediated communication pre- and post-asylum were explored in this chapter. Previous research has found that in a pre-asylum context, digital media was used for asylum seeking, to find information on gay culture, and to build relationships online with other gays living in secret; interpersonal communication was used to find and initiate escape routes (Rodriguez, 2019). In a post-asylum context, digital media was used to connect with loved ones in the homeland, as well as to find other LGBTIs in the queer diaspora and build relationships offline. Furthermore, digital media, particularly YouTube, was used to create more positive categorizations of gay identity. Digital media and physical location worked in tandem to help the gay refugees/asylees acculturate and shape their identity. The positive categorizations in the queer diaspora fostered a shared collective identity with other LGBTIs that "offered scope for the reconstrual and reevaluation of gay identity and its position within the identity structure in relation to the other components of identity" (Jaspal & Cinnirella, 2012, p. 233).

The gay refugees/asylees in this chapter evidence that identity is not rigid and fixed. Rather, identity is fluid and is influenced by the representations and interactions individuals experience throughout their lives. Gay refugees/asylees perform social identity based on those experiences, representing themselves in a way that is congruent to the respective social group they choose to interact with. In person, in the physical space of the queer diaspora, they were able to perform a gay social identity, an identity fostered by representations of, and represented toward, LGBTI individuals in the queer diaspora of San Francisco. They decidedly socialized with LGBTIs from their own Middle Eastern cultures and avoided those who were non-LGBTI. This enabled the gay refugees/asylees to still preserve their cultural identity without the pejorative categorizations of their sexuality.

The cultural facet of the gay refugees/asylees' identity was also preserved using digital media in a very similar fashion. Facebook was found to be a major source of tension for self-representation and fostered dual performances of social identity. Some interviewees had only one Facebook page and filtered what they posted according to their audience. They refrained from posting any gay content that their friends, family, and native governments could see. One individual had two Facebook pages and posted content specific to either his "straight" identity or his "gay" identity. This finding reifies previous research on digital disconnecting by highlighting that diasporic LGBTIs avoid explicit and implicit references to their sexuality on Facebook (Dhoest, 2019). Additionally, this chapter complements that research by evidencing that disconnection is not just limited to digital spaces; rather, it occurs in both the offline spaces of the queer diaspora and online on social media. Facebook and gay dating apps, particularly, provided the gay refugees/asylees with the option to engage with individuals of their choosing, present the facet of their identity that best coincided with those individuals' categorizations of the gay refugees/asylees, and decide whether to interact with them in physical spaces. Digital media is not just a source of categorizations that are identified with to shape identity; it is a space to control how those identifications are represented to others, in hopes of shaping positive audience-specific categorizations.

This process between online and offline identity negotiation exemplifies Jenkins's (2000, 2014) conceptualization of internal and external moments of the dialect, evidencing that categorization and identification are iterative processes, always in motion, influencing one another. The process also highlights that a gay identity is never fully identified, and that both negative and positive categorizations of being gay are always in flux and present for gay refugees/asylees who flee from global areas where being gay is precarious. There exists a liminal space within the social identity process where gay refugees/asylees partially internalize a gay identity and perform it in front of selective audiences. However, they still consider and partially internalize negative categorizations of a gay identity and refuse to perform it in front of family, friends, and other individuals or entities who may find it deviant. This liminal space is genuinely where identity negotiation takes place.

The chapter's study is limited in its scope to generalize these findings to a universal gay refugee/asylee audience. It is also important to note that the interviewees in the study all identified with a Western identity of being gay or queer, whereas other refugees/asylees who are cisgender men who have sex with other cisgender men may not. Nonetheless, the study provides a profound and meaningful narrative of the lived experiences of gay refugees/asylees post-asylum in the queer diaspora of San Francisco and explicates the roles that digital media and physical space play in the identity negotiation process. These experiences help inform those within and outside of academia to better understand how social identity is directly informed by representations seen, as well as created, on digital media.

REFERENCES

Abdi, S., & Van Gilder, B. (2016). "Cultural (In)visibility and Identity Dissonance: Queer Iranian American Women and Their Negotiation of Existence." *Journal of International and Intercultural Communication, 9*(1), 69–86.

Alinejad, D. (2017). *The Internet and Formations of Iranian American-ness: Next Generation Diaspora*. London: Palgrave Macmillan.

Alonso, A., & Oiarzabal, P. J. (2010). *Diasporas in the New Media Age: Identity, Politics, and Community*. Reno: University of Nevada Press.

Blumer, H. (1969). *Symbolic Interaction: Perspective and Method*. Hoboken: Prentice-Hall.

Butler, J. (1990). *Gender Trouble: Feminism and the Subversion of Identity*. New York: Routledge.

Cover, R. (2002). Re-sourcing Queer Subjectivities: Sexual Identity and Lesbian/Gay Print Media. *Media International Australia, 103*(1), 109–123.

Crenshaw, K. (1991). "Mapping the Margins: Intersectionality, Identity Politics, and Violence against Women of Color." *Stanford Law Review, 43*, 1241–1299.

DeCuir-Gunby, J. T., Marshall, P. L., & McCulloch, A. W. (2011). "Developing and Using a Codebook for the Analysis of Interview Data: An Example from a Professional Development Research Project." *Field Methods, 23*(2), 136–155.

Dhoest, A. (2019). "Intersections and (Dis)connections: LGBTQ Uses of Digital Media in the Diaspora." In *The Handbook of Diasporas, Media, and Culture*, J. Retis & R. Tsagarousianou (pp. 385–400). Hoboken: Wiley-Blackwell.

Eng. D. (1997). "Out Here and Over There: Queerness and Diaspora in Asian American Studies." *Social Text, 15*(3/4), 31–52.

Faugier, J., & Sargeant, M. (1997). "Sampling Hard to Reach Populations." *Journal of Advanced Nursing, 26*(4), 790–797.

Fortier, A. M. (2002). "Queer Diaspora." In *Handbook of Lesbian and Gay Studies*, edited by D. Richardson & S. Seidman (pp. 183–197). Los Angeles: Sage.

Georgiou, M. (2006). *Diaspora, Identity and the Media: Diasporic Transnationalism and Mediated Spatialities*. New York: Hampton Press.

Goffman, E. (1959). *The Presentation of Self in Everyday Life*. New York: Doubleday.

Hall, S. (1990). "Cultural Identity and Diaspora." In *Identity*, edited by J. Rutherford (pp. 222–237). London: Lawrence & Wishart.

Hall, D. E., & Jagose, A. (Eds.). (2012). *The Routledge Queer Studies Reader*. New York: Routledge.

Ilesanmi, O. O. (2009). "What Is Cross-Cultural Research?" *International Journal of Psychological Studies, 1*(2), 82–96.

Jaspal, R., & Cinnirella, M. (2012). "Identity Processes, Threat, and Interpersonal Relations: Accounts from British Muslim Gay Men." *Journal of Homosexuality, 59*(2), 215–240.

Jenkins, R. (1994). "Rethinking Ethnicity: Identity, Categorization and Power." *Ethnic and Racial Studies, 17*(2), 197–223.

Jenkins, R. (2000). "Categorization: Identity, Social Process and Epistemology." *Current Sociology, 48*(3), 7–25.

Jenkins, R. (2002). "Different Societies? Different Cultures? What Are Human Collectivities?" In *Making Sense of Collectivity: Ethnicity, Nationalism and Globalisation*, edited by S. Malesevic and M. Haugaard (pp. 12–32). London: Pluto Press.

Jenkins, R. (2014). *Social Identity*. 4th ed. New York: Routledge.

Karim, K. H. (2004). "Re-viewing the 'National' in 'International Communication': Through the Lens of Diaspora." *Journal of International Communication, 10*(2), 90–109.

Ling, R., Fortunati, L., Goggin, G., Lim, S. S., & Li, Y. (2020) "An Introduction." In *The*

Oxford Handbook of Mobile Communication and Society, edited by R. Ling, L. Fortunati, G. Goggin, S. S. Lim & Y. Li (pp. 3–14). Oxford: Oxford University Press.

Manalansan, M. F. (2003). *Global Divas: Filipino Gay Men in the Diaspora*. Durham: Duke University Press.

Manalansan, M. F. (2006). "Queer Intersections: Sexuality and Gender in Migration Studies." *International Migration Review, 40*(1), 224–249.

Mandaville, P. (2003). "Communication and Diasporic Islam. A Virtual Ummah?" In *The Media of Diaspora*, edited by K. H. Karim (pp. 135–147). New York: Routledge.

Massad, J. A. (2002). "Re-orienting Desire: The Gay International and the Arab World." *Public Culture, 14*(2), 361–385.

Mead, G. H. (1934). *Mind, Self and Society* (Vol. 111). Chicago: University of Chicago Press.

Miconi, A. (2020). "News from the Levant: A Qualitative Research on the Role of Social Media in Syrian Diaspora." *Social Media+ Society, 6*(1). 1–12.

Morse, J. (2000). "Determining Sample Size." *Qualitative Health Research, 10*(1), 3–5.

ORAM. (2012). *Rainbow Bridges: A Community Guide to Rebuilding the Lives of LGBTI Refugees and Asylees*. San Francisco: ORAM. https://reliefweb.int/report/world/rainbow-bridges-community-guide-rebuilding-lives-lgbti-refugees-and-asylees.

Ormsbee, T. J. (2010). *The Meaning of Gay: Interaction, Publicity, and Community among Homosexual Men in 1960s San Francisco*. Washington, DC: Lexington Books.

Owen, W. F. (1984). "Interpretive Themes in Relational Communication." *Quarterly Journal of Speech, 70*(3), 274–287.

Papaioannou, T., & Olivos, H. E. (2013). "Cultural Identity and Social Media in the Arab Spring: Collective Goals in the Use of Facebook in the Libyan Context." *Journal of Arab & Muslim Media Research, 6*(2/3), 99–114.

Puar, J. (1998). "Transnational Sexualities: South Asian (Trans)nation(alism)s and Queer Diasporas." In *Q&A: Queer in Asian America*, edited by D. Eng & A. Hom (pp. 405–422). Philadelphia: Temple University Press.

Puar, J. (2013). "Rethinking Homonationalism." *International Journal of Middle East Studies, 45*(2), 336–339.

Rahman, M. (2010). "Queer as Intersectionality: Theorizing Gay Muslim Identities." *Sociology, 44*(5), 944–961.

Reich, S. M., Subrahmanyam, K., & Espinoza, G. (2012). "Friending, IMing, and Hanging Out Face-to-Face: Overlap in Adolescents' On-line and Off-line Social Networks." *Developmental Psychology, 48*(2), 356–368.

Riggins, S. H. (1992). "The Media Imperative: Ethnic Minority Survival in the Age of Mass Communication." In *Ethnic Minority Media: An International Perspective*, edited by

S.H. Riggins (pp. 1–20). Thousand Oaks: Sage.

Rodriguez, N. S. (2017). "San Francisco's Queer Diaspora and the Gay Middle Eastern Refugee/Asylee." *JOMEC Journal, 11,* 111–126.

Rodriguez, N. S. (2019). "Western Media's Influence on Identity Negotiation in Pre-asylum 'Gay' Men." *Intercultural Communication, Identity, and Social Movements in the Digital Age,* edited by In M. U. D'Silva & A. Atay (pp. 29–47). New York: Routledge.

Sandelowski, M. (1995). "Sample Size in Qualitative Research." *Research In Nursing & Health, 18*(2), 179–183.

Savaş, Ö. (2019). "Affective Digital Media of New Migration from Turkey: Feelings, Affinities, and Politics." *International Journal of Communication, 13*(22), 5405–5426.

Schimel, L. (1997). "Diaspora, Sweet Diaspora: Queer Culture to Post-Zionist Jewish Identity." In *PoMoSexuals: Challenging Assumptions about Gender and Sexuality,* edited by C. Queen & L. Schimel (pp. 163–173). Jersey City: Cleis Press.

76crimes.com. (2022). "68 Countries Where Homosexuality Is Illegal." https://76crimes. com/76-countries-where-homosexuality-is-illegal/.

Siapera, E. (2014). "Diasporas and New Media: Connections, Identities, Politics and Affect." *Crossings: Journal of Migration & Culture, 5*(1), 173–178.

Sparks, G. (2016). *Media Effects Research: A Basic Overview.* 5th ed. Boston: Cengage Learning.

Tajfel, H., & Turner, J. C. (1979). "An Integrative Theory of Intergroup Conflict." *The Social Psychology of Intergroup Relations, 33*(47), 74.

White House, Office of the Press Secretary. (2011, December 6). "Presidential Memorandum—International Initiatives to Advance the Human Rights of Lesbian, Gay, Bisexual, and Transgender Persons" [Press Release].

Ward, C., Bochner, S., & Furnham, A. (2001). *The Psychology of Cultural Shock.* 2nd ed. New York: Taylor & Francis.

You Are a Marked Body

Caught in the Fires of Racialization as an
Arab Woman in the American Academy

Noor Ghazal Aswad

I remember playing with the kids in our neighborhood in Newcastle upon Tyne, who also happened to be my close friends at school. I imagine I was probably ten years old or so. It was a weekday. Three of my school friends rang the door, and my mother agreed to let me play with them with the caveat that we stay near our house. "Your mother is so overprotective!" they would tell me. This day, my mother answered the doors in jeans and a sleeveless crocheted white top. Her hair was short and dark, and her beautiful green eyes watchful as always. "Wow, she looks so normal!" one of my friends told me. It was the first time they had seen her without a headscarf. My mother, born and raised in Syria and who had moved to England when she married my father, wore the Islamic headscarf whenever out in public. My parents had raised us in the Islamic faith, and we would spend weekends with our Arab and Muslim friends, be it going to the movies, visiting the mosque, or sharing dinner together. I was jarred at the insinuation that she had somehow seemed abnormal all this time in my friends' eyes. I was silent as it dawned on me that people did not always see us as we saw ourselves.

Hence began the practice of seeing myself in other people's eyes, a "twoness" or double consciousness of sorts (Du Bois, 1903). I look back to that moment as formative—forever seared in my consciousness. I have decided, some twenty years later, to respond to their oppositional and interrogational declarations of my mother's normality. Today, I bring my own embodied experience as an "othered" being to consciousness by tracking and tracing vignettes from my academic journey. Using multiple layers of consciousness, I connect the personal to the cultural to the political. More specifically, I mark moments of otherization as a diasporic graduate student during my doctoral journey in the American academy.

Autoethnography is the "postcolonial turn" that ethnography has taken by recentering the researcher as integral to the field (Chawla & Rodriguez, 2008; Clair, 2003). The power of theorizing through experience cannot be undermined, permitting intricate understandings of cultural nuance and embodiment in hegemonic frameworks (Anzaldúa, 1987; Collins, 2000). As such, I draw on my lived experience in a raced, gendered, and classed body not to generalize my voice to others but to open a dialogue on the positionalities we occupy within hegemonic systems. By theorizing experiences of the flesh, I join other critical cultural and feminist scholars who have located the personal within broader matrixes of domination (Ahmed, 2004; Anzaldúa, 1987; Calafell, 2013, 2014; Collins, 2000; Juárez, 2019). An autoethnographic performance paradigm privileges the body as a way of knowing (Anzaldúa, 1987), particularly in histories of colonialism that cannot be divorced from the body (Calafell, 2014). The body, as a set of signifiers, is prioritized as a text by which to read and theorize systems of oppression (Yep, 2013). As Chávez puts it, "bodies are not simply read, but rather in their construction as foreign, they are translated" (2009, p. 23). Such paradigms allow one to move from the theoretical study of flattened discourse to textual fragments rich with context. This rhetorical reflexivity "seek[s] out these sites of tension, displacement, and contradiction between the Being There of performed experience and the Being Here of written texts" (Conquergood, 1991, p. 193).

We must acknowledge the imperative to scrutinize the implications of the situatedness of our knowledge structures. Too often we have been divorced from how race is constructed *in situ*. Therefore, this chapter is a response to calls for rhetoricians to examine the everyday experiences of historically marginalized people (Ono & Sloop, 1995). The production of racial knowledge is "one of the least critiqued arenas in which 'race' is produced" (Crawford, 2007, p. 1). With this in mind, this chapter focuses on the academy, not merely as a site of instruction but also as a political and cultural site of contestation over knowledge, canons, and voices that embody and transcribe race.

Though the way in which the academy produces, reproduces, and reinforces hierarchical norms has been explored at length in the literature, these accounts have come primarily from Latina/o/x, African American, and Asian perspectives (Calafell, 2013, 2014; Chawla & Rodriguez, 2008; Collins, 2000; Hendrix, 2011; Moore, 2017; Thomas & Hollenshead, 2006). There exists scant literature from the perspectives of postcolonial Arab and/or Muslim academics, though there have been a few noteworthy recent efforts in this regard (Ghabra, 2015; Ghabra & Calafell, 2018; Yousuf & Calafell, 2018). Therefore, this chapter addresses how racial hierarchical norms are produced, reproduced, and reinforced within pedagogical spaces focused on intersectionality and racial justice issues through examining the experience of an Arab/Muslim diasporic graduate student in the United States.[1]

The Academy as a Border Zone

In this chapter, I conceptualize the academy (and the attending spaces that taper from it) as a material border in which symbolic constructions that regulate and define others are legitimized and reproduced. I do so by homing in on the "border effects" of discourses that transcend the physical space of the academy, that is, the material consequences of knowledge production in the academy on bodies "of color." Borders are not just "where oceans meet land, where rivers divide nations, and where fences stand" (Ono, 2012, p. 31). Instead, borders move with migrants into the social spaces in which they live, be it in the workplace, home, or otherwise. Anzaldúa theorizes borderlands as present "wherever two or more cultures edge each other, where people of different races occupy the same territory, where under, lower, middle and upper classes touch, where the space between two individuals shrinks with intimacy" (1987, preface). These unnatural boundaries form a dividing line constructing identity intersections, embodiments, and coalitions (Johnson, 2012).

As such, the academy is conceived as a domestic border within the nation, where logics of internal colonialism—defined by Tuck and Yang (2012) as the biopolitical and geopolitical management of people, land, flora, and fauna—are present. I argue that the academy, in the process of racialization, actively otherizes diasporic students by casting them outside the border even when "located physically within the borders of the nation" (Flores, 2003, p. 380). Insofar as the academy is in the business of representing others through critical discussions of race, the degree to which these people appear as others becomes a function of how we detachedly constitute them under the academy's terms. Though the pivotal work of the academy in the critical scholarship on race cannot be undermined, I argue there is an ambivalence and quiescence with which such knowledge must be accompanied.

Caught in the Crossfire

Autoethnographies are often perceived as nonnormative (Calafell & Moreman, 2009), standing out in predominantly "white" narratives of being. I proceed, acknowledging that spaces of privilege and disempowerment are consequential when coming to a research project such as this. I explore the details of the personal not only to show how fragments of identity exist simultaneously in disadvantaged and privileged positions, but to set the backdrop against which the vignettes of my time in the American academy can be read. Through a distillation of experience, and an intensification of the personal, I build on my previous work to explore how we might build solidarity across divisive boundaries (Ghazal Aswad, 2021). At this juncture, I reflect on the many subjectivities I embody: educated, financially comfortable, traveled, British, multilingual, white-skinned, and able-bodied. I also touch on my history of immigration, (lack of) American citizenship, and my "marked" presence as a Muslim woman, which potentially collide with these identities. I come from a relatively privileged background as the daughter of two educated parents. My father is a well-known and successful physician, one of a handful of surgeons in the United Arab Emirates specialized in cervical cancer. Though my grandfather was a pharmacist, four of his five children were doctors in what is considered the family's profession. My grandmother came from the well-off Chamma family, known to own several villages, factories, and businesses, which left her personally wealthy and independent from a young age.

My father fled Syria during the uprisings of the 1980s, often referred to as "the events," which culminated in the Hama massacre where over twenty thousand people were killed. He escaped in secret, on the hunch of being falsely informed on by a colleague who had a vendetta against the family. He had just finished his final year of medical school, though he had not yet received his degree. My grandmother would recall the dramatic night in which the army came to their home searching for my father the day after he had left. He escaped to Austria with five hundred *liras*, selling newspapers on the street in Austria until he was able to arrive safely in England. He would not return to Syria for another fifteen years.

Though I was born and raised in England, we visited Aleppo in Syria at least twice a year, an ancient city from the second millennium BCE strategically located at the crossroads of several trade routes. We would spend summers at the Citadel, absorbing the hustle and bustle of the busy city, at the Old Souk, or drinking tea at my grandma's veranda with family and friends. Gold-domed mosques coexisted with Armenian cathedrals, Maronite Churches, and even synagogues. It was a miraculous place. At twelve years old, my parents uprooted the family to move to the United Arab Emirates. Although I continued my schooling there for many years, in a sense, we were all only temporary inhabitants. I would eventually migrate to the United States, pursuing my graduate education first in the Midwest and later in the mid-South.

The complexity of my group identification is at times complicated by my ethnicity. Though of Syrian descent, my family has origins in Turkey from the area of Mardin and Erzincan, and I often grew up hearing of my great-grandmother's great Turkish beauty. My hometown Aleppo borders Gaziantep in Turkey. As such, many northern Syrians share Turkish ancestry, which is unsurprising considering the whole region had once been under Ottoman rule. My history could be said to make me a person whose national or cultural identity is somehow miscellaneous, by virtue of birth, religion, language, migration, parentage, and overseas education (Clifford, 1986). My "membership" in many apparently conflicting groups may make my loyalties, and even my identity, seem arbitrary, if not always problematic. For this and other reasons, I have at all times been placeless, yet filled with belonging to various places, languages, and cultures. Despite the immense pride I have in my roots, it comes at the cost of a global unmooring and fluidity of identity that even I struggle to place. An identity that has never been perfectly acculturated but instead is in a "constant process of negotiation" (Bammer, 1994), infinitely dispersed and indefinitely displaced.

In what follows, I connect these narratives of ethnic and spatial belonging to my bordering experiences at the American academy. As pedagogical borders shifted beneath my feet, I found my embodied history clashing with prescribed American racial hierarchies within a U.S. colonial imaginary, buckets of my "whiteness" or "color" into which I must fit. My diasporic attempts to place my "interstitial" positionality were made ever more challenging (Bhabha, 1996)—I was often caught in the crossfires, negotiating the counternarratives of a hegemonic "common-sense" identity placed upon me in pedagogical spaces.

Innocence and Rose-Colored Glasses

Coterminous with the rise of the unabashedly racist and sexist era of president Donald Trump, there were rising concerns about the whiteness of the communication discipline. Chakravartty and colleagues' (2018) watershed essay "#CommunicationSoWhite" highlighted ongoing racial inequality and colonial legacies in terms of the production of disciplinary knowledge in the field. For all intents and purposes, the communication discipline has been at a crossroads, wrestling with its pedagogical, research, and public commitments. With this in mind, in this chapter I juxtapose my embodied reality within the pedagogical discussions of the discipline to explicate how racial hierarchies reify and perpetuate limited categories of race through praxis emanating from academic spaces.

I was not introduced to "whiteness" as an academic concept until my doctoral studies at the University of Memphis. Doctoral programs are not often academic microcosms of the cities they exist in, but Memphis was certainly different. Our program was noticeably more diverse than other departments, and the campus as a whole was of a majority-minority composition (Office of Institutional Research, 2019). As such, discussions surrounding race, class, gender, and identity were rampant in every class, in stark opposition to my time in the Midwest, where such awareness had been nonexistent.

My time in Memphis became crucial to my exploration of critical race theory. I soon found the inventory of related terms accumulate in my consciousness. Intellectual exchanges on race began infiltrating even my most intimate friendships. I was lucky to find myself amid a particularly strongly outspoken cohort. One colleague in particular was far more tuned in to these conversations than I. She was powerful in expressing her ideas, and I was in awe of her. We would lingeringly mull over class discussions as we walked to our car after evening classes, engaging in hours of unfiltered conversations where we would flesh out things we would not have dared to in class. We turned to the topic of our intersectional embodiments and our place in the academy. Our conversations become struggles, where we both were still uncertain of our relationality to all of this. One time, I exclaimed, "But I am White!"

All my life, out of necessity, that was the box I had ticked. I was not alone in this. Most Arab Americans, in the absence of a Middle Eastern or North African category, identify themselves as white (Rojas, 2019).[2] The U.S. census continues to define white as "a person having origins in any of the original peoples of Europe, the Middle East, or North Africa" (U.S. Census Bureau, 2018). This is also a reflection of the extent to which Arab Americans see themselves as part of dominant group in a global context, rather than a minority group (Ajrouch & Jamal, 2007). Further, a semiotics of whiteness among some Arabs, such as Lebanese/Syrians, allow for some to be white-passing, though in my case my hijab was a marker of difference (Ahmed, 2011; Ghazal Aswad, 2020).[3] In these discourses, the hijab becomes not only a visual marker of religion but an emblematic marker of racial difference (Yousef, 2020).

My colleague told me, "Hey, I don't want to take that away from you, but you are not white." She insisted my hijab, as well as my name, were "telling." Her characterization of my comments stung, as if I had been coveting something that was not mine. I explained Arabs were Caucasian, the definition of white. She was surprised at this, but maintained I was of the "Black and brown folk."

No doubt intended as an acknowledgment of shared experiences (Vega & Chávez, 2018), in that moment I was hurt. I felt as if I was being put in my place. For some reason, the neat categorization failed to capture the particularities of my diasporic experience. In an essentializing moment, the plethora of embodied experiences of women of various races, classes, identities, and sects became reducible to one knowable story: a single story of otherness. I laugh now looking back at this conversation, at how naïve I was. Though grateful for my more mature understanding of the complex nature of these discussions, I still yearn for the innocence I had then, for the time when I saw life with rose-colored glasses.

Bordering Declarations of Race in Embodied Spaces

In the third year of my doctoral studies, a friend of mine joined the doctoral program after many years of leaving academia. We became close, and I was relieved to have an ally whose positionality closely mirrored mine. Before long, we found ourselves sharing insights and comparing notes on our experiences in the department. At a departmental event that I was unable to attend, she told me one of the white male students in my cohort was debating the relative whiteness of various students. He offered himself up first, stating why for various reasons his whiteness might be questioned. He then proceeded to discuss the degrees of my whiteness. "Noor, on the other hand, though she speaks well, her hoojab and accent make her less white in the eyes of some."

I was disturbed. I keenly felt the inquisitive surveillance of my diasporic body that these comments betrayed. I was unsure how I felt about the entitlement inherent in his analyzing the levels of my perceived whiteness, an immigrant in a space that was at times alienating and foreign. His location in the conversation was epistemically salient, considering that some privileged positionalities are discursively dangerous (Alcoff, 1991). I noticed the politics of declaration, in which enunciations of his own whiteness became good practice, reproducing white privilege in "unforeseen" ways (Ahmed, 2004). Indeed, though whiteness must "be seen" to resist the power of whiteness (Dyer, 1997, p. 45), this occurs at the risk of non-whiteness then being marked, defined, declared, and assigned as its counterpart. In these pedagogical spaces, race becomes not only a theoretical object of study but something to be tracked and assigned to others in a "neutral" manner.

Pedagogical spaces become border zones that "designate, produce, and/or regulate the space of difference" (DeChaine, 2009, p. 44). Despite the intentional politics of critical race studies as loyal to a politics of inclusion (Flores, 2016), pedagogical spaces in which critical race is discussed at times lend themselves to the further marginalization of immigrant scholars through the parceling out of whiteness to them. This is rooted in the assumption that racism is based in ignorance, and that through more knowledge, anti-racism is achieved (Hage, 2000). Moreover, I began to find problematic how the all-encompassing terms of "whiteness" and "people of color" were utilized, with little thought of the doctrinal consequences of how these terms restrict conceptions of identity.

Simultaneously, I was reminded of the ever-present "gaze of the white male" and the historically constituted subject-position from which I was being studied (Morrison, 2012). While these pedagogical spaces intend to promote social change by challenging interlocking and distinct forms of oppression, inadvertently othered bodies are interpellated as "subjects" of analysis. The student's cutting demarcation of my perceived whiteness seemed an authenticating announcement of my otherized place in society, empowered by his pedagogical sense of being learned on these issues. The academy became a border space, unintentionally legitimizing flawed racial categorizations and ahistorical ways of thinking about others. These norms are presented as clear-cut and readily identifiable, when they are not only imperfect but narrowly constructed within the culture of the United States (Keating, 1995). Here, I borrow Walter Mignolo's words,

> When you feel that you have been classified, that you are not what you think you are, you become part of the gaze of the classifier. The awareness of dwelling in the border brought immigrant consciousness and that affected my body. (Mignolo & Walsh, 2018, p. 251)

Though I am not suggesting that anti-racism must transcend race to avoid the reification of race (Gilroy, 2000), I advocate for a recognition of the material impacts of reductionist conceptualizations of race in our embodied discourses with one another. The following questions arise: Where is the cognizance of our role in (in)advertently perpetuating the histories of these terms and using them with effect and affect against others? Has whiteness become an object to be determined and assigned according to various metrics or calculations? Is this the new whiteness that is "self-conscious and critical" (Cohen, 1997), or is the study of whiteness sanctioning an elitist and educated white normativity? Does being versed in critical race theory entitle one to place others as artifacts of discourse, to be analyzed socially, politically, ideologically, and religiously? Does it entitle us to make spectacles of their identities? Are attempts to classify others according to racial hierarchies perpetuating colonizing practices?

American Racial Hierarchies in the Colonial Imaginary and Skewed Paradigms of Intersectionality

"So Noor, in Syria, do y'all consider yourself White?" I paused, uncertain how to answer. Aside from a phenotypic preference for whiteness (a colorism of sorts), Syrians generally did not define themselves in those terms. "No, we consider ourselves Syrian," I exclaimed.

The starting point of the conversation was not where I would have liked it: we were on different planes completely. The epistemological and ontological claims implicit in the articulation of the question shackled my agency in responding. On reflection, I realized that instead of a nuanced discussion on cultural and ethnic heritage, pedagogical discussions of race in the classroom were encouraging a recentering, rather than decentering, of American notions of identity with a U.S. colonial imaginary. As opposed to opening up spaces for agentic articulations of identity, race's normativity was obscuring even the possibility of a world where my whiteness did not have be pondered upon.

I was caught between structures, conscious of the tension between how I relate to myself and how my friend wanted to engage in solidarity with me. Was critical race theory as a pedagogical site of study causing us to "get stuck" on whiteness (Dyer, 1997) as opposed to an exploration of the distinct historical formations of other identities? In the words of Nigerian writer Chimamanda Ngozi Adichie, the many overlapping stories of the diaspora are "reduced to a single narrative" (Adichie, 2009). Theories of race were abundant in the texts I read, but the apparent universalization with which they were presented troubled me. Race is a highly contingent and mutable social construction (Haney-López, 1994), but in pedagogical practice, these abstract concepts were being "copied and pasted" ahistorically contrary to the critical work intended to dismantle oppressive conditions of power. The presumed certainty and unquestioning nature in which they were consolidated and deployed transcendently echoed the hierarchization of particular knowledges, cultures, and histories (Dei et al., 2006). More specifically, stagnant U.S. racial hierarchies are reductively applied to others naturalizing the self-proclaimed supremacy of American racial norms, the host nation-state.

"So, would you consider yourself White?" I ask my cerebral brother, a third-year medical student residing in London who spends his weekends reading the *Iliad* and *Odyssey* in addition to other historical antiquities. He visits us annually in Memphis, and I cherish our discussions. I have been living insularly in the United States and in my own mind for so long that I am eager to see how my brother identifies. He responds:

> No, absolutely not. I am Arab. The slight paleness of my skin has nothing to do with whiteness. But, I think whiteness is different things in different countries. In Switzerland for example, you don't call Swiss people white. Because Swiss people, though they are white, are not American white people, are they? I think the idea of whiteness is an American thing. Or at least, something in American scholarly circles. (personal communication, June 22, 2019)

My brother's words echo in my mind for weeks. The impulse to place immigrants within the larger cultural narrative of the United States appears unavoidable (Ghazal Aswad, 2019, 2020; Ghazal Aswad & de Velasco, 2020), and the academy is certainly not immune to these forces. The particularity of American society is habitually "imposed, in apparently de-historicized form, upon the whole planet" (Bourdieu & Wacquant, 1999, p. 41). The practice of mapping the geography, race, and culture of one place on to another is a well-documented Orientalist tendency (Bourdieu & Wacquant, 1999). However, these tendencies are interrupted when immigrants resist their placement in a U.S.-centric worldview that discounts the historical singularities of their existence. The comfortable reinforcement of my "place" in monolithic racial categories belied the fact that race is a sociohistorical trope not to be inscribed across all cultures or geographies. The placement of whiteness atop U.S. racial hierarchies, while ignoring the specificities of other social markers, is another symptom of the sweep of U.S. colonialism oblivious to the agency and privilege of those originating from outside of the United States.

These racial placements fell into what I term "skewed paradigms of intersectionality" oblivious to other intersecting axes of my diasporic body, the material effects of which I felt every day. Recently, academics have called for an examination of the consequences of an isolationist attention to race (Vega & Chávez, 2018). Indeed, the microscopic concentration on race in these pedagogical spaces obscures other facets of my intersectionality, such as my lack of American citizenship. I was regularly confronted with precarity as a result of it, be it when considering how to maintain legal status in the country or when traveling within the nation's borders or abroad. Being an immigrant lends a clandestine element to all aspects of one's life, and I often feel the threat of control and surveillance. Noncitizenship had cast a long shadow over every detail of my life in the United States, though it continued to be an ancillary concern within discussions of intersectionality.

For all the grand narratives of U.S. individualism, characterizations of my racial status flattened any consideration of the multiplicity of my identity, placing me within predetermined constructions of American racial identity and minority canon formation. The academy became a border zone of cultural negotiation and contestation, regulating belonging within the national U.S. imaginary. The treatment of these racial hierarchical norms as sacrosanct betrayed a blind spot that obfuscates other realities of existence outside the United States. It relays diasporic identities as naturally falling into immutable racial categories applicable to all bodies. As such, pedagogical discussions of race in the academy risk binding diasporic students within preprepared racial molds, without concern for their histories. After all, whose histories were being centered in these categorizations?

Invisibility and Selective Solidarity

I recall my professor casually stating in class one day, "Noor, you are a marked body." I took pause, shuddering at the implicit meaning of the words. Though pedagogical discussions of my marked body were likely intended as an intellectual exercise recognizing my marginalized positionality within the academic canon and in society, they were stifling in their limitedness in capturing the realities of my life. The majority of the time, pedagogical spaces completely neglected the place of Arab-Muslims in American society, or interpellated them into alien spaces with which I did not identify under "other racialized immigrant groups." The storied and historied bodies of Muslims were rarely theorized within rhetorical studies, or even within discussions of intersectionality (Yousuf & Calafell, 2018). Moreover, few discussions directly attended to the structural violence against Muslims as a mode of white supremacy. While these topics may have been touched on, they exist only at the periphery of these conversations. Though I felt an affective connection with these discourses of otherness, I also felt an outsider to them. As put by Brah, "each border embodies a unique narrative, even while it resonates with common themes with other borders"

(1996, p. 203). As such, I frequently was a spectator to other prominent players as they worked out how they would coexist with one another.

The sense of invisibility culminated when I shared with a white female colleague of mine that I was thinking of writing an autoethnography regarding my experience as an Arab-Muslim woman in the academy. Instead of encouraging words, she looked at me quizzically, stating, "I would advise you to avoid getting into a competition with the African American community on those kinds of issues. I do not mean to preach, but anti-Blackness really is the axis around which all these discussions should revolve." The insinuation was that I was engaging in a power struggle and that doing so would insert myself in a diabolical "oppression" competition with others. I was acquainted with the essentialist Black/white paradigm and its pervasive impact on racial discourse (Alcoff, 2003; Delgado, 1996; Perea, 1997), but I had not expected to suddenly be "in" it. I was unnerved that the specificities of my experience were not worthy of examination, and how my voice was being constituted a priori.

I reminded myself that solidarity with the Arab American community was not to be taken for granted. Upon reflection, I noted how again, a well-intentioned "white" body was positioning itself as a gatekeeper intellectualizing how my experiences should take form. I decided to persevere even more strongly to delegitimate intellectualizations of what diasporic experiences should look like. Omitting the postcolonial experiences of Arab American immigrants contributes to marginalization of these communities (Naber, 2000). And so, through this chapter, I have begun the tensive process of bringing "double consciousness" to term, placing myself at the front of the "gaze," rather than as the recipient of its hegemonic force.

Conclusion

This chapter was written in the summer of 2019 amid growing awareness of the colonial legacies of our academic spaces. As I wrote in an apartment in Istanbul over the Bosphorus, a pivotal "political moment" reverberated across the field, namely the publication of a statement by the editor of the respected disciplinary journal *Rhetoric and Public Affairs*, Professor Martin J. Medhurst, a distinguished scholar of the discipline, calling out the threat of identity to the "scholarly merit" of the discipline in response to concerns about the racial homogeneity of the

Distinguished Scholars (Dutta, 2019). In the aftermath of the editorial, a huge backlash erupted, aptly described as a "bleeding" of the communication discipline (Tracy, 2019). At the time, an essay of mine, submitted to the same journal a few months prior, had received a coveted response: "revise and resubmit."[4] I was in a state of both personal and professional uncertainty, unsure how to act as prominent academics began withdrawing their work from the journal. And so, this chapter became imbued with a renewed urgency, situated as it is from the perspective of a diasporic student "caught in the crossfires" of the "going-ons" in the academy in its search for a racial utopia.

As an immanent critique, this chapter illustrates how pedagogical spaces valorize American notions of identity within a U.S. colonial imaginary, "muddling" the borders at which racial hierarchies are drawn. The academy actively imposes, in interstitial moments, U.S. racial hierarchies in a manner so easy, so settled, as to be diminutive of diasporic students. Critical discourses of race, though aiming to alleviate oppressions, at times operate oppressively toward diasporic identities by drawing on and sustaining discourses of race. In doing so, the academy is complicit in the material production and reproduction of hegemonic racial classifications, at the cost of a contemplation of the dynamic and layered histories of others.

In conclusion, I implore scholars to be mindful of the importance of engagement with the material effects and affects of how racial constructions are deployed toward others to avoid the reproduction of alienating colonial logics. This is not in any way a disauthorization of the study of critical race theory, which is essential to combating racism, but rather an injunction for greater reflexivity on our own parochial priorities and the geopolitical and sociocultural subjectivities of others.

NOTES

1. The term "pedagogical spaces" is used several times in this chapter. With this term, I am referring specifically to pedagogical spaces informed by intersectionality, critical race, social justice, and anticolonialist theories.
2. Though this may be the case for Arab Americans residing in the United States, it is important to note this does not (necessarily) apply to Arabs living in the Middle East, as will be discussed later in this chapter.

3. Ajrouch and Jamal's (2007) study on Arab Americans found that Lebanese and Syrians were more likely to identify as white than other Arabs, such as Iraqis or Yemenis.

4. The essay was eventually accepted for publication after intense discussions around the best course of action (see Ghazal Aswad & de Velasco, 2020).

REFERENCES

Adiche, C. N. (2009). "The Danger of. Single Story" [Video]. TED Conferences. https://www.ted.com/talks/chimamanda_ngozi_adichie_the_danger_of_a_single_story/comments.

Ahmed, L. (2011). *A Quiet Revolution: The Veil's Resurgence, from the Middle East to America.* New Haven: Yale University Press.

Ahmed, S. (2004). "Declarations of Whiteness: The Non-performativity of Anti-Racism." *Borderlands*, 3(2), 104–126.

Ajrouch, K. J., & Jamal, A. (2007). "Assimilating to a White Identity: The Case of Arab Americans." *IMR: The International Migration Review*, 41(4), 860–879.

Alcoff, L. (1991). "The Problem of Speaking for Others." *Cultural Critique*, Winter (20), 5–32.

Alcoff, L. (2003). "Latino/as, Asian Americans, and the Black-White Binary." *Journal of Ethics*, 7(1), 5–27.

Anzaldúa, G. (1987). *Borderlands: The New Mestiza.* San Francisco: Spinsters/AuntLute.

Bammer, A. (1994). *Displacements: Cultural Identities in Question.* Bloomington: Indiana University Press.

Bhabha, H. K. (1996). "Culture's In-Between." In *Questions of Cultural Identity*, edited by S. H. & P. Du Gay (pp. 53–60). Thousand Oaks: Sage Publications

Bourdieu, P., & Wacquant, L. (1999). "On the Cunning of Imperialist Reason." *Theory, Culture & Society*, 16(1), 41–58.

Brah, A. (1996). *Cartographies of Diaspora: Contesting Identities.* New York: Routledge.

Calafell, B. M. (2013). "(I)dentities: Considering Accountability, Reflexivity, and Intersectionality in the I and the We." *Liminalities: A Journal of Performance Studies*, 9(2), 6–11.

Calafell, B. M. (2014). "Performance: Keeping Rhetoric Honest." *Text and Performance Quarterly*, 34(1), 115–117.

Calafell, B. M., & Moreman, S. T. (2009). "Envisioning an Academic Readership: Latina/o Performativities per the Form of Publication." *Text and Performance Quarterly*, 29(2),

123–130.

Chakravartty, P., Kuo, R., Grubbs, V., & McIlwain, C. (2018). "#CommunicationSoWhite." *Journal of Communication*, 68(2), 254–266.

Chávez, K.R. (2009). "Embodied Translation: Dominant Discourse and Communication with Migrant Bodies-as-Text." *Howard Journal of Communications*, 20(1), 18–36.

Chawla, D., & Rodriguez, A. (2008). "Narratives on Longing, Being, and Knowing: Envisioning a Writing Epistemology." *International Journal of Progressive Education*, 4(1), 97–111.

Clair, R. P. (2003). *Expressions of Ethnography: Novel Approaches to Qualitative Methods.* Albany: SUNY Press.

Clifford, J. (1986). "Partial Truths." In *Writing Culture: The Poetics and Politics of Ethnography*, edited by J. C. & G. E. Marcus (pp. 1–26). Berkeley: University of California Press.

Cohen, P. (1997). "Labouring under Whiteness." In *Displacing Whiteness: Essays in Social and Cultural Criticism*, edited by R. Frankenburg (pp. 244–282). Durham: Duke University Press.

Collins, P. (2000). *Black Feminist Thought: Knowledge, Consciousness, and the Politics of Empowerment.* New York: Routledge Press.

Conquergood, D. (1991). "Rethinking Ethnography: Towards a Critical Cultural Politics." *Communication Monographs*, 58(2), 179–194.

Crawford, C. L. (2007). *Breaking Down "Race": A Radical Retheorization of Racial Formation Theory.* Montreal: Queen's University.

DeChaine, R. (2009). "Bordering the Civic Imaginary: Alienization, Fence Logic, and the Minuteman Civil Defense Corps." *Quarterly Journal of Speech*, 95(1), 43–65.

Dei, G., Asgharzadeh, A., Bahador, S. E., & Shahjahan, R. A. (2006). *Schooling and Difference in Africa: Democratic Challenges in a Contemporary Context.* Toronto: University of Toronto Press.

Delgado, R. (1996). "Rodrigo's Fifteenth Chronicle: Racial Mixture, Latino-Critical Scholarship, and the Black-White Binary." *Texas Law Review*, 75(5), 1181–1202.

Delgado, R., & Stefancic, J. (2017). *Critical Race Theory: An Introduction.* 2nd edition. New York: New York University Press.

Du Bois, W. E. B. (1903). *The Souls of Black Folk.* Oxford: Oxford University Press.

Dutta, M. (2019). "Whiteness, NCA, and Distinguished Scholars." *Culture Centered Blogspot.*

Dyer, R. (1997). *White.* New York: Routledge Press.

Flores, L. A. (2003). "Constructing Rhetorical Borders: Peons, Illegal Aliens, and Competing Narratives of Immigration." *Critical Studies in Media Communication*,

20(4), 362–387.

Flores, L. A. (2016). "Between Abundance and Marginalization: The Imperative of Racial Rhetorical Criticism." *Review of Communication*, 16(1), 4–24.

Ghabra, H. (2015). "Disrupting Privileged and Oppressed Spaces: Reflecting Ethically on My Arabness through Feminist Autoethnography." *Kaleidoscope: A Graduate Journal of Qualitative Communication Research*, 14(1).

Ghabra, H., & Calafell, B. M. (2018). "From Failure and Allyship to Feminist Solidarities: Negotiating Our Privileges and Oppressions across Borders." *Text and Performance Quarterly*, 38(1–2), 38–54.

Ghazal Aswad, N. (2019). "Biased Neutrality: The Symbolic Construction of the Syrian Refugee in the *New York Times*." *Critical Studies in Media Communication*, 36(4), 357–375.

Ghazal Aswad, N. (2020). "Fragmented Paradigms of Transculturality: Negotiating Equivocal Agency in Refugee Representations in Refugee Resettlement Organizations." In *Negotiating Identity and Transnationalism in Middle Eastern and North African Communication and Critical Cultural Studies*, edited by H. Ghabra, F. Z. Alaoui, S. Abdi & B. M. Calafell (pp. 31–48). New York: Peter Lang Publishing.

Ghazal Aswad, N. (2021). "Radical Rhetoric: Towards a Telos of Solidarity." *Rhetoric and Public Affairs*, 24(1–2), 207–222.

Ghazal Aswad, N., & de Velasco, A. (2020). "Redemptive Exclusion: A Case Study of Nikki Haley's Rhetoric on Syrian Refugees." *Rhetoric and Public Affairs*, 23(4), 735–760.

Gilroy, P. (2000). *Against Race: Imagining Political Culture beyond the Color Line*. Cambridge: Harvard University Press.

Hage, G. (2000). *White Nation: Fantasies of White Supremacy in a Multicultural Society*. New York: Routledge.

Haney-López, I. F. (1994). "Social Construction of Race: Some Observations on Illusion, Fabrication, and Choice." *Harvard Civil Rights-Civil Liberties Law Review*, 29(1), 1–62.

Hendrix, K. G. (2011). "The Growth Stages and Maturation of an Outsider-within: Developing a Critical Gaze and Earning the Right to Speak." *Qualitative Inquiry*, 17(4), 315–324.

Johnson, J. (2012). "Bordering as Social Practice." In *Border Rhetorics: Citizenship and Identity on the US-Mexico Frontier*, edited by R. Dechaine (pp. 33–47). Tuscaloosa: University of Alabama Press.

Keating, A. (1995). "Interrogating 'Whiteness,' (De)constructing 'Race.'" *College English*, 57(8), 901–918.

Mignolo, W., & Walsh, C. (2018). *On Decoloniality: Concepts, Analytics, Praxis*. Durham:

Duke University Press.

Moore, M. R. (2017). "Women of Color in the Academy: Navigating Multiple Intersections and Multiple Hierarchies." *Social Problems, 64*(2), 200–205.

Morrison, T. (2012). "Toni Morrison on Love, Loss, and Modernity." *Telegraph.*

Naber, N. (2000). "Ambiguous Insiders: An Investigation of Arab American Invisibility." *Ethnic and Racial Studies, 23*(1), 37–60.

Office of Institutional Research. (2019). University of Memphis. https://www.memphis.edu/oir/.

Ono, K. (2012). "Borders That Travel." In *Border Rhetorics: Citizenship and Identity on the US-Mexico Frontier,* edited by D. R. DeChaine (pp. 19–32). Tuscaloosa: University of Alabama Press.

Ono, K., & Sloop, J. M. (1995). "The Critique of Vernacular Discourse." *Communication Monographs, 62*(1), 19–46.

Perea, J. F. (1997). "The Black/White Binary Paradigm of Race: The Normal Science of American Racial." *California Law Review, 85*(5), 1213–1258.

Rojas, L. (2019, February 25). "'Are We White?': SoCal's Arab-Americans Debate Which Box to Check on the Census." *LA-ist.* https://laist.com/news/are-we-white-socals-arab-americans-debate-which-box-to-check-on-the-census.

Thomas, G. D., & Hollenshead, C. (2006). "Resisting from the Margins: The Coping Strategies of Black Women and Other Women of Color Faculty Members at a Research University." *Journal of Negro Education, 70*(3), 166–175.

Tracy, S. (2019). "The Communication Discipline Is Bleeding." sarahjtracy.com.

Tuck, E., & Yang, K. W. (2012). „Decolonization Is Not a Metaphor." *Decolonization: Indigeneity, Education & Society, 1*(1), 1–40.

U.S. Census Bureau. (2018). "2020 Census Program Memorandum Series." https://www.census.gov/programs-surveys/decennial-census/decade/2020/planning-management/plan/memo-series.html#:~:text=The%202020%20Census%20Memorandum%20Series,and%20documenting%20important%20historical%20changes.

Vega, K. S., & Chávez, K. R. (2018). "Latinx Rhetoric and Intersectionality in Racial Rhetorical Criticism." *Communication and Critical / Cultural Studies, 15*(4), 319–325.

Yousef, S. (2020). "Re-articulating the "Good Muslim" in Times of Trump: Islamophilia and the Muslim Woman in the Women's March Poster." In , *Negotiating Identity and Transnationalism in Middle Eastern and North African Communication and Critical Cultural Studies,* edited by H. Ghabra, F. Z. Alaoui, S. Abdi & B. M. Calafell (pp. 31–48). New York: Peter Lang Publishing.

Yousuf, S., & Calafell, B. (2018). "The Imperative for Examining Anti-Muslim Racism in Rhetorical Studies." *Communication and Critical/ Cultural Studies*, *15*(4), 312–318.

Epilogue

Walid Afifi and Michael Lechuga

T he chapters in *Migrant World Making* demonstrate that there is rich scholarship on the experiences of migrants from within migrant communities. However, the fields of rhetoric, communication, and media studies are relatively late in recognizing the unique skills of knowledge producing, sense making, and time traveling that migrating people must possess in order to survive. The editors and contributors of this volume have described these processes as "migrant world making"; however, we suggest that "making" a world for migrants is really just the beginning. Migrant worlds need to be sustained so that those transnational folks holding tensions that pull from competing directions can find comfort in their transition. Migrant worlds need to be honored, not hidden in the shadows. Migrant worlds need to be invested in, not exploited.

First, we have seen in this volume how migrants make worlds for themselves where so often they are expected to fit into a place that has been molded by colonial, nationalist, and capitalist forces. Many of the chapters in this volume describe this struggle that migrants face in being able to act as agents in their own and social environments. In online activism for social justice, in the web pages of humanitarian organizations, in the vernacular discourses of protestors, and even in the voices of scholars making homes in the academy, we have seen how migrant world making can be tedious, emotional, confusing, and sometimes dangerous. We have seen that not being who others expect you to be is a common experience, and that we can honor those who build rich and vibrant migrant worlds despite the pressures to assimilate into nationalist cultural, political, and social norms.

Second, migrant world making spans temporalities, meaning that the past-to-present-to-future progression that is characteristic of Western thought does not necessarily apply to migrants making worlds in new places. Memory, presence, and hope are inseparable from one another, as seen in this volume through migrants' experiences and expressions. The forces of colonialism, capitalism, and nationalism pressuring migrants to assimilate often erase the cultural richness of the past in favor of a stratified future where migrants live on the fringes and in the shadows of the contemporary world. For example, refugees who are forced to migrate to places like Colorado must resist the social stigmas that come with being labeled a refugee. Many migrants do not choose to move but still must grapple with the expectations that nationalist ideologies impose on them. Often, migrant world making for these groups means hope for a return to a past that may or may not ever come. For others, like pro-migrant activists and scholars, migrant world making means remembering our cultural roots while creating a future that values migrant worlds.

Third, the contributors to this volume teach us that migrant world making is material. This means that as migrants build a home in a new place, they bring with them the cultural bonds that are rooted in a land left behind. Culture, after all, is how groups articulate their relationship to a homeland, even if that homeland is a distant memory. In many cases, migrants turn to online spaces of belonging that often provide a virtual site for connection with members of diasporas to share strategies for world making or just reminisce about a connection to a shared homeland. In other cases, Latina/o/x migrants like those in the Southwest United States are finding ways to reclaim space for political and social recognition by shedding light on the ways that colonialism robs people of their connection to place. This tension, though, is not just felt by economic migrants. As we have seen, climate devastation and authoritarianism are creating more and more instability in the world, growing the number of migrants and refugees who are building worlds in new places. Even nations are not permanent, and the precarity that migrants face today could be a situation any of us might face in the coming decades.

Finally, throughout *Migrant World Making*, we have seen how migrants are multimodal communicators who speak many languages, on multiple platforms, and in various capacities and temporalities, to navigate the regimes of nationalism that have been erected by colonial and capitalist enterprises. These skills—many of which are showcased by the contributors and research participants of this volume—are used not only by migrating peoples throughout nation-states, but also by many migrating academics to navigate the cultures of institutions of higher education in which many of us work. These skills should be honored and recognized.

Along with recognition, though, we ask, what more can be done? Drawing scholarly attention to the fact that these experiences exist and impact the ways we understand communication might not be enough. Thus, we take this opportunity to talk about what more can be done on two levels. First, we implore our discipline to question our research practices to consider how migrant voices are ignored when we engage in knowledge-production practices that uphold colonial and nationalist paradigms. Second, we consider how those in the respective fields might stand in solidarity and cooperate with others who are trying to organize for better lives for migrating peoples in the places where we work, live, and practice community.

Championing Migrant World Making

Migrant world making is different for everyone. This volume has illuminated many of the ways migrants communicate their belonging amid challenges in the face of transition, uncertainty, and rejection. Rather than expound on the multitudes of ways migrants make worlds, though, this volume ends by considering what readers might do to champion the efforts of migrants and institutional and political organization that already support migrant world making: engaging with humanitarian and political groups that support migrants while calling for an end to austere bordering practices that impede migrants from finding their homeplace.

Championing Migrant Experiences

According to the United Nations' "World Migration Report 2020," there are an estimated 282 million migrants globally, which is almost a hundred million more than twenty years ago, and is already surpassing some estimates for migration totals by 2050 (United Nations International Organization for Migration, 2019). That number translates to approximately one in every thirty people. Worldwide, two-thirds of the migrant population are estimated to be "migrant workers," which make up nearly 20 percent of the workforce in high-income countries. Thirty-one million migrants are children. Because of their lack of protection and their high poverty rates, among other factors, migrants face a wide variety of risks to life and well-being. For example, in a five-year period (2014–2018), the UN recorded 30,900 deaths of migrants during their attempt to reach their destination, a number that is likely a far underestimate. Another 40,190 migrants were reported in a UN-maintained system to assist victims of human trafficking, again likely a large undercount of the number of migrants who face exploitation (United Nations, 2019).

It must be clear, though: while the numbers of people who migrate in precarity today are at record numbers, each experience of migrating peoples has value. Oxfam's "I Hear You" project gives us a glimpse into some of these migrant experiences (Oxfam, 2016). In one such narrative, a young Syrian woman has spent four years in a refugee camp and is desperately clinging to a rapidly fading dream to return to a university and ultimately become a lawyer, while emphasizing how she cannot lose hope. Another refugee was a stay-at-home mother, reminiscing about her children's school accomplishments and their affinity of watching her and her husband's wedding video, along with many aspects of what might be considered routine family life, completely absent since their escape from a destroyed home. As Oxfam demonstrates, elevating the individual stories of migrants and refugees (even when many of those who are featured are unable to reveal their identities due to safety concerns) illuminates the numerous techniques and technologies that migrating peoples develop to sustain their lives while moving between nations.

Additionally, the COVID-19 pandemic has had an especially negative impact on migrant communities. The *Atlantic* reported on the impact of the pandemic on the undocumented community in the United States, already living in isolation (Caplan, 2020). What happens, one might ask, when people experiencing symptoms of the virus cannot turn to the medical system out of fear of deportation? Caplan elaborates:

> The pandemic compounds the vulnerability and sense of precariousness that had always loomed among the undocumented community. . . . People are waiting until the very last minute to call an ambulance or go to the hospital . . . because they're fearful their names will go to the government if they're tested for COVID-19. (2020, para. 13)

By the time many affected people do call for help, it is usually too late.

In another report conducted by the Jan Sahas Migrant Laborers Collective, the group describes the effect that COVID-19 policies in India have had on the internal migrant population (Jan Sahas, 2020). A survey of over 3,500 of the nearly 55 million daily wage workers showed that over 55 percent earn between $2–6 per day, on average, as primary income for four-person families (2020, p. 12). After India instituted a 21-day lockdown in March 2020, even these meager wages disappeared for most migrant laborers. Further 42 percent of those surveyed indicated having no rations to sustain their families for even one day, let alone extended time without pay (p. 32). Nearly 80 percent feared they could not continue to pay debt that they had taken on to work, and 50 percent of those believed they would be victims of violence as a result (p. 13). One-third of those they interviewed were stuck in destination cities without the ability to pay for a return to their homes. The authors described one such example:

> As part of our survey, one of the workers we reached out to was Saurabh. Along with a group of 16 people (including 5 women and 6 children), he was stranded and starving near Badshahpur (Haryana), which is around 15 kilometres from Gurugram, without any food or essentials. All of them were construction workers from Madhya Pradesh, who have been without work [for a week]. Usually paid on a weekly basis, none of them were paid wages for their last week's work which was abruptly interrupted by the lockdown. Left with no money or food, Saurabh was requesting for any possible help. (Jan Sahas, 2020, p. 11)

As was the case around the globe, the spread of COVID-19 widened the gap between those who benefit from globalization's economic exploitation and those who are bound to it.

· One last example of the exploitation of migrant workers we offer is the *kafala* (sponsorship) system in Jordan, Lebanon, and the Arab Gulf states. It is a legal system that covers the treatment and rights of foreign migrant workers in these countries, replacing local labor laws. Under this system, the state gives local individuals or families sponsorship permits to employ foreign migrant workers and the sole rights to terminate or extend their work visas. The sponsor also covers travel expenses, which creates a form of bonded labor that many domestic workers cannot escape. The system is ripe for exploitation, and several organizations, including Human Rights Watch, have reported on the many ways in which is it used as a form of modern-day slavery. Reports of abuse include the common practice of confiscating laborers' passports, along with acts of violence, imprisonment, and sexual and physical assaults, sometimes resulting in deaths. Lebanon alone is home to over 250,000 foreign domestic workers, the vast majority of whom are women working in private households and migrating from Africa or Asia. Amnesty International (2019) conducted interviews with thirty-eight of them between 2018 and 2019. The following is only a portion of their summary report:

> Among the live-in domestic workers, only five out of the 32 said that they were allowed to keep their passports with them. Ten of the women said their employers did not allow them to leave the home; some even said that their employers went as far as locking them in when they left the home. . . . The majority of women interviewed reported being subjected at least once to humiliating and dehumanizing treatment by their employers and six women reported being subjected to severe physical abuse. Most women interviewed reported that their employers had not provided them with the appropriate medical care when they needed it. Amnesty International interviewed six women who either had suicidal thoughts or had attempted suicide as a result of their exploitative living and working conditions, their isolation and the violence to which they were subjected. (Amnesty International, 2019, p. 5)

In each of these examples, we see how institutions are finding ways to leverage their resources to both uplift the voices of migrants and improve their lives. These organizations (visible mostly because of their size and scope) mobilize aid for migrant groups who are often exploited within the confines of the colonized and economically globalized world, and at times amplify the voices of migrants to make the case that our current efforts aren't enough. So, one might ask, "How frequently do these critical voices of migrants get listened to and heard in the field of communication studies? Moreover, how frequently do scholars engage in practices that both amplify the voices of migrating communities and channel resources to organizations that improve migrants' lives?"

Championing Migrant Research and Researchers

To help answer the first question, we turned to unpublished data from an investigation that resulted in the coding of all articles published across a nearly six-year period (from January 2013 until June 2018) in nine communication journals (*Communication Monographs, Human Communication Research, Journal of Communication, Journal of Applied Communication Research, Journal of International and Intercultural Research, Communication and Critical/Cultural Studies, Communication, Culture, and Critique, Howard Journal of Communication*, and the *Asian Journal of Communication*).[1] For the purposes of this chapter, we searched through the 1,581 article titles in that corpus for references to the words "migrant," "immigrant," "refugee," or "undocumented" (Afifi & Cornejo, 2020). Only twenty-eight (1.8 percent) of all publications in that period matched the search criteria. Thirty-three percent of those publications involved analyses of the ways that media framed migrants' experience or the way that white-majority residents of a country reacted (typically, in terms of feeling threatened) to migrants. In other words, only 1.2 percent of all studies published across a nearly six-year period in nine of our journals lifted the voices of migrants. Moreover, only six of those appeared in journals that did not specialize in culture (0.8 percent of the 733 articles appearing in those four journals during this period). To be blunt: migrant voices are ignored in our discipline's "mainstream" flagship journals. So, the answer to the first question is *very infrequently*; our communication scholarship says almost nothing about the lives of migrants. Our discipline, like so many of the structures within which migrant communities live, appears satisfied with perceiving and treating the 282 million migrants as invisible.

What would theorizing about communication look like if we took seriously the lived experience of migrant domestic workers in the kafala system, or the undocumented migrants in the United States, or the millions of migrant laborers in India? What knowledge has our discipline produced, to which their experiences have contributed? When very space has been created for those with migrating experiences, we render their lives meaningless in relation to our understanding of communication outcomes. Perhaps if we take the challenge of championing migrant communities more seriously in our discipline, we might start with major structural changes, including creating an infrastructure in which community-engaged (public) scholarship is recognized and rewarded; changing promotion and tenure documents in ways that rewards contributions to co-constructed knowledge beyond book or journal manuscripts; developing a roster of manuscript reviewers who have expertise in, and commitment to, a wide range of community-centered scholarship; and considering the creation of a journal that publishes a variety of scholarly outputs that emanates from work in communities. Why focus on community-engaged scholarship as a thruway to elevating migrant voices? Because the work that it takes to access migrant communities as a trusted ally is not sufficiently recognized, let alone elevated, within the typical reward structures in our discipline. Developing this infrastructure is the first step in integrating migrants and migrant voices in co-productive community scholarship.

To start the work of championing migrant world making, we begin by working on our discipline—but the work does not stop there. Those academics invested in migrant knowledge production and communication might use our voices to honor the lives of migrants, not just in scholarship but in the day-to-day experiences of migrating people in the cities and towns around the globe. We ask for a commitment to migrant knowledge production and communication that goes beyond scholarship and becomes an ethos extending beyond the research, teaching, and service commitments many of us embark on in our professional lives. This volume has shown that creating strong collaborative networks between nonprofit organizations and other nongovernmental agencies that work with migrant communities and members is possible for scholars. Such networks often reduce barriers for scholars interested in working with migrant communities, and would provide rich opportunities for collaborative and reciprocal knowledge creation and application.

As *Migrant World Making* has demonstrated, inclusion does not happen by just being in the same spaces as migrants, like using public transport together or sharing workplaces. It starts when migrants and local communities meet in a common space with an intentional interaction that brings cultures into dialogue with one another. Again, it is mostly nonstate actors such as nonprofit organizations leading the charge in shortening distances between migrant and nonmigrant groups. Among these, Casa Scalabrini 634, a program of Agenzia Scalabriniana per la Cooperazione allo Sviluppo in Rome (Italy), is an inspiring example. By providing a space of welcoming and activities capable of inter-connecting lives and creating a common sense of belonging, CS634 supports its beneficiaries—including single persons and families with children—in becoming autonomous and integrated into Italian society. It is a valuable and concrete example of creating the culture of encounter and building more resilient communities through the successful inclusion of migrants and refugees at the local level. De Sanctis and Khrebtan-Hörhager's chapter is an example of the kind of work that champions migrant world making in communication studies.

Championing Abolitionism

Cisneros (2021) suggests that scholars and critics engaged in migrant activism commit to a telos of abolition—one that acknowledges the freedom of peoples to freely move across borders, to safely remain in places where their presence is politicized, and to easily return to places they have left. He asks that those studying migrants and the border control mechanisms that capture them adopt an "abolitionist vision," one that can imagine an "end to (1) capitalist exploitation and nation-state violence that contribute to human displacement . . . , (2) architectures of political exclusion and labor exploitation caused by border regimes . . . ; and (3) the displacement of people and theft of land of the settler colonial present" (p. 96). An abolitionist telos described by Cisneros would remove many of the barriers facing migrants who are making their worlds in precarious situations precisely because of the anti-migrant attitudes and infrastructures throughout the world today. In many cases, the best thing we as scholars and critics can do to champion migrant world making is to get out of the way. And as we do, we can begin to remove the obstacles that have been constructed to keep migrants from realizing their "freedom to stay, freedom to move, and freedom to return" (Cisneros, 2021, p. 96).

Liberation theology might provide another insight into the approach that we can adopt if we are to appreciate and respond to the migrant experience from an abolitionist telos. Brown makes the following critical observation:

> Juan Luis Segundo, a Jesuit from Uruguay, warns us that unless we agree that the world should not be the way it is, we can never understand what liberation theology is all about. If we are satisfied with the world as it is, there is no point of contact, because the world that is satisfying to us is the same world that is utterly devastating to them. (1993, p. 44)

It is precisely that task which is at hand for us if we are to champion the voices of migrant communities within our discipline. This book has been an intervention in the pursuit of that task, and this chapter is a call to action with that same goal. We see that the spirit of liberation theology can be translated to the fields of rhetoric, communication, and media studies as a way to stop the prescriptive use of our theories and methods to "solve problems." This conception of liberation must start with thinking how the theories and methods in our fields have been used to erase the experiences of those not living in the same worlds as our own. We must reckon with the role our discipline has played in rendering the world the way it is, knowing that it relies on the vast economic, political, and social exclusion and exploitation of Others. Finally, we must make the epistemic shift to no longer be satisfied with the world as it is, and reflect that change in our work.

We end with one final example of a group championing migrant world making. Freedom University is a "modern-day freedom school" in Atlanta, Georgia, in the United States. For many, a college education is not easily accessible or affordable (Freedom University, 2020). This is especially true in the state of Georgia where its board of regents in 2010 prohibited undocumented students from attending the state's top universities. Not long afterward, Freedom University opened its doors with a mission to educate and empower undocumented students who have been locked out by the state. Freedom University is a local grassroots project brought to life by a broad coalition of undocumented students, immigrant rights activists, local nonprofit organizations, and professors at the University of Georgia. With a volunteer faculty, the university provides a curriculum that includes the social sciences and humanities, fine arts, biological and life sciences, and SAT and college preparation. Described by students as a place where they walk in undocumented but leave unafraid, Freedom University provides a space for undocumented students to gain a college education from an institution with a mission of liberation (Freedom University, 2020). In other words, it's a place where migrants make worlds for themselves and with the support of the communities around them.

In all, *Migrant World Making* is an invitation to experience what it is like to build new worlds. In the face of growing hyper-nationalism, global economic crisis, environmental catastrophe, and the ongoing coronavirus pandemic, it is almost certain that we will see an increase in the number of people who must uproot to find a more suitable life—perhaps this will be one of us. We honor today's migrants, who build a world with the hopes for a better future in a new place while holding the rich memories of a connection to a homeplace. To that end, we might stop seeing migrant communities as abject victims of nationalism and start seeing them as stewards of the knowledge all humans may need in the coming generations to survive the vastly changing global landscape.

NOTE

1. The analysis was restricted to journals that published primarily empirical research, thereby excluding some leading journals in the fields (e.g., *Quarterly Journal of Speech*).

REFERENCES

Afifi, W. A., & Cornejo, M. (2020). [Coding of titles from published articles in #CommsoWeird project]. Unpublished raw data.

Amnesty International. (2019). "'There House Is My Prison': Exploitation of Migrant Domestic Workers in Lebanon." https://www.amnesty.org/en/documents/mde18/0022/2019/en/#:~:text=Search-,Lebanon%3A%20'Their%20house%20is%20my%20prison'%3A%20Exploitation%20of,migrant%20domestic%20workers%20in%20Lebanon&text=Lebanon%20is%20home%20to%20over,of%20these%20workers%20are%20women.

Brown, R. M. (1993). *Liberation Theology: An Introductory Guide*. Louisville, KY: Westminster/John Knox Press.

Cisneros, D. (2021). "Free to Move, Free to Stay, Free to Return: Border Rhetorics and a Commitment to Telos." *Communication and Critical/Cultural Studies*, *18*(1), 94–101.

Freedom University. (2020). "History & Timeline." https://www.freedom-university.org/history.

Imagining America. (2020). "We Envision." https://imaginingamerica.org/who-we-are/

we-envision/.

Jan Sahas. (2020). "Voices of the Invisible: Rapid Assessment on the Impact of COVID-19 Lockdown on Internal Migrant Workers, Recommendations for the State, Industry, and Philanthropy." *People's Archive of Rural India*. https://ruralindiaonline.org/en/library/resource/voices-of-the-invisible-citizens/.

Kaplan, E. (2020, May 27). "What Isolation Does to Undocumented Immigrants." *Atlantic*. https://www.theatlantic.com/family/archive/2020/05/isolated-undocumented-immigrant/612130/.

Oxfam. (2016, December 6). "Oxfam Joins with Margot Robbie, John Cho, Gael García Bernal, Minnie Driver, and More to Launch 'I Hear You' Project in Support of Refugees." https://www.oxfamamerica.org/press/oxfam-joins-with-margot-robbie-john-cho-gael-garcia-bernal-minnie-driver-and-more-to-launch-i-hear-you-project-in-support-of-refugees/.

United Nations International Organization for Migration. (2019). *World Migration Report 2020*. Geneva: International Organization for Migration. https://publications.iom.int/system/files/pdf/wmr_2020.pdf.

Contributors

Walid Afifi is a professor in the Department of Communication at University of California, Santa Barbara. Afifi's program of research revolves around uncertainty and information-management decisions and has led to the development and refinement of the Theory of Motivated Information Management. That work has increasingly focused on immigrant communities and/or communities experiencing trauma.

Noor Ghazal Aswad is an assistant professor at the University of Alabama. Her research interests revolve around social movement rhetorics, racial rhetorical criticism, and rhetorics of immigration and identity.

Victoria A. Cisneros is a two-time alumna of California State University Fresno's Department of Communication. Her research interests include rhetorical criticism, social justice, and feminist rhetoric. Cisneros is the marketing strategist for Fresno State's office of University Brand Strategy and Marketing.

Leda Cooks is a professor in the Department of Communication at the University of Massachusetts. Cooks's research interests revolve around power, identity, body, food, and culture, particularly as they are connected to discourse and performance.

Veronica De Sanctis is a project manager for research and communication at Scalabrini International Migration Institute and holds a PhD in history from Sapienza Universita di Roma.

Sergio Fernando Juárez is an assistant professor of Intercultural Communication at Loyola Marymount University. Juárez's areas of research include critical pedagogies within the field of communication and development of equitable educational practices within institutions to better value multiple forms of intelligence and knowledge. In 2021 he received the Activism and Social Justice Pedagogy Award by the Social Justice & Activism Division of the National Communication Association. Juárez is an incoming associate editor of the National Communication Association's peer-reviewed journal *Communication Education.*

Minkyung Kim is an assistant professor in the Department of Communication at the University of Illinois Urbana-Champaign. Kim's research focuses on organizational-level communication and its impacts on community resilience and social well-being. Specifically, she studies nonprofit organizations serving vulnerable populations and how they leverage and navigate macro-level communication processes like interorganizational networks to maximize their capacity for community impact. She also explores symbolic, material, and mediated artifacts as forms of organizing and how such processes empower culturally and politically marginalized communities.

Julia Khrebtan-Hörhager is an associate professor in the Department of Communication Studies at Colorado State University. Her research and teaching interests are in intercultural and international communication, European studies, conflict, cultural memory, international cinematography, and critical media studies.

Melanie Kwestel is a doctoral candidate in the Department of Communication at the School of Communication and Information at Rutgers University. Her research looks at how marginalized groups organize to reach economic goals within corporate networks and the role that certification NGOs play in conferring legitimacy on both corporations and activist groups representing workers and producers.

Michael Lechuga is an assistant professor in the Department of Communication and Journalism at the University of New Mexico. Lechuga researches and teaches cultural studies, rhetoric, migration studies and settler colonialism studies.

Eunbi Lee is assistant professor in the Department of Communications and New Media, National University of Singapore. Lee's research focuses on storytelling in communication and performance studies and transnational feminisms. Especially, Lee examines how storytelling from Asian and migrant massage/sex workers becomes cultural and political actions for transnational feminist movements and social justice.

Anjana Mudambi is an assistant professor in the Department of Communication at University of Wisconsin–Milwaukee. Her research focuses on critical analyses of discourses of marginalized groups, with an emphasis on how South Asian Americans have engaged, reproduced, and challenged dominant, hegemonic discourses. In addition, some of her recent work has looked at undergraduate students' discourses in the context of improving our scholarship and praxis around critical intercultural communication pedagogy.

Nathian Shae Rodriguez is an associate professor in the School of Journalism and Media Studies at San Diego State University. Rodriguez's research focuses on minority representation in media, specifically LGBTQ and Latinx portrayals and identity negotiation, as well as pop culture, identity, issues of masculinity, and pop culture pedagogy.

Fernanda R. Rosa is an assistant professor in the Department of Science, Technology, and Society at Virginia Tech. Her research interests include internet governance and design, social justice, and the Global South.

Natasha Shrikant is an assistant professor in the Department of Communication at the University of Colorado Boulder. Her research highlights the importance of social interaction as a form of communication that constitutes social identities and inequalities. Using discourse analysis and ethnography, she analyzes interrelations of identity, culture, and ideology in interaction. Her publications focus on Asian American identity, refugee identity, and race/ism in interaction, particularly in organizational contexts.

Arthur D. Soto-Vásquez is an assistant professor in the Department of Psychology and Communication at Texas A&M International University. Soto-Vásquez studies the relationship between digital media, popular culture, and identity making. Soto-Vásquez's recent work has focused on U.S. Latinx political communication.

Corinne Mitsuye Sugino is an assistant professor of communication studies at Gonzaga University. Her research interests lie at the intersection of Asian American racialization and histories of protest, false discourses of multicultural inclusion, comparative racialization, and rhetorical studies.